Images of Nurses
on Television

Philip A. Kalisch, Ph.D., is Professor of History, Politics and Economics of Nursing at The University of Michigan. He earned his baccalaureate and master's degrees from the University of Nebraska and his Ph.D. from The Pennsylvania State University.

Beatrice J. Kalisch, R.N., Ed.D., F.A.A.N., is currently Shirley C. Titus Distinguished Professor of Nursing, Chairperson of Parent-Child Nursing, and director of the graduate program in Parent-Child Nursing at The University of Michigan. She earned her B.S.N. at the University of Nebraska and her master's and doctoral degrees from the University of Maryland.

The Drs. Kalisch have conducted a number of studies in the history and politics of nursing over the past 10 years. They are coauthors of several books, including *Politics of Nursing, Nursing Involvement in Health Planning,* and *The Advance of American Nursing.* They have also coauthored many articles for such journals as *Nursing Research, Nursing and Health Care, Nursing Forum, American Journal of Nursing,* and *Nursing Outlook.* They have served as Visiting Distinguished Professors at The University of Alabama and The University of Texas. Currently they are coprincipal investigators of a USPHS research grant to investigate the image of the nurse in the nation's news media.

Margaret Scobey, M.A., a graduate of The University of Tennessee and The University of Michigan, was a research associate in the Nursing in the Mass Media Research Project. She has coauthored several articles on various aspects of nursing within the social and cultural contexts of history for such journals as *Nursing and Health Care, Journal of Nurse-Midwifery,* and *Armed Forces and Society.* She is currently a Foreign Service Officer with the U.S. State Department.

Images of Nurses on Television

Philip A. Kalisch, Ph.D.
Beatrice J. Kalisch, R.N., Ed.D., F.A.A.N.
Margaret Scobey, M.A.

Springer Publishing Company
New York

Copyright © 1983 by Springer Publishing Company, Inc.

All rights reserved

No part of this publication may be reproduced, stored in a retrieval system, or transmitted in any form or by any means, electronic, mechanical, photocopying, recording, or otherwise, without the prior permission of Springer Publishing Company, Inc.

Springer Publishing Company, Inc.
200 Park Avenue South
New York, New York 10003

83 84 85 86 87 / 10 9 8 7 6 5 4 3 2 1

Library of Congress Cataloging in Publication Data

Kalisch, Philip Arthur.
  Images of nurses on television.

  Bibliography: p.
  Includes index.
  1. Nurses in television. 2. Television programs—United States—History. I. Kalisch, Beatrice J. II. Scobey, Margaret. III. Title.
PN1992.8.N87K34 1983 791.45'09'09352613 82-10772
ISBN 0-8261-3870-5

Printed in the United States of America

Contents

Preface		*vii*
1.	Nursing Myths and Medical Realities: Early Images of the Television Nurse, 1950s	1
2.	The Freezing of an Image, 1960s	18
3.	Close-Up: Major M.D.s and Minor R.N.s in the 1970s	41
4.	Stock Footage: Nurses and Physicians in Short-lived Medical Dramas, 1970s	60
5.	Sounds of Laughter: Nurses in Situation Comedies of the 1970s	81
6.	Suspended Moments: Nurses in 1970s Action–Adventure Series	101
7.	Mixed Bag: Two Classics, One Early Demise, and Two Lightweights	114
8.	Montage: Fragmentary Images of Television Nursing	137
9.	Join Us Tomorrow: Nurse Characters in Daytime Drama	159
10.	Perspectives on the Image of Nursing on Television	176
Bibliography		*201*
Appendix: Television Series and Series Pilots Pertaining to Nurses and Physicians		*207*
Index		*212*

Preface

The following study* chronicles and analyzes the development of the image of nurses and nursing on television. The future of the nursing profession depends, to a large extent, upon popular attitudes and assumptions about the contribution of nurses to the nation's welfare. The sources of public opinion are many and varied, but television is, without question, the single most important source of information in the United States. Nurses assume an impressive share of the health care responsibility in America. Furthermore, the nursing care responsibilities and contributions extend far beyond the corridors of hospitals. Nurses provide service and leadership in the field of community health, and nurses with advanced preparation are increasingly assuming responsibilities that were traditionally carried out only by physicians. The scope and variety of nursing practice reflect, to some extent, the changed educational preparation of nurses since World War II. More and more nurses are college graduates, and many proceed to advanced degrees in both nursing studies and associated fields. Even as nurses expand and improve their function in the health care system, many experts realize that the potential of the nursing profession has yet to be tapped.

The reality of contemporary nursing practice, however, finds little or no reflection in the largely fictional world of television broadcasting. Insofar as television programming presents a microcosmic view of American society, the role and image of nurses in that society are distinctly underplayed. To be sure, romantic and misleading presentations of nursing have appeared in all of the mass media: in novels, magazines, film, radio, and newspapers. Yet no medium of communication comes close to matching television in its power and influence.

---

*This study was supported by Research Grant NU 00579 from the U.S. Public Health Service, Health Resources Administration, Bureau of Health Professions.

U.S. News and World Report, in its ninth annual survey of "Who Runs America," ranked television as the institution third in influence only to the White House, and large business (May 10, 1982). The size of television audiences combined with the repetitive nature of television series and inherent values make it imperative that the student of modern American society understand the nature and content of television programming.

Whether deservedly or not, television is generally regarded as aesthetically inferior to film and literature for a number of reasons: The advertising function of television usually insures the prevalence of the lowest common denominator; the poor resolution and the small size of the television screen diminish the intensity of the life portrayed upon it; the breakdown of time into relatively small program units compresses experience into highly simplified terms; and the constantly shifting stream of images tumbles the momentous and the trivial together in indiscriminate succession, homogenizing them in the process. For researchers, television's chief significance as a medium has resided in its sheer mass; in its rapid infiltration of everyday American life; and in the fact that its images, for all their transience, smallness, sameness and mediocrity, have been transmitted, year after year into the consciousnesses of hundreds of millions of viewers.

The consistent misrepresentation of reality on television in regard to the world of medicine and health care affects not only nurses but also the general public. It seems without doubt that the source of a good deal of the public's dissatisfaction and frustration with the medical profession and health care system stems from the huge gap that separates real medicine from fictional television medicine. The confusing, impersonal, frightening experiences of most patients in large hospitals contrast markedly with their expectations derived from watching TV doctors cure and comfort their patients. Real hospitals and doctors cannot deliver the warm, paternal, reassuring care provided so easily by a Marcus Welby or a Joe Gannon. And, unlike most TV dramatizations of diseases and surgeries, in real life people suffer and die from ailments beyond the scope of the doctor's knowledge. Nurses and the public may also suffer from the persistently stereotyped views of the nursing profession; if nursing resources are to ever be fully utilized within the health care system, there must be some effort made to re-educate the public and the decision makers about the role and the contributions that nurses can make to the nation's health.

Before nursing leaders and educators can try to change the image of nursing on television, they must understand it in its entire historical context. To this end, the following study proposes to document the way in which nurses have been presented on television from the early days of broadcasting to the present. Although this study differs significantly in depth and scope from other studies on the content of television programming such as Gerbner et al., Greenberg, and McLaughlin, it does share many of the analytical tools used in those studies. This study on the image of nursing on television offers an exhaustive, longitudinal examination of the problem. Scholarly works on the content of television programming have generally been based upon a single season of programming or on a sample of programs taken over a few seasons. The following study of nursing and television is based upon a complete survey of all television shows that have ever featured nurses; it is limited only by the destruction or unavailability of some evidence. It is felt that this broad examination will provide a richness and texture rarely found in the more limited and purely statistical studies. Furthermore, this study of the image of nursing on television has included both an intense subjective or qualitative examination of the materials as well as the more conventional objective and statistical description of the presentation of nursing on television. It is anticipated that the conclusions of the nursing image research will contribute substantively to the current study of the content of television programming; in particular it should provide valuable information for those areas concerned with the depiction of sex roles and occupational roles in television programming.

1
Nursing Myths and Medical Realities: Early Images of the Television Nurse, 1950s

The medium of television, which so quickly captivated American audiences in the 1950s, offered a wide variety of programming that reflected its infant development. Networks tried to transfer popular radio series to the new medium with mixed success. Often settings and scenery mimicked the devices used on the proscenium arch stage, indicating that television producers had not yet found production methods that were tailored to the camera's flexibility. Variety hours and dramatic anthologies were the staple of nighttime broadcasting in these early years. The general hospital–medical drama, so familiar to contemporary audiences, also began in the 1950s, but belonged to the anthology format so that there were no regular, continuing characters. Consequently, most of the presentations of nursing characters occurred on a one time only basis. Nurse characters also appeared in news and documentary shows and in situation comedies.

Certain recurring themes and attitudes in television programs did impinge upon the image of the medical and nursing professions, despite the infrequency of serial characters. A reverential tone toward physicians and the medical world colored almost all dramatic renderings of medical themes. The generalized treatment of women in domestic, romantic, and maternal roles also influenced the portrayal of nurses on television. Nurse characters rarely emerged as technically skilled or autonomous professionals; yet the overall image of the profession was positive because nurses were invariably treated with sympathy and respect. The decade of the 1950s, for the purposes of this study, actually spans the years, 1952–1959: In 1952 the first network, prime-time medical show appeared, *City Hospital;* and in 1959, *Hennessey,* the last new medical show of the 1950s, premiered. Several production companies created medical or nursing shows that appeared in syndication; these will be examined in a separate section on syndicated series; but occasionally reference will be made to these series in discussing the 1950s shows.

Programmers clearly recognized the didactic power of television, and they broadcast purely informational shows for the welfare of the audience. The care of infants and children was a popular subject in the years just after the war. Local stations often aired syndicated or locally produced shows such as *Life with Baby* (1955), in which Red Cross Nurse Beatrice Norden discussed routine child care, or *Baby Time* (1955), in which W. W. Bauer, M.D. and Jane Warren, R.N. informed mothers about such normal infant and child development care as what to do with a teething baby. In these shows, the nurse appeared as an educator of mothers and was in a collegial relationship with the physician.

In 1955 NBC presented a show starring Dr. Spock who advised problem-ridden parents. That same year, ABC broadcast a general medical documentary series called *Medical Horizons*. This show offered weekly reports on the advances of medicine, narrated by host Don Goddard who explained a particular disease or medical problem each week and interviewed doctors, hospital staff, and patients on location in real hospitals and clinics across the country. For example, on December 19, 1955 the series covered twelve hours in the life of a hospital nurse and examined her work in caring for the sick, educating some patients, training student nurses and participating in public-health matters. The CIBA drug company sponsored a syndicated series in 1955, re-run on ABC in 1958, entitled *March of Medicine,* narrated by Ben Grauer and Eric Sevareid. In addition to reports on new treatments and surgical procedures, this series also emphasized basic research on such subjects as obesity, arthritic and rheumatic diseases, and prenatal care.

The story of nurse Genevieve de Galard-Terraube, the "Angel of Dienbienphu," captured the attention of TV journalists in the early 1950s. In addition to Dave Garroway's interview of her for *The Today Show* on July 26, 1954, during her tour of the United States, the mystery anthology *Danger* presented an hour-long dramatization of the day-to-day events in the battle of Indochina at the garrison of Dien Bien Phu including Mme. Galard-Terraube, the only woman attending the wounded at Dien Bien Phu. In all of these news stories, documentaries, and informational programs, the image of nursing was, at the very least, realistic because real, working nurses were used.

Informational and documentary shows were not, however, the most memorable TV programs of the 1950s. "The golden age of television" referred to the now legendary dramatic anthologies such as *Playhouse 90, Studio One,* and the *Armstrong Circle Theatre,* all of which broadcast live, original screenplays. To these more famous shows must be added the dozens of sixty- and thirty-minute dramatic shows that offered a new story every week. These anthologies filled the network schedule throughout the 1950s and varied between general drama and specialized subject matter. Generally speaking, the longer, ninety-minute productions used the best writers, actors, and directors, while the shorter productions less consistently achieved a high quality. With the exception of *Medic,* nursing appeared in these shows only when the playwright chose to introduce a nurse character or to explore a nursing theme. From these dramatic anthologies, two representative episodes that dealt with nurses will be presented: *Best of Broadway* (NBC) offered the Kaufman and Hart play, "The Man Who Came to Dinner," in 1954 and *The Jane Wyman Show* (ABC) did "An Echo of the Past" in 1956.

Before these examples are examined, it must be noted that other shows did occasionally feature nursing. On *Top Plays of 1954*, Irene Dunne portrayed "Sister Veronica," a supervising nurse who concerned herself with the health and problems of her many patients. *Playhouse 90*, in a 1957 production, "Four Women in Black," told the story of four missionary nuns headed west to build a hospital in Tucson; the show starred Helen Hayes. A 1958 episode of *Perry Mason* was "The Case of the Fugitive Nurse." *The Jane Wyman Show*, 1956–1958, presented three other stories featuring nursing in addition to the one to be highlighted below. *The Loretta Young Theatre* did a play about a nurse in 1957, "Three and Two Please," along with several others in the show's eight year run from 1953 to 1961. In 1959 *Playhouse 90* aired Arthur Hailey's "Diary of a Nurse" which starred Inger Stevens and served as the prototype of the 1962 television series *The Nurses*.

Best of Broadway's television adaptation of "The Man Who Came to Dinner" brought an already popular property to the small screen on October 13, 1954. The storyline, when reduced to capsule form, loses much of its effervescence because so much of the play's charm stems from the witty dialogue and repartee among the various zanies and intruders. The premise of the show rests upon the presence of portly, Falstaffian, vituperative New York critic, Sheridan Whiteside, in the middle-class Ohio home of the Ernest Stanley family. Whiteside has injured his back after an accidental fall off the Stanley porch (this back injury, which keeps him in a wheelchair, explains the presence of the nurse, Miss Preen); in retribution he plans lawsuits from their living room and takes over the entire house, exiling Mr. and Mrs. Stanley to the upstairs rooms. Whiteside would be happy to depart when, after a few weeks, his doctor announces that his back was not injured after all except that Maggie Cutler, Whiteside's attractive secretary and aide-de-camp, has fallen in love with a local journalist and playwright and intends to settle down in Ohio. Whiteside stays on to break up Maggie's romance.

Unfortunately, Whiteside's empire begins to crumble before his very eyes with everyone threatening and abandoning him, until his comedian friend, Banjo, arrives and helps to restore everyone to good humor, or at least grudging cooperation. Then Whiteside takes his leave, only to fall once more—and thus returns to begin again.

The nurse, Miss Preen, received scant attention. Although her part was small, her reputation was much greater. She was the main inspiration for Sheridan's nastiest insults during the course of his month-long stay at the Stanley home. At various times he said to her:

"You move like a broken down truck horse."

"You have the touch of a sex-starved cobra."

"Go and read the life of Florence Nightingale and learn how unfitted you are for your profession."

In addition, both the first and last lines of dialogue in the play were spoken in reference to Miss Preen. The play's first words, uttered by Whiteside offstage were, "Great, dribbling cow," and then he followed the jittery Miss Preen as she ran to fetch her patient's corn flakes. The last words, heard from a newly fallen Whiteside, were: "Miss Preen! . . . Miss Preen! . . . I want Miss Preen back."

Miss Preen serves as the most consistently comic character in the drama, not by what she does or says but by what is said about her and done to her. Her self-sacrificing obedience to her patient, all in the name of nursing, made her the perfect object of Whiteside's wit. In her professional concern for his welfare, she alone made no attempt to defend herself from his rudeness and temperament. ZaSu Pitts, who had frequently portrayed nurses in 1930's movies, played the outraged but obedient nurse as a rather hapless comic figure. Miss Preen wore a full uniform, appearing as a buttoned-up and starchy representative of the nursing profession. The audience assumed, both from Miss Preen's persona and from her own admission, that nursing has been her entire life; no personal information about her life ever emerged, not even her first name. As she told Whiteside before she quit, "I became a nurse because all my life, ever since I was a little girl, I was filled with the idea of serving a suffering humanity." This sense of missionary zeal in relieving human misery made her impervious to personal slights and discomfort, at least until she encountered Sheridan Whiteside. The audience also sensed that Miss Preen (the name even sounds repressed) had very little experience with the opposite sex. Interestingly, a silly flirtation from Banjo represented the final straw; she patiently obeyed Whiteside's orders, listened to his insults, and even took care of a flock of penguins for him, but when her sense of feminine virtue was assaulted by Banjo, she packed her bags and left.

Preen's strengths lay in her vast reserves of patience and dedication to her profession. Clearly she considered her patient's irrational whims and petulant outbursts to be part and parcel of her responsibility as a nurse, and she made not a single defense.

Miss Preen's most serious flaw was that she had no sense of humor. She took her patient's insults and orders in total seriousness; other victims of his insults realized that Sheridan was for the most part kidding, and they gave back almost as well as they received. But Miss Preen failed to see the absurdity and humor in the situation. She wrung her hands, swallowed hard, expressed shock in her facial expressions, all to indicate unease with the ludicrous establishment surrounding Sheridan Whiteside. When Banjo arrives in Act 3, she answers the door for him and is immediately swept off her feet and covered with kisses and professions of love. She screams her protests and demands her release. After putting her down, he continues his mock passion by slapping her fanny and inviting her to his room.

Through this antic episode, Miss Preen saw nothing vaguely entertaining about Banjo's entrance. She had been mortally insulted, her sense of decorum totally outraged. Clearly she believed that to relax and to enjoy the comedy around her would be unfitting for her professional identity.

It is difficult to say how Miss Preen's personality traits affected her professional performance because so little attention was given to her nursing responsibilities. The audience saw that she fulfilled her duties to her patient to the letter of the law; she delivered his medications, transported him from one room to the other, and made concerned remarks about his general health (by warning him away from a box of candy). She lacked the flexibility, however, to ride with the unorthodox situation; Miss Preen's nursing abilities seemed restricted to routine and normal assignments. Of course in her defense, Sheridan Whiteside could have provoked Florence Nightingale to marry Jack the Ripper.

Miss Preen's nursing experience with Whiteside changed her entire view of the human race; she swore to do all in her power to exterminate mankind. Only a nurse with such a single-minded devotion to her profession could have been so totally disoriented by working for Whiteside; a woman with a fuller knowledge of the world and an interest in life beyond the sickroom may have been able to, if not appreciate, at least tolerate Sheridan Whiteside's brand of humor. Preen, although essentially a comic character, inspired little audience sympathy because she allowed herself to be victimized. In addition, her humorless view of her job made her unable to participate in the hijinks around her.

The character represented a common stereotype of the professional nurse: a prim, humorless spinster whose idea of doing good does not include laughter and fun. After all, sickness is serious and levity out of place. As a private duty nurse, Miss Preen also demonstrated many of the problems experienced by professional nurses who work in private homes; that is, the menial service such as cleaning up and carrying trays of food.

An example of a nurse character from the more common type of dramatic anthology, the weekly half-hour drama, occurred in the *Jane Wyman Theatre* production of "An Echo of the Past," starring Miss Wyman as an Army nurse, Meg, who works in an evacuation hospital near Dover during the Second World War. A patient, Jim Ewing, who Meg loved before the war, arrives at the hospital with eye injuries and remains bandaged for the duration of the story. In a flashback, Meg relives her last meeting with Jim Ewing, before the war when she was a successful, sophisticated New York socialite who occasionally sang at fashionable nightclubs and moved from one party to the next. Jim was a midwestern architect who lived in the city and attended the social whirl much less frequently. They soon fell in love, but when Jim asked her to marry him and move back to Minneapolis, she refused. She claimed that she could never give up the bright lights for life in middle America. Meg lost track of her frivolous existence, became a nurse, and entered the army to help others. Back in the present, Meg is unsure of Jim's feelings toward her and decides not to reveal her identity to him. She enlists the other nurse to keep her name a secret. Throughout his recovery and recuperation, he and the nurse become good friends. She helps him walk outside, and they exchange confidences about their pasts. Meg intends to identify herself just before he is to be evacuated to a larger hospital. She hopes he wants to re-establish their former relationship. Just as she is about to tell him, she notices an attractive young woman at his bed—his wife. She runs from the ward, tears in her eyes but determined not to break down; after all, one cannot return to the past.

This episode presented the nurse in a very positive light. The men in the ward admired and liked their nurse. However, her services for them were usually of a supportive, comforting, even romantic nature rather than professional. For example, she flirted with the young soldiers and sang a lullaby to one young man every night; she tucked the patients into their cots and turned out the lights. This maternal/romantic role suggested that the nurse's true value to these patients was to assuage their loneliness and homesickness, not a negligible responsibility but surely one that did not require several years of nursing education. In addition, Meg's reason for entering nursing, "to do something unselfish for the first time in my life," contributed to the idea that nursing is, per se, a self-sacrificing, self-effacing profession, one in which young women can do penance for past misdeeds. Despite these qualifications, Miss Wyman portrayed a sensitive, intelligent, mature young woman who served as a nurse and who did a lot of good for her patients.

Ford Theatre, another anthology drama series of the 1950s, began as a monthly series of live, hour-long dramatic plays in 1948. In 1952, the series became a filmed series of half-hour plays. One of these, which appeared in May 1956, entitled "Behind the Mask," featured a rather interesting story of a physician and the nurse who loved him.

The story opens as a stranger enters a small town pharmacy looking for George Robles, the local rich man and owner–operator of the area's main economic industry, an oil field. Very quickly in the course of the story, the stranger successfully performs an emergency appendectomy. At the conclusion of the surgical procedure, Norah, the nurse (Barbara Hale) arrives and immediately sees that the patient has survived the ordeal easily; she compliments the doctor, addressing him as Dr. Scott Stanley, an ex-Army physician, the name printed on his medical bag.

Everyone is impressed with Dr. Stanley's surgical feat, and soon Stanley is established as town doctor (head of a small hospital) with Norah as his nurse. She takes it upon herself to display his diplomas, which makes him angry; he suggests that she is suspicious of his identification. The nurse assures him that she is not suspicious of him; she lights his cigarette and flirts with him, fusses happily about her little nursing station, and takes a wifely tone with the pharmacist who has made a delivery. She obviously takes a proprietary interest in the doctor's business affairs, assuming herself to be a partner and hoping that she will soon be more than a partner.

Through a series of events, eventually it is discovered that "Dr. Scott" is in fact a former medic, Johnny Carter, who assumed the role of doctor in the army when the real "Dr. Scott" died. However, just as he confesses, Robles brings in his wife Alice who cannot breathe. Despite Norah's and Robles' shock, they plead with "Dr. Stanley" to do what he can because qualified medical help is so far away. Norah stops him from berating himself and offers to help him do the tracheotomy because she has seen it done many times before. The operation is a success; Johnny removes the obstruction and the patient's recovery is assured. Although Mr. Robles does not intend to press charges, Johnny knows that he will go to prison for practicing medicine without a license. However, he plans to become a doctor after prison, and Norah promises to wait for him.

This melodramatic and rather unconvincing story of a fraudulent doctor and the nurse who loves him presents Norah as a sympathetic and attractive young woman, but her subservient professional role to a man who is not even a doctor seems to reflect poorly upon her nursing expertise. Although it would be possible for a man to learn sufficient medical skills to pass himself off as a doctor for a while, it seems very odd that the nurse who worked closely with him would not notice that her physician employer was unfamiliar with routine hospital practices. Furthermore, at the critical point, when Alice Robles needed emergency surgery and Johnny announced his deceit, the nurse immediately offered to help him. Clearly she had more experience with the procedure than he, yet she offered to help him do a procedure with which he was unfamiliar. The point of view is clear: Even a fraudulent doctor is preferable to an experienced registered nurse. After the successful conclusion of the procedure, all the thanks and congratulations went to the fake doctor, and the nurse contributed to this adulation. In addition, Norah seemed more interested in pursuing the doctor than he did her. Rather than express even the slightest outrage at Johnny's endangering the lives of others because of his desire to be a physician, she immediately began defending him to himself and promised to wait for him while he spent his years in prison.

Thus, both professionally and personally, nurse Norah represented the ideal American woman of the 1950s: a handmaiden who puts her boyfriend/husband's interests above her own in all matters. As in so many shows of the decade, this image of nursing was meant to be positive, yet, in its assumptions about the proper role of women, it clearly indicated that nurses were at best loyal and self-sacrificing assistants to physicians.

The medical drama series, based on the exploits of one or two doctor-heroes surrounded by a regular sustaining cast, did not really find a niche in television schedules until the early 1960s with the introduction of *Ben Casey* and *Dr. Kildare*. However, three forerunners of the genre did make some impression on television audiences of the 1950s. Both *City Hospital* (CBS) and *The Doctor*

NBC) followed the established radio interpretation of the physician's role as a wise man rather than a skilled technician. *Medic* (NBC), which ran for two seasons, broke the mold of doctor-as-counselor and established the necessity of technical realism and accuracy that so informed all later medical dramas.

City Hospital premiered on CBS in March 1952 and ended in October 1963. The show was done simultaneously for television and radio; the radio series was already on the air in January 1952 and lasted for several years. Thematically, it fell somewhere between radio's famed *Dr. Christian* and the first real television medical show, *Medic*. The Dr. Christian formula emphasized the physician as a wise old man and counselor to his patients; Dr. Christian gave little evidence of expertise with newfangled medical technology and rarely used medical terminology. *Medic*, as will be seen below, introduced television audiences to the esoteric and highly complicated world of modern medicine, where doctors conversed in their own language and were technicians as well as wise men, while nurses were relatively unimportant and certainly less omnipotent. Dr. Barton Crane in *City Hospital* used convincing medical language, talked to specialists, recommended specific operations, and precisely identified diseases. However, his forte came from his ability to discover underlying emotional problems or suppressed fears or angers that affected the lives of both his patients and his friends. For example, in one episode Dr. Crane takes an interest in the engagement of his friend Dr. Don Burke to an attractive widow, Laura, who has a young daughter. Don admits to Crane that there are some problems despite their love. Ever since they decided to get married, Laura has become much more protective of her daughter, hesitant to trust her to Don's supervision, and reluctant to set a wedding date. The crisis is reached when the daughter develops an appendicitis, and Laura refuses to let Don, the hospital's best surgeon, do the operation. At this point Dr. Crane takes Laura aside and insists that she tell him the source of her conflict. Finally Laura reveals that she has unconsciously been equating Don with her late husband, a thoroughly immature and unreliable man. When she recognizes this fact and the fact that she really does consider Don mature and trustworthy, she allows him to do the surgery on her daughter; presumably Don and Laura will live happily thereafter.

The presentation of nursing was quite negligible in *City Hospital*. The largest nursing role occurred in a story about a physician accused of murdering his patient. An elderly woman patient of Dr. Sampson had entered the hospital for a gallbladder operation, but Sampson postponed the surgery in order to obtain a cardiac evaluation. The nurse, Miss Kirby, had been in the patient's room when she suffered a heart attack; Miss Kirby immediately went to fetch Dr. Sampson with the news of that attack; he took one look at the patient and sent the nurse for amyl nitrate. When Miss Kirby arrived with the drug, the patient had already died. In subsequent discussion of the incident a great deal was made of the fact that the physician was alone with the woman before her death and that the nurse could not confirm the doctor's diagnosis of heart disease. Although the nurse did not lie, she did nothing to help the physician's case. Furthermore, it was clear that Miss Kirby immediately doubted Sampson's integrity when she learned that the patient left a large bequest to the doctor and that the doctor had had recent financial reverses. In this very brief presentation of a nurse, the writers developed her as an easily suggestible woman who could be manipulated into offering testimony that might hurt the physician. Furthermore, the nurse was not shown as having much skill or expertise. Although she did recognize an attack, she did nothing to initiate emergency treatment; rather, she left the patient in order to search for the doctor. Her only tasks were to fetch items. In all, the nurse seemed to be a very limited health professional, unable to act on her own in the most negligible tasks. In none of the other episodes, did the nurse play any role at all; occasionally a doctor might tell Miss X to make a phone call or to carry out some other trivial matter for him.

The Doctor appeared on NBC from August 1952 until June 1953, and reran in syndication in 1956. Each drama centered on situations of high emotional stress rather than on physical ailments. Warner Anderson, the host-narrator, not only discussed each story's theme before and after the drama but also starred in a few of the episodes. Aside from Anderson, all the other actors and actresses in *The Doctor* changed from week to week. The dramatic conflict in these stories apparently arose from hidden or unknown emotional problems, much as those dealt with by Dr. Crane on *City Hospital*.

In 1954 NBC introduced the first popular health care series, a thirty-minute dramatic anthology series entitled *Medic*. The series combined a carefully researched documentary style with uneven dramatic production. Richard Boone as Dr. Konrad Styner introduced each episode and occasionally appeared in the narrative. Usually, however, the series presented totally different casts. The only continuity in the series was provided by the medical theme and the creative force of James Moser who researched and wrote many of the episodes. Moser first distinguished himself by writing for the Jack Webb production *Dragnet;* both *Medic* and *Dragnet* emphasized that stories were taken from actual case histories and, through the use of voice-over narration, presented a rather documentary approach to the subject at hand.

This first medical television drama established standards of realism and accuracy that have rarely been matched in later health care series. Each episode was carefully scrutinized by a special committee of physicians and given the imprimatur of the Los Angeles chapter of the American Medical Association. Many scenes were shot on location in California hospitals, and real nurses and physicians appeared in background scenes. The show included footage of a thoracotomy, and a caesarean section. This last ("The Glorious Red Gallegher," March 12, 1956) offended the sensibilities of the sponsor, and the network did not try to resell advertising for the series; the show died after two successful seasons.

The central theme of *Medic* was the reverential portrayal of physicians as the new priests of the modern world. Each episode began with a dedication to the physician, "Guardian of Birth . . . Healer of the Sick . . . Comforter of the Aged," and described the qualities of the worthy physician as three: "the eye of an eagle, the heart of a lion, and the hand of a woman." Physicians appeared as the repository of wisdom and the only sure guides through the unintelligible world of disease and modern miracle cures. Several episodes dealt with historical tributes to medical heroism or milestones in medical research. Still, although the portrayed physicians almost always saved their patients, the series did not present the physician in the superheroic, omniscient terms that characterized later health care dramas.

Although *Medic* was remarkably realistic and covered unattractive topics with an honesty not usually associated with the world of dramatized medicine, many aspects of the show's philosophy revealed it to be very much a product of its time, especially in its attitude toward women. No episode ever featured a female physician in a prominent role. In general women characters seemed weaker and less rational than did the male characters. For example, in the show which examined the case of a forty-five year old woman experiencing the symptoms associated with menopause, the woman's attending physician, Dr. Konrad Styner, lectured the distraught patient against looking at her condition the "way you women used to." Never once did he attempt to elicit the woman's feelings or fears. He decided immediately that he knew what she was feeling and how best to treat her. This female character was cherished by her family, portrayed sympathetically, and yet somehow she was treated as an inferior.

Nurses who appeared in *Medic* ranged in age from the early twenties to the early sixties and were not exceptionally pretty, although they were generally attractive, neatly dressed, and well groomed. Nurses were never used as romantic foils or as objects of sexual jokes and comments. Moreover, the physicians almost always treated the nurses respectfully, even formally. For example, Dr. Styner called his office nurse of many years, "Miss Mitchell." When seen in the background, nurses appeared to be handing instruments in surgery, preparing blood for transfusion, charting and doing paper work at the nursing station, transporting patients, and carrying trays in the hallway. In most of the episodes, nurses contributed very little to the dramatic narrative or to the resolution of a patient's problem. Two episodes specifically addressed the role of nursing in modern health care: "The Glorious Red Gallegher" and "Mercy Wears An Apron."

"The Glorious Red Gallegher," which contained the offending segment of a caesarean section, was timed to coincide with the 100th anniversary of the origin of modern nursing. The producers chose a charming elderly actress, Hope Emerson, to play the lead role of an Irish-brogued obstetrical nurse facing retirement at age 61. This nurse, Clara Mary Gallegher, was meant to personify the best traditions in the nursing profession. Toward the end of the show, Konrad Styner narrated a moving passage about the value of nurses:

> For the next 24 to 48 hours the patient will require constant and expert nursing care and so will her newborn son . . . . Youth and adult alike are staking their lives on the knowledge, skill, and efficiency of the figure in white who attends them, the registered nurse. Clara Mary Gallegher is one of these . . . typical, not at all, for the task of nursing is not limited to a single ward, or a single hospital, or even a single climate. But Clara Gallegher in her instinctive compassion for a body broken or diseased, her complete and utter devotion to the care of the sick must be typical of the young and constant courage that gave birth to a new pledge and rebirth to an old profession on a battlefield in the Crimea, exactly one hundred years ago almost to the month. The profession is nursing. The pledge is the Florence Nightingale oath. The words are simple and unassuming, yet uttered by a hundred voices they have a hundred meanings. For vows such as these did not flourish in sound or on the printed page but only in action. The truth and substance of the pledge lie within the person and can be various as the human heart and mind and body are various.

Despite the laudatory nature of this homage to nursing, the virtues that were emphasized in the narrative were the traditional qualities of self-sacrifice, generosity, and comfort. Clara Mary Gallegher, while totally sympathetic, served primarily as a substitute mother/grandmother for her patients. Her final act as a nurse was that of self-sacrifice: she gave up her retirement travel plans in favor of sheltering a homeless mother and babe.

"Mercy Wears an Apron" presented a different side of the nursing profession: public health nursing. This episode, which told the story of a public health nurse's contributions to a paraplegic's rehabilitation, featured a nurse acting autonomously (though the narrative made it clear that the nurse was working under a physician's orders). The image of the profession was quite positive, with the nurse given all the credit for the man's eventual return to an active, normal life. However, this single episode might be important because of its uniqueness. Other presentations of nurses in the series were less glowing.

The writers of *Medic* clearly intended to characterize nurses as valuable members of the health care delivery system; but they valued the age-old attributes of the nurse as a maternal comforter and handmaiden of the physician. The profession of nursing was a noble calling because it required self-abnegation, humility, generosity, and charitable deeds from its members.

Situation comedies of the 1950s rarely dealt with medical problems; perhaps it was not considered in good taste to associate humor with medicine. Only *Hennessey*, which appeared from 1959 to 1963, combined a medical format with a humorous situation, and even in this show the comic elements of the plots rarely touched issues of medical practice. Three nurse characters did appear in successful comedies: Nancy Remington of *Mr. Peepers,* Martha Hale of *Hennessey,* and Donna Stone of *The Donna Reed Show*.

The typical *Peepers* plot featured the hero engaged in often quixotic ventures.

The humor of *Peepers* apparently resided in Wally Cox's (as Peepers) meek, self-effacing manners which often belied a soul and heart of heroic dimensions. Most plots revolved around ordinary events or situations made humorous by Peepers' reactions. For example, one plot from 1954 found the biologist to be the object of affection of a rare butterfly. Another found Peepers attending a friend's wedding in the wrong type of suit. The third and final year of the series featured the domestic life of Peepers and his new bride, the former Nancy Remington, school nurse. In fact, the wedding of Peepers and Nancy was one of the first media events: Newspapers and magazines ran photographs of the couple in formal wedding attire and printed mock formal invitations to the wedding. Thereafter, the young couple's search for an apartment, their in-law troubles, and other such marital problems constituted the main thematic material.

Mr. Peepers and Nancy had a long-standing romance before the third year. However, the school nurse's role in the series was as Peepers' girlfriend only. She almost never received attention as an individual or in a professional capacity, and Nancy's role as school nurse contributed little to the plot development. For example, the episode of April 25, 1954 entitled "The Engagement," in which Nancy and Peepers became engaged, while portraying Nancy in the school setting, never even uses the word nurse, and there is no indication as to what Nancy's work at the school is.

The image of nursing as projected by Nancy Remington would have reinforced other nursing images of the 1950s. Nurses were kind, sweet, and marriage oriented. In addition, Nancy apparently projected a naivete and innocence which made her the perfect match for Peepers' mildly bumbling persona. Patricia Benoit, who played Nancy Remington, looked to be in her early twenties, had short dark hair, and seemed to be the typical, wholesome girl next door who still lived with her parents.

In *The Donna Reed Show* probably only the most attentive and loyal fans knew that Donna Stone had been a registered nurse prior to her marriage to Dr. Alex Stone, pediatrician. In the over 274 thirty-minute episodes of the series, Donna's nursing identification appeared in only a handful of installments. During the eight year run of the series on ABC, Donna spent most of her time catering to the whims of a boyishly handsome husband and two attractive yet problem-prone teenagers. *The Donna Reed Show* followed in the tradition of *Father Knows Best* and *Ozzie and Harriet* in its presentation of strong, happy, middle-American family life. The show focused on Donna's aptitude and wiles in dealing with her family's problems. Her feminine intuition played a great part in her success, and her sensitivity as a mother often made Alex's years of experience in pediatrics fade into insignificance. On many occasions Donna shared her successful strategies in the battle of the sexes with her daughter Mary, who often needed her mother's help in learning how to attract a boy's attention or in landing an important date. Alex apparently never hired a nurse or secretary to help in his practice. On at least two occasions Donna became involved in his practice by trying to collect overdue accounts. Once she substituted for her husband's office nurse although the nurse had never previously appeared nor did she later appear. In one episode Mary identified her mother to a reporter who was interested in a story on the successful motherhood of Mrs. Stone, "graduate nurse." However, Donna's nursing background seemed to have no bearing on her activities as a wife and mother; that is, there were no suggestions that her nursing education prepared her for motherhood or helped her to cope with solving the problems of her family. Her skills as wife and mother were firmly imbedded in her compassionate nature and feminine intuition. Donna operated on illogical and even irrational motives that stemmed from her emotions; yet she succeeded in winning her point more often than did her husband who argued his side logically and rationally. If perspicacious viewers did think of her as a former nurse, they would have had to conclude that in the late 1950s a nurse easily gave up her nursing career for the more challenging role of wife and mother coping with the washing machine and the children's predicaments. They would also have had to note that former nurses could be formidable problem-solvers and go-getters because of their feminine intuition and charming ways.

The last series of the decade that featured a nurse character was the Jackie Cooper production *Hennessey,* which starred Cooper as an unassuming physician and naval lieutenant based in San Diego; Abby Dalton co-starred as a nurse, Lieutenant Martha Hale, who worked in Hennessey's dispensary. Lieutenant Charles J. "Chick" Hennessey appeared as a boyish, fallible, nervous, and, at times, confused young doctor. The three year series, 1959 to 1962, revolved around the often ill-fated experiences of Lieutenant Hennessey as he became involved with naval base personnel or other characters whom fate or his Commanding Officer, Captain Shafer, threw in his path. He might have lacked self-confidence in a situation, but he never failed to provide counsel or sympathy to those in need. The regular characters in this series also included Martha Hale who served as Chick's sidekick, girlfriend, and all-around helpmate, described by one of the producers as "an honest, straightforward nurse type with a kind of antiseptic attractiveness for men." Nurse Hale, although fond of Hennessey and even of Captain Shafer (the superior officer), never let an opportunity pass to prove her feminine prowess at outwitting them. The storylines varied from nearly slapstick situations in which Hennessey faced improbable problems that demanded extraordinary solutions to more thoughtful shows in which Chick exercised his considerable compassion and goodwill on behalf of a needy friend. The only change in the format of the series came in the final season when the romance between Chick and Martha picked up steam, culminating in their wedding at the end of the season.

Critical and popular response to the series was favorable; by mid-season of the first year, *Hennessey* ranked ninth in the Nielsens (*Dennis the Menace* was first). The show's attraction probably was due to Cooper's winning portrayal of the bumbling yet boyish Hennessey. For example, in "Hennessey and the Lady Doctor," Hennessey had to host a female psychologist's visit to the base; the most humorous scene occurred when Chick could not get his jeep out of the golf course. He was typically ineffectual, and Schafer was typically disgruntled. Again, Chick's confrontation with the lady psychologist fulfilled the viewer's expectation of the boyish and innocent Cooper/Hennessey's inability to handle the aggressive, sophisticated woman. His predictable failure, not his comic lines, generated the humor. Stereotypical actions and reactions delivered by the regular characters were the meat and potatoes of the series. Martha Hale, the pert, bright, Navy nurse, depended upon the battle of the sexes humor prevalent in the 1950s for her character's contribution to the comedy; she sought to prove female intuition triumphant over male logic. The image of nursing in *Hennessey* rested upon the character of Martha Hale; only on a few occasions did other nurse characters enter the storyline.

"Scarlet Woman in White" featured a young, pretty nurse who interpreted her nursing role with a great deal of sexual connotation. The network censors worried about the character's sexually suggestive conversations with several men characters and about the identification of sexually provocative behavior with the nursing profession. In an exchange of letters between the network and the sponsor's representatives, the sponsors made clear that they did not want to offend the nursing profession by suggesting that nurses typically behaved in sexually provocative ways, but the show still presented a highly unfavorable image of the nursing profession. In this episode, a recent nursing school graduate, flirtatious, cooing Harriet Barnes (Yvonne Craig), had attracted many admirers in one of the hospital wards, and some men beg Hennessey not to discharge them. Chick alone doesn't fall for her flirtation, especially when he observes that another nurse, dowdy Ethel Peterson, has been hurt and humiliated by all the attention given to Harriet. Martha Hale informs Chick that all the nurses are talking about Harriet's carrying on and are expressing only petty and jealous thoughts about the offending nurse. Ethel comes to Chick for sympathy and to request a transfer. Chick hints to Harriet that she should change her ways, to no avail. A more direct confrontation with the nurse succeeds, and in the course of their discussion Hennessey learns that Harriet behaved outrageously because she felt she was ignorant. All ended well, when Chick brought about the needed change in Harriet's demeanor. When Shafer sees the reformed Harriet with longer skirts and less suggestive hairstyle, he mutters, "Why did you do it, boy?" Martha, curious and jealous about Chick's involvement with Harriet, tricked the two doctors into thinking that Harriet might have poisoned some candy sent in gratitude for Chick's advice. In all, the nurses appeared to be gossip-ridden, ineffectual, jealous, petty women who relied on a physician to set a young nurse straight. Nowhere in the episode was it suggested that the profession had certain standards which Harriet was flouting or that any nursing supervisors took an interest in the young girl's actions.

Even without this pointed although unintentional negative image of nursing, the character of Martha Hale repeatedly reinforced the idea that nurses were jealous, illogical, and manipulative. Martha Hale worked with Chick in the dispensary, but her role never involved her in patient care. She faithfully checked charts, fetched records, or handed over a syringe, but the viewer never found her doing skilled work or really contributing to a patient's health. Although Martha was an attractive, healthy looking, California blonde who was intelligent and unafraid of showing it, more often than not she displayed her intelligence in making sassy retorts which would burst the pretentions of Shafer or Chick. However, when Martha did contribute to someone's welfare it was usually by dint of her feminine intuition. Although Martha did not play the scatterbrained "Lucy Riccardo" type of woman, she did primarily use her wits and charm and illogical female strategies to disarm the men around her. Chick emerged as the only consistent problem solver in the series; his sympathy and openmindedness attracted others to him. No one sought Martha for help; she only became involved as an assistant to Chick, even though at times she outwitted him. The viewer probably found Martha Hale an attractive, sympathetic character and concluded that good nursing was based on feminine intuition, and that nurses were typically full of guile and charm.

In addition to these major nurse characters in situation comedy series of the 1950s, nurses appeared in non-medical comedy shows too. For example, in an episode of *Amos 'n Andy,* entitled "Hospitalization," nurses appeared in the background of a hospital sequence. Of course, *Amos 'n Andy,* sympathetically remembered by nostalgia buffs and with shuddering horror by civil libertarians, kept firmly focused upon its regular cast of characters, with very little attention fixed upon incidental characters; thus the role of nursing in this episode was very slight indeed.

The plot of "Hospitalization" revolves around one of George "Kingfish" Stevens' frequent schemes to make money and lands Andy in a hospital through a series of comic events. Though the story takes place within a hospital setting, no nurse appeared anywhere in this episode, except in the background. The nurses were used as a source of sexual interest. Calhoun finds himself almost eager for hospitalization when he sees the nurses. The dominant, albeit limited, image of nurses was that they provide romantic interludes for hospitalized patients. The only positive note about the nurses in this episode was that they were all black, as was the physician. Although *Amos 'n Andy* may have been offensive and totally unrealistic in its presentation of black Americans, at least it was consistent and presented a black community replete with black doctors, lawyers, nurses, and businessmen.

In summary, it might be noted that nurse characters on television in the 1950s were never intentionally distorted. Unlike more current television imagery, nurses of the 1950s never appeared to be sexually experienced or promiscuous. The great attention given to the character of Harriet Barnes in "Scarlet Woman in White" as late as 1959 indicated a high degree of concern with maintaining a positive moral image of the profession. Nurses such as Martha Hale on *Hennessey*, Nancy Remington on *Mr. Peepers,* and Donna Stone on the *Donna Reed Show,* had romantic or nearly romantic relationships with male protagonists, but the explicit sexual contact between these nurses and their boyfriends/husbands stayed within the strict boundaries of television morality; the maximum sexual contact was limited to brief, passionless kisses infrequently exchanged. No "linen closet" jokes were made about nurses, and none of the series or episodes implied that nurses were anything but proper ladies.

More often than not, nurses in the 1950s shows were portrayed as sympathetic women and good nurses, but the qualities lauded almost always came from the traditional womanly treasurehouse of virtue: Good nurses were intuitive, sympathetic, empathetic, self-sacrificing, self-effacing, generous, and comforting. Although occasional references were made to a nurse's education and skill, as for example in *Medic,* the actual depicted nurses revealed few skills. Nurses were never portrayed as dumb, uneducated, or inarticulate, but neither were they admired for their academic or professional qualifications. Nurse characters often gave up their profession for marriage and family. Donna Stone quit the profession after marriage; undoubtedly Martha Hale quit nursing after marrying Chick for in the late 1950s two naval officers could not be married. One suspects that marriage spelled the end of Nancy Remington's career as a school nurse. Producers rarely presented real portraits of a modern nursing practice. Lines of authority between nurses never emerged. Often physicians handled nursing-related problems. Perhaps worse than this aspect of the presentation of nursing, nurse characters rarely appeared to be friends with each other. For example, on *Medic,* in "All My Fathers, All My Mothers," dissension arose among the nurses on the floor with regard to the treatment of the little girl patient; the supervising nurse had harsher, more disciplinarian approaches to the child's care, yet never exercised any authority over the other nurses. "The Glorious Red Gallegher" did show an older nurse sharing some confidences with a younger nurse, but given the nurse's nearly legendary service and dedication, there was no indication of nurses getting together to celebrate her retirement after forty years as a nurse. The worst impression of relations among nurses appeared on the *Hennessey* episode, "Scarlet Woman in White," when the nurses engaged in vicious gossip about a fellow nurse and seemed unable to deal with the nurse's flouting of nursing standards.

Some contrasts to this feminine, domestic image of nursing did occur. The documentary-style films shown on some of the short-lived series such as *Medical Horizons* and *March of Medicine* briefly depicted the real work of nurses. Occasionally *Medic* included shots of nurses doing skilled tasks and receiving credit for intelligent judgments and decisions. Often local child care programs featured nurses speaking intelligently upon questions of pediatric health; of course this further associated nursing with motherhood and domestic concerns. On balance, nurses on television in the 1950s appeared to be wholesome and intelligent women who demonstrated the best if stereotyped features of femininity.

2
The Freezing of an Image, 1960s

After the controversial cancellation of *Medic* in 1956, the networks waited a good five years before attempting another prime-time health care drama. This time they hit pay dirt with the popular *Ben Casey* (ABC) and *Dr. Kildare* (NBC). In the euphoria of success, programmers attempted to capitalize upon the newly found medical mania by introducing other health care or hospital theme dramas, yet none of the other series could be judged an unqualified success. CBS, left out of the first season's winnings, aired *The Nurses* in 1962. Both NBC and ABC developed psychologically oriented spin-off series from their hit shows: *The Eleventh Hour* (NBC) and *Breaking Point* (ABC). Although neither *The Nurses* nor the two psychology dramas achieved the success of *Ben Casey* and *Dr. Kildare*, they did make their mark upon television audiences, and some of them received good critical response. The only situation comedy with a medical–nursing theme to premiere in the 1960s was *Julia*, remembered more for its use of a black leading lady than for the quality of its production.

The most influential purveyors of the image of modern hospital life, medicine, and nursing in the 1960s were the twin doctor shows, *Ben Casey* and *Dr. Kildare*, with their respective heroes, Vince Edwards and Richard Chamberlain. In their heyday—1961 to 1965—these programs engendered a classic U.S. fad, with all the marketing hoopla including Ben Casey shirts and jokes and publicity campaigns associated with money-making items. Reporters and gossip columnists hankered after every word uttered by the taciturn Edwards and took great delight in repeating the story of his childhood in a tough Brooklyn neighborhood and his years of struggle as an aspiring actor. These same reporters wrote saccharine sweet articles on Richard Chamberlain, assuring his many fans that he was just as squeaky clean in person as he was on the small screen.

The predecessor for the *Kildare* series came from a group of successful MGM feature films of the 1930s, and *Ben Casey* probably grew out of producer James Moser's experience with his earlier series, *Medic* (1954–1956). Yet the producers of these series really followed the same set of values as portrayed and appreciated in the television western; the western drama may have been recently and temporarily abandoned in the early 1960s, but television had not forgotten the public's love for a western hero—a loner, with few material or human ties, on an eternal quest for justice. The atmosphere found in the settings—California hospitals—resembled the western frontier in that they were worlds apart, isolated from routine society and civilization and ruled by their own peculiar laws. The Grim Reaper stalked the corridors, and Ben/Jim, using his knowledge and skills rather than a six-gun, challenged him to a shoot-out once a week.

Both *Ben Casey* and *Dr. Kildare* relied upon the wise old mentor/idealistic young doctor format as the vehicle for transmitting thematic information. The older physician was often the voice of values, ethics, or moral questions involved. For example, in a two-part episode of *Dr. Kildare* from the third season ("Tyger, Tyger"), the young doctor fell in love with an epileptic surfer. The girl thrived on challenge and danger, and Jim compared her to the Tiger in William Blake's poem. Rather than let the viewer recognize any symbolism or character development associated with the poem, early on in the story the writers had Gillespie interpret for Kildare the submerged premise of the poem: "... not to interfere with nature."

The main differences between the two series were based in the personalities of the two protagonists. Ben Casey was a brooding, arrogant, angry chief resident in neurosurgery. His choice of specialties emphasized his personality; as a surgeon, he cut into the problems of his patients and preferred radical, definitive handling of those problems. Ben Casey was self-confident and intolerant and he bullied reluctant patients into accepting his prescribed treatments and recalcitrant physicians into seeing things his way. The wishes of a patient or his family carried little weight with this neurosurgeon who alone knew the best and only course of treatment.

Richard Chamberlain as Dr. Kildare, played first an intern and later a resident in internal medicine. The combination of his lesser experience and his choice of specialties allowed Kildare a greater scope of emotional reactions to incidents and health problems. Kildare did not always immediately know the right answers and often became emotionally involved in his attempt to find the right answer for a patient or friend. Kildare used gentle reasoning and charm rather than angry denunciations to persuade. Kildare was not above light-hearted frolics and fun and, unlike Casey, he often engaged in personal relationships with both colleagues and patients.

Despite these important differences, the two series shared a similar intention: to idealize the role of the physician in society. Both Zorba and Gillespie pontificated upon the responsibilities and sacrifices required of doctors; both series made frequent reference to the great financial sacrifices involved in becoming a doctor; both downplayed the doctor's future earning power. The young protagonists appeared to be ubiquitous, almost always on-duty and living at the hospital, and both series tended to downplay the role of nursing in a modern hospital. There were some differences between the two series, however, in their treatment of nursing and nurse characters. In general, *Dr. Kildare* presented nurse characters more frequently than did *Ben Casey* but often with less than desirable characteristics. When either of the shows did use a nurse as a featured character, her conflicts were almost always personal rather than professional. None of the mechanics of a nursing service in a large urban hospital ever emerged in the context of an episode; the nurses were simply present with whatever task they were seen doing, with no identification of their rank, specialty, or education.

The treatment of nurses and the image of nursing in *Ben Casey* could not be judged as positive. Although nurses were never disparaged or insulted on the show, the minimal attention given the role of nursing in a series set within the confines of a large general hospital was enough to persuade the viewer that nurses did very little and made no perceptible contribution to the welfare and recovery of patients. Out of 153 episodes, only ten featured nurse characters other than the ubiquitous and colorless Miss Wills. Of these ten, only six prominently featured nurse characters; in almost none of these cases were the nurses characterized as valuable professionals or good problem-solvers.

In "A Disease of the Heart Called Love," nurse Lydia Mitchum (Shelley Winters), an unmarried woman in her 40s, discovered herself to be pregnant. Lydia was a well-respected, beloved nurse at the hospital, on a first-name basis with the physicians, but she was also a lonely divorcee with few contacts outside her work. The father of her child was a playboy-type resident named Charlie. When she developed pre-eclampsia, she was rushed into the hospital emergency room where, for some reason, neurosurgeons Zorba and Casey advised her on her obstetrical condition and recommended that she terminate the pregnancy. Lydia refused. Later, Casey tried to convince Lydia to give up the baby for adoption and she agreed—work and motherhood were described as irreconcilable. In a dramatic climax, Lydia delivered prematurely and nearly died. Upon her recovery she changed her mind and decided to keep her baby.

The image of nursing from this episode suggested that nurses derive no self-esteem from their careers, and that their careers are incompatible with a fulfilling role as a mother. Lydia overcame her own feelings of inferiority and asserted her right to keep her child, although the motivation for this change of heart was rather unclear. For a conventional, conservative divorcee of the early 1960s to keep an illegitimate child would have required extraordinary self-confidence and courage—precisely what Lydia had lacked all her life. By the end of the episode, Lydia emerged as a strong individual, but the viewer remained ignorant of the source of her strength. She did not receive inspiration from her lover or her friends, and she had no past history of self-assertion. In all, the character was sympathetic, but she did little to enhance the image of nursing.

Throughout the Casey episodes, nurses were doomed to disaster which Casey straightened out. In "Goodbye to Blue Elephants and Such," a nursing student who was sexually assaulted could not identify her attacker as a result of amnesia associated with the shock of the event. In "Imagine a Long Bright Corridor," Ben had to prove his mettle to veteran nurse Phelps of the nighttime emergency room. In "Light Up the Dark Corners," a nurse fell in love with a terminally ill patient. Predictably in these episodes, Ben would bully and argue with the nurse if she seemed remiss in her duties or if she misinterpreted her obligations. In none did a nurse character exhibit self-control or the ability to handle her own problems.

In a few other episodes, nurse characters contributed slightly to plot development. In "Kill the Dream, But Spare the Dreamer," a beautiful nurse, in love with her physician–employer for years, begged Ben to help the man. Her true love, the doctor, refused to marry her because, as he said in a bit of memorable *Ben Casey* dialogue:

> I was married to a nurse, just like you. And she was a romantic, dedicated dreamer, just like you. (Pause) Sure. They say it's good for a doctor to marry a nurse because she understands what a difficult life a doctor has. . . . She's supposed to understand the long hours, and the failure and the death. (Pause) Well, that's unadulterated bunk.

Thus was an entire profession dismissed as a group of romantic, dedicated dreamers who could not even fulfill their divine mission—to make understanding wives for physicians.

The nurses appeared to be attractive young women who wore very neat, tailored, and well-fitting uniforms, although the uniforms were not designed to emphasize sex appeal. Occasionally their sex appeal was enhanced by tight fitting sweaters and suggestive sounding dialogue, but these characteristics appeared when the nurses were off duty. ("A Few Brief Lines for Dave"). Despite their physical charms, the nurses never attracted the romantic interest of the regular physicians on the staff. Ben never had a romantic involvement with a nurse, although he had them with nearly every other type of female professional: physician, reporter, social worker, biochemist, ballerina, school teacher, and lots of rich young socialites.

Nurses seen in the background of *Ben Casey* performed very unspecific actions, although they usually appeared to be working at something. In one episode a nurse sat at a desk outside Zorba's office and acted as a secretary. The most common props given nurses were clipboards and trays (medication, equipment, even food)). The viewer never knew exactly what the nurses jotted down on their clipboards, but they were assiduous in doing so. None of the machinery of a nursing service ever appeared in the series; that is, no head nurses, supervisors, nursing directors, rotation schedules, nursing rounds, or shift changes were ever noted. Typical of this unspecific identification of nursing duties and of the scant attention paid nurses was the characterization of Miss Wills (played by Jeanne Bates), the only regular nurse character who appeared in nearly every episode throughout the five year run of the series. Miss Wills was always on duty—day or night, rain or shine. The cynic might conclude that the producers decided to save money by using one all-purpose nurse for multiple low level tasks.

Miss Wills was totally nondescript. In five years of programming, the viewer never heard her first name. She was in her late thirties to early forties, blond, attractive and friendly, but not sexy, sophisticated, or overly intellectual. She always appeared in uniform, even at a staff party where everyone else was in street clothing. She always acted quickly and competently but never on her own. Occasionally she smiled, but she never laughed. She might become annoyed, but never angry. Ben and Zorba treated her respectfully but never solicited her opinion or behaved in a friendly, informal manner with her. At times Miss Wills went out of her way to do Ben a favor. For example, in "Pas de Deux" she and other staff members surprised Ben with an impromptu farewell to his departure for San Francisco for a medical convention.

In general, the nurses on *Ben Casey* were treated as attractive and respectable emissaries of the physicians. Ben often sought help or counsel from his mentor Zorba, but it would never have occurred to him to find help from a nurse. He simply gave them orders, usually politely. Nor did the nurses seem to have their own world of nursing matters. Nurses rarely interacted; Miss Wills seemed to have no friend on the nursing staff; Lydia Mitchell in her time of woe never sought friendship or help from another nurse, but instead went to Ben, Maggie, or Zorba. Nurses rarely gave orders to other nurses or to orderlies, and there was no apparent hierarchy among them, except perhaps between students, volunteers, and the registered nurses.

The image of nursing certainly received no positive support from this series, but then neither did women in general. Dr. Maggie Graham, the attractive and kind anesthesiologist who was mildly attracted to Ben, never achieved the status of her male colleagues. The viewer never had a sense of Maggie's duties beyond answering Ben's calls for anesthesia. With the exception of the operating room sequences, Maggie stood around the nursing station waiting for Ben to say something. Most young females who appeared as patients fell immediately in love with Ben, and many women set their hearts on marrying the elusive neurosurgeon. Very few intelligent, assertive, confident women appeared in any of the episodes reviewed. While if nurses were ignored and misrepresented in the series, the misrepresentation appeared to stem from the writers' more general assumptions about women.

The *Dr. Kildare* series often favored nurses with small bits of dialogue, either between nurses or with a physician or patient; however, their tasks patterned those in *Ben Casey:* emissary and handmaiden duties. Nurses did lots of observing from corners of treatment rooms, a good deal of walking in the hallways, and plenty of standing at the nursing station. They did very little identifiable work and no tasks involving professional discretion or decision making. A few nurse characters appeared recurrently on the show: Nurse Fain (Jean Innes); Nurse Conant (Jo Helton); and Nurse Springer (Lee Meriweather). In the first year, at least six nurse characters were given supporting actress roles; in the second year, eleven nurses were so featured. In the third year, twelve nurses were featured; and in the fourth year, eighteen nurse characters received such cast credits. In the final year, in addition to the almost weekly appearance of Nurse Zoe Lawton (Lee Kurty), Kildare's romantic interest, at least ten additional nurse characters were given some small roles in the episodes.

Generally the nurses were quite young (18 to 25) or in their mid-forties or older, giving the impression that women in their late twenties and thirties abandoned nursing to marry and bear children. The identification badges of many of the older nurses bore "Miss" rather than "Mrs.," implying that the older nurses never had the opportunity to have families, and that many young nurses who did become mothers never went back to nursing. The nursing students and young registered nurses were, without exception, very pretty, while the older nurses were quite prim but usually attractive. Female doctors appeared in some of the episodes, and although they were as pretty as the nurses, they looked more serious and intelligent. One female medical student wore glasses and her hair pulled back to the nape of her neck; none of the nurse characters affected such disciplined hairdos.

Some of the images of nursing, although secondary to the storyline, were quite negative. Often the nurse seemed unsophisticated and intellectually stunted. In "To Walk in Grace" two nurses, cutely identified as "Currier and Ives," gossipped and discussed a romatic novel; one later called Dr. Kildare a "dreamboat." Kildare discovered them chatting and reprimanded them for reading drivel. In a four-part episode from the last year, Nurse Horgan disapproved of a patient, a professional billiards player, and she let her self-righteous opinions be known to all around her. Miss Paulson in "An Ungodly Act" was portrayed as a stereotypical middle-aged spinster who was frustrated, petty, and even vindictive. She thoroughly disapproved of pretty nurse Leah's budding romance with Kildare, but worst of all she refused to admit a dying child to the hospital.

Occasionally a positive image of nursing emerged within the context of an individual episode. For example, in "Quid Pro Quo" a staff nurse accompanied intern Tomlinson in his first examination of an asthmatic patient; she noted the intern's growing panic while she remained quite calm. The intern assumed the patient to be dying and hastily summoned Dr. Kildare. When Dr. Kildare entered the treatment room, he winked at the nurse, assuming she knew the patient to be in no danger, and she suppressed a smile. In this same episode, a nurse reviewed the blood sugar findings on a patient and realized that the report had to be inaccurate; her assessment of the report saved a patient from receiving the wrong treatment. In "A Sense of Tempo" a retired nurse had returned to work because of a short-term emergency; Mrs. Margolis was described as an efficient and compassionate woman, able to anticipate a patient's needs. One patient remarked: "I have a growing suspicion that Mrs. Margolis might be telepathic." Indeed, that was exactly what she turned out to be. Because she was such a competent and compassionate nurse, she was treated with a good deal of respect and affection by the physicians. Gillespie even called her by her first name, and she felt free to discuss her patients with him. Mrs. Margolis, like nurse Lydia on *Ben Casey,* was portrayed as a special case of being a nurse deemed worthy of friendship with doctors.

Although young Dr. Kildare was usually respectful and friendly with the nurses, he also treated them with a certain condescension. For example, in "Do You Trust Your Doctor?" Kildare snapped at a nurse when he ordered her to summon a physician; she started to question his order but he cut her off and crisply told her: "Just do it please!"

Before the last season, most of Kildare's serious romantic interests were with such non-nurse characters as a pretty surfer, a Roman aristocrat, and a divorced businesswoman. In the final year, when the producers wanted to create a permanent romance for the handsome doctor, they naturally chose a nurse because of the ease of introducing her into many of Kildare's professional interests. Zoe Lawton, R.N. (Lee Kurty) supposedly worked as a head nurse at Blair General Hospital, although her responsibilities seemed no different from other Blair nurses—taking messages, running errands, and the like. Because of her close involvement with Kildare, she did discuss patients' medical and personal problems with him on several occasions, but she never made much of a contribution to the outcome of a patient's condition. The only professional action she seemed to take with regard to a patient's welfare occurred in the four-part episode "Fathers and Daughters" in which she carefully supervised a prizefighter's first steps after a long confinement to bed; she seemed to keep a close eye on this patient's movements. There was no indication that she had outlined a systematic program for this patient's therapy, but she did seem responsible for his movements.

Zoe's most important contribution to the image of nursing was her attractive appearance. Her blond hair was cut in a pert, pixyish style; she had dark eyes, straight white teeth, and a curvaceous figure—a typical California girl for the typical California boy. She was reputed to be a good nurse, and her identification as Head Nurse at a relatively young age—about 25—marked her as a successful woman. Most of her interactions with Kildare consisted of lighthearted, romantic banter. Kildare's interest in Zoe rarely became intense. His earlier flings seemed to embroil him in much more serious soul searching about his identity and his purpose in life. Apparently Zoe, being a nurse, posed no problems for Kildare because she fit so easily into his established life and professional role. In one four-part episode, "A Few Hearts, A Few Flowers," Zoe did become infatuated with an exciting playboy–author (Ricardo Moltalban) and this caused Kildare some restless moments and perhaps a little jealousy.

There were at least twelve episodes of *Dr. Kildare* which featured nurses as protagonists. Representative of them was an episode entitled "The Exploiters" from the third season. This story described the difficult relationship between nurse Jean Dennis and her lower class family. Jean's only complaint about nursing was that it did not pay enough to allow her to send her brother to medical school. She seemed content enough with her choice and was reputed to be an efficient and compassionate nurse, but she noted that her brother, who wanted to be a physician, was the only member of her family with a chance to make something of himself, suggesting that nursing was inferior to medicine. In a family crisis about money, Jean became increasingly upset and Drs. Kildare and Gillespie provided the needed sympathy and generosity to help her through her family crisis. None of the other nurses seemed capable of giving Jean the support she needed.

The producers and writers of these two series probably did not intend to malign the nursing profession or to slight the contribution of nurses to patient welfare. However, in order to keep the dramatic focus on Kildare and Casey, the stories simply ignored the role of nursing in modern hospital life. In addition, the attitude toward women in general relegated female characters to the position of dependent, weak, problem-prone types who offered great opportunities for the heroes to display their problem-solving expertise. *Dr. Kildare* was perhaps less guilty of this bias because several strong female characters did appear in the series: Pat, the surfer, in "Tyger, Tyger;" Sister Benjamin in "Fathers and Daughters;" and even the comic heroine Ellen in "Goodbye Mr. Jersey." Because *Dr. Kildare* gave greater attention to nurses in unimportant dialogue, the series also presented more stereotypically unpleasant or inane nurse characters. The large audiences of these popular series gained little positive feeling for the nursing profession and perhaps developed a disregard for nursing skills as a result of their weekly involvement in the crises ridden Blair General and County General Hospitals.

The Eleventh Hour (NBC's attempt to follow up the success of *Dr. Kildare* and *Ben Casey* in 1962 to 1964) and ABC's *Breaking Point* in the 1963–1964 season both failed to capture the public's fancy. As one critic who predicted the demise of *Breaking Point* noted, the series was "too honest for its own good. This is the kind of honesty that seems to offend the kind of viewer who does not want some problems touched, for no other reason than that he does not want to understand them." Both series addressed such important, contemporary social problems as chronic depression; emotional disturbances in children; the trauma of rape; mental retardation; capital punishment; racial struggles; alcoholism; promiscuity; wife-beating; and sex education. Long before feminist issues received much public attention, *The Eleventh Hour* explored post-natal depression; a mother's anger toward her child; a Marilyn Monroe-type death; a woman's inability to face the responsibility of supporting herself and her child after she is divorced by her husband; and a few episodes on women who break down domestic and familial chains in order to mature and to develop their own personalities.

Both series adopted the winning *Casey/Kildare* format of the wise, older physician's relationship with a less experienced young doctor. However, in neither was the leading man so adored as Vince Edwards or Richard Chamberlain. The dramatic focus of each episode remained securely aimed at the conflicts and problems of the patients; the psychiatrist protagonists served mainly as reference points and guides rather than as heroes on white horses who solved everyone's problems within sixty minutes.

Nurses appeared more prominently in *Breaking Point* because the two leading men were staff psychiatrists at a hospital and thus spent more time in hospitals. The psychiatrist/psychologist team of *The Eleventh Hour* operated primarily from their private offices and rarely admitted patients to the hospital (seven of the thirty-two first season shows and four of the twenty-nine second season entries had at least some hospital setting). Generally speaking, the two series did little to enlighten the viewer on the role of nursing in the care and treatment of psychiatric patients. Because the private treatment session between psychiatrist and patient is a very routine and normal occurrence, the exclusion of nursing was at least more understandable than in the Casey/Kildare shows where nurses were kept out of routine hospital situations in which they would normally appear.

In a typical episode of *Breaking Point,* nurses and nursing played a minor yet positive role. In "The Tides of Darkness" nurses contributed little to the final recovery of a fourteen-year-old girl from the emotional trauma associated with rape; however, the nurses were presented in a positive light. Thompson at one point ordered round-the-clock psychiatric nursing coverage for the girl and requested a particular nurse if she were available. The psychiatrist appreciated the special skills and education of the nurses, even if the nurses were not shown to do anything with the patient beyond comforting and reassuring her.

The nurses seen in the background of *Breaking Point* were, like the nurses in other series, well-starched and unimportant, though they were presented, at least, as competent observers. The physician characters of *Breaking Point* did not project the arrogant, god-like attitudes found in *Ben Casey* but listened sympathetically to patients and led the patients to their own solutions.

As noted above, *The Eleventh Hour* offered the viewer fewer opportunities to see nurses working around psychiatric patients because of the limited hospital settings and the lack of nurses who functioned as therapists in community settings. In "The Bride Wore Pink," for example, a nurse sat quietly in the shadows of a patient's room. The only nurse character ever featured in this series was Diahann Carroll who played an obstinate, compassionate veteran nurse who helped a once handsome man restore his self-confidence and learn to accept his facial disfigurement caused by fire ("And Man Created Vanity," October 23, 1963). In another episode of this series, Dr. Bassett tried to help a successful black businesswoman cope with the emotional conflicts she encountered with her estranged husband, an angry black activist who considered his wife to be a traitor to the cause. The story offered no pat solutions to this complicated and often bitter situation but did explore the two-sided question: Who is to say how the battle is to be fought? Although the woman patient did spend a few days in the hospital under Dr. Starke's care, no mention was made of a nursing character. If the public learned anything about the image of nursing from this fine series, it was that nursing personnel have little involvement in the care of mentally ill or emotionally disturbed patients.

CBS entered the health trend in the fall of 1962 with its sixty-minute drama *The Nurses*. The executive producer of the series, Herbert Brodkin, patterned the show more on his award winning show *The Defenders* than on the *Kildare/Casey* competitors. Indeed, the series bore the distinctive stamp of Brodkin's influence; the original idea for a continuing series based upon the conflicts and crises in the nursing staff of a modern hospital came to Brodkin as a result of two episodes of *Playhouse 90:* "Diary of a Nurse" and "No Deadly Medicine." The technique employed by Brodkin and company to pursue a moral credo of exploring causes of sin rather than condemning it, found its expression as social realism: A moral issue, often controversial in nature, is tightly argued from different points of view. Brodkin insisted upon technical authenticity for the series and employed two New York registered nurses, Florence McManus and Sandra Pascual, to not only check the sets and equipment used, but also to consult on the scripts and motivations of characters. The series had a polished, thoughtful (if not thought-provoking) appearance.

The storyline for *The Nurses* in the first two seasons followed the personal and professional lives of two nurse characters in Alden General Hospital in New York City: head nurse Liz Thorpe (Shirl Conway) and student nurse Gail Lucas (Zina Bethune). Liz's experience, wisdom, and realistic view of human experience often corrected the high-minded, idealistic, and spontaneous enthusiasms of her young protégé Gail. Recurring characters included two staff nurses; a student nurse Kelly (Joanna Miles); a young intern Lowry (Stephen Brooke); and Liz's beau Dr. Anson Kiley (Edward Binns). The patients and staff of Alden General revealed a racial and occupational mix found in a large metropolitan area. Although the series reflected the technical advice received from the consulting nurses, the dramatic conflict emphasized moral and ethical choices rather than urgent, life-saving interventions. The series remained rather vague about specializations and staff assignments. For example, the floor which Liz Thorpe supervised housed a combination of pediatric, medical, and surgical patients. Anson Kiley, the recurrent physician character of the first two seasons, never declared a specialty. By keeping these details rather vague, the writers could introduce the regular cast into almost any type of health care situation.

When the show was rechristened *The Doctors and The Nurses* in the third season, Liz Thorpe and Gail Lucas (finally a graduate nurse) became supporting characters for two new members of Alden's medical staff: Dr. Ted Steffan (Joseph Campanella), the supervisor of residents, and Dr. Alex Tazniski (Michael Tolan), the iconoclastic, idealistic, and brilliant young resident. During this final season, the writers tended to feature the threat or results of violence and crime. Of twenty-eight third season episodes, at least three dealt with suicide, three with murder, one with brutal violence and one with the occult. In the previous seventy-two episodes, only one incident of murder, one of attempted suicide, one of violence, and one of the occult reached the eighth floor of Alden General.

The switch to a joint doctors/nurses format came as a surprise to the two leading actresses, Shirl Conway and Zina Bethune, who claimed that they had not been consulted or forewarned of the change. Stimulus to revamp the series originated with CBS's self-styled program bureaucrat, Michael Dann, who claimed that he didn't "feel altogether secure" about the show as early as 1960 because "it was a completely female-oriented show . . ." Brodkin himself admitted the difficulty of finding good stories for a pair of nurses. Shirl Conway accepted the change philosophically but did deplore the new title. "Out of sheer diplomacy, I think it should be called *The Nurses and the Doctors*. The producers have made a lot of money out of the nursing profession, and it would have been more politic to give the nurses top billing" (*TV Guide*, March 8, 1965, p. 10). Despite the network's belief that two male leads could improve the ratings, the series failed to attract a larger audience.

The decision to cancel *The Doctors and The Nurses* seemed to have been as much an indication of changing network programming policy as of the series' unimpressive ratings. As producer Brodkin noted, many shows with lower ratings were renewed by CBS for the 1965–1966 season. CBS also terminated Brodkin's award winning *The Defenders* and the troubled *For the People* (a mid-season replacement in 1965) at the same time. CBS executives claimed this kind of drama was not popular. Brodkin disagreed with the network's rationale and interpreted the collapse of his three shows as a rejection by CBS of social realism in dramatic form. Brodkin said, "They rationalize that a series made in New York can't be successful because the public doesn't want to see "The New York Look". . . . When you translate this expression—it's reality, as opposed to fiction—realism as opposed to phony Hollywood stories—bright, happy, pretty, all-American stories about Never-Never Land. There's a CBS West Coast group which thinks of these realistic shows as being seamy, ugly, shot-in-the-alley stories with unattractive content" (*TV Guide*, September 27, 1965, p. 19).

Critical response to *The Nurses* reflected the critics' own prejudices as much as the show's true value. In addition, the sometimes good/sometimes bad reviews pointed out the unevenness of the episodes—at least to viewers of the early 1960s. Gilbert Seldes found the show uninteresting "because I don't really believe it" (*TV Guide,* February 21, 1963, p. 21). That is, the critic felt that the show gave a false impression of modern hospital life because it focused only on unusual episodes rather than the "routine hours when nothing happens." On the other hand, this same reviewer in *TV Guide,* February 24, 1962, said of another hospital-based drama: "What happens in *Ben Casey* is exciting, whether it's true to life or not." (p. 1). Underlying the often blanket criticisms of the series seemed to run a general disdain of female-dominated drama; what may be unbelievable and melodramatic in such male-dominated series as *Dr. Kildare* and *Ben Casey* was termed exciting, while *The Nurses* was relegated to the status of a daytime soaper.

In retrospect, the overall dramatic quality of *The Nurses* has not been matched in recent years by any sixty-minute series and certainly not by the 1970s rash of medical-oriented shows. The show created well-developed, unified, original dramas which addressed serious ethical and moral concerns. Thematically the show pursued a rather consistent path, as writers sought to surprise or shock viewers out of making automatic assumptions about the guilt or innocence of characters based on deceptive first impressions. The plots more often than not carried the viewer into the gray realm of moral ambiguity—what was right turned out to be wrong and vice versa. Nor did the resolutions of the stories always satisfy the viewer's desire for neat endings and moral absolutes, although justice was usually served. For example, "For the Mice and the Rabbits," a second season episode written by Art Wallace, concerned veteran nurse Carrie Bruner (Geraldine Fitzgerald), who took it upon herself to not administer a prescribed experimental drug to a young patient of whom she was very fond. The nurse read the literature on the drug and was not convinced that the possible advantages outweighed the risks involved. As it turned out, the nurse's fears proved correct, and dozens of patients who took the drug experimentally suffered serious physical consequences. The nurse reassured the despondent physician who ordered the drug administered to the patient, saying that he need not worry about the effects on the patient in question. Despite the physician's relief that the patient did not receive the drug, he and the nursing administration dismissed Miss Bruner for failing to follow a doctor's orders.

In "Frieda," a first season episode written by Albert Rubin, a sympathetic, dedicated nurse (Vivian Nathan) turned out to be a former Nazi who participated in concentration camp medical experiments and who was drummed out of nursing by an unsympathetic refugee who denounced her. Although justice was served in her expulsion from her job—who could condone the Nazis?—the viewer was left with unresolved, positive feelings for the former Nazi.

The role of protagonist rotated in the first two seasons among Liz Thorpe, Gail Lucas, several one-time-only nurses, and occasionally non-nurse characters. In the first two seasons, a nurse (Gail, Liz or other nurse characters) figured prominently in about twenty-five episodes, while in about eight shows, non-nurse characters, usually patients, were featured, although either Gail or Liz also shared a major portion of the attention. Of the twenty-eight shows in the third year, at least thirteen featured physicians as the protagonists. Only three episodes focused primarily on Liz and only one on Gail.

The moral conflicts which characterized the dramatic exposition frequently centered upon the incongruities between personal background or preferences and the responsibilities of the nursing profession. The nurses presented seemed in constant pursuit of the golden mean: the right proportion of sympathy and concern with the right proportion of distance and objectivity. The imbalance might affect either professional or personal involvements; that is, work-related difficulties might affect the nurse's personal life, or, personal problems might jeopardize proper completion of nursing duties. More often than not, nurses were shown trying to handle personal problems which did or might affect their work. Gail Lucas was especially prone to mixing her personal opinions into professional matters. Another common way the series approached moral, ethical issues was to present three nurse characters who differed from each other in their approach to common problems.

Liz Thorpe, beautifully developed by actress Shirl Conway, was the most memorable character from the series. In the days before women's lib became a cliché, Liz represented the best in emancipated womanhood; feminine, compassionate, even girlish at times, Liz brought a sense of authority, discipline, and professional excellence to the nursing profession. The universal admiration of Liz by patients, physicians, and other nurses emphasized that here indeed was the ideal nurse. Liz Thorpe's appearance, background, and personality contributed to her appeal as a woman and protagonist of the series. Although in the earliest episodes of the series Liz wore shapeless, tailored white uniforms, prudish looking pinned up hair, and unattractive, ever-present glasses, at some time before mid-season, the producers softened her appearance and increased her attractiveness. By "The Third Generation," Liz Thorpe looked like an attractive, feminine woman in her mid-forties. Bit by bit, Liz's personal history emerged: She studied nursing at Alden General Hospital, quit nursing when she married, and returned to work after her husband died. Childless, Liz lived alone in an attractive, comfortable, but modest apartment, enjoyed reading, the outdoors, and socializing with friends; on many occasions she was seen smoking and drinking, much in keeping with the personality of a sophisticated New Yorker. Men found Liz attractive; in addition to her long-term romance with Anson Kiley, staff physician, Liz gave evidence of dating other men and enjoying a satisfying social life. Although her involvement with Anson Kiley was never explicitly examined, limited evidence hinted that they were sexually involved.

Liz's personality revealed a complex woman; often she appeared to maternally guide Gail through the crises of youth and inexperience; in addition, Liz had a soft heart for broken-winged sparrows and lost kittens. The patients most in need of extra care received Liz's tenderest ministrations. However, Liz's sharp tongue and acerbic wit kept her from becoming too saccharine. Liz did not suffer fools easily and often lost her temper with the inefficient or the unwelcome. When a long-awaited orderly arrived on the floor and asked for her, Liz tartly remarked, "Oh, I'm not Mrs. Thorpe. Mrs. Thorpe grew old and retired waiting for an orderly." Her main contribution to the image of nursing was her role as arbitrator of disputed issues and finder of compromises and solutions; Liz represented the golden mean—the right balance between compassion and objectivity, between involvement and distance, between idealism and pragmatism. While others about her lost their heads, Liz pursued the middle course, usually. Whenever she did err, it was always on the side of too much compassion, too much generosity, or too much involvement. When Liz did make mistakes, she recognized them herself and corrected them.

The series' other leading nurse character, Gail Lucas played by Zina Bethune, had less depth and believability than did Liz Thorpe. The eighteen-year-old nursing student served as the show's official idealist who thought with her heart and acted on her generous impulses. Excused by her lack of experience and redeemed by good intentions, Gail blundered her way through two years as a student at Alden Hospital's School of Nursing and became a staff nurse there in the third season. In her starched pinafore and cap Gail looked the part of the naive ingenue. Big blue eyes, long blonde hair pinned primly under her cap while in uniform, and open facial expressions characterized this nurse's physical appearance. Compared to the new nursing student Barbara Bowers (Elizabeth Ashley), second-year student Gail Lucas looked like a rookie. Because of the emphasis on Gail's inexperience and innocence, the character acquired a unidimensional quality that bothered many critics and Zina Bethune who once complained that Gail had no background: Who were her parents?; Where did she come from? One episode ("Where Park Runs Into Vreeland") introduced Gail's mother at the end of the second season, but otherwise Gail's identity remained firmly tied to her student nursing. "Circle of Choice" did present Gail as being a dancer as well as a nurse, but in the end she chose nursing over a ballet career. Gail had a nearly asexual quality, although serious romances did more than once interfere with her work. In the second season Gail seemed to have a running romance with equally blonde, handsome, and innocent-looking intern Ned Lowry, but no episodes revealed so much as a kiss between them.

Professional nursing groups and individual nurses found Gail the most disconcerting aspect of the series; the student made too many blunders and errors to have been tolerated in a real hospital. In addition, Gail rarely appeared in the classroom nor did she receive clinical instruction. At most Gail learned from mistakes and listened to Liz's instruction. Gail showed poor judgment, doing things that second- and third-year nursing students would probably not do. For example, in "Show Just Cause Why You Should Weep" (second season) Gail read from a patient's chart in the obvious hearing of non-professionals and even identified the patient for them. In "A Private Room," Gail blurted out to patients in a ward that a fellow patient had a terminal disease.

Gail was impulsive, intense, and loyal to her ideals, however mistaken they may have been. Because Gail always acted out of compassion, concern for the downtrodden, and because lack of experience could always be considered, she never carried the burden of incompetence. In "Show Just Cause" Liz rather severely reprimanded her for spreading information to non-professionals and failing in certain other matters of protocol, but at a hearing to determine Gail's fault, Liz stood up and defended her to the hospital trustees and administrators because Gail was, after all, a promising young woman with much to offer the profession. The fact that Gail's accuser happened to be guilty of child abuse also helped her out of the slander charge. Gail's virtues, aside from her compassion and concern for others, stemmed from her stubborn insistence that truth and justice would win the day. For example, she refused to believe that she would be dismissed from nursing school because of her unprofessional handling of a particular case, because, after all, the real issue was whether or not a mother and father were abusing their son. There was a *deus ex machina* quality to Gail's predicaments; just in the nick of time, someone or something would happen to establish her veracity or at least to save her from herself. Unlike Liz Thorpe, Gail often turned to others for help, comfort or counselling—usually she turned to Liz.

Other Alden General staff nurses who appeared in minor roles showed neither the virtuosity of Liz nor the exaggerated idealism of Gail Lucas. They appeared to be ordinary folks, competent and happy in their work, but untroubled by the larger issues of life. Verna Ayres (Hilda Ayres) was an attractive black nurse in her thirties who often played confidante to a troubled Liz; occasionally Verna took action on her own, as when she tried to persuade Kiley to protect Liz's reputation by leaving her alone. Ollie Sutton (Diana Sands), another young, black nurse, appeared to be a typical human being, affected by the criticism of others but able to recognize her own errors. For example, in "The Imperfect Prodigy," Ollie took an opportunity to criticize Dr. Tazinski to the hospital administrators, but realized to her chagrin that she had overdone it. The nursing students who shared Gail's work appeared to be happy, hard-working young women who gave little thought to the larger meaning of their careers; they seldom suffered the introspective pangs of Gail Lucas.

In the show's efforts to explore various aspects of the human condition, nurse characters were often used to convey a message, not so much about nursing as about humanity in general. Many of these featured nurses displayed negative qualities or emotional disturbances, but each show resolved the matter in such a way as to indicate that the situation was unusual in the nursing field or at least not tolerated by nursing professionals. Often well-known actresses played the parts of troubled nurses who usually ended up bringing their problems to Liz Thorpe.

The relationship among nurses almost always expressed friendship, affection, mutual respect, and loyalty to each other. The most important friendship existed between Liz Thorpe and Gail Lucas, but this friendship did not stand on an equal footing since Gail clearly needed Liz's help and guidance more than Liz needed Gail's dubious contributions. Apparently, the viewer supposed that Liz saw something of her own girlish idealism and enthusiasm in Gail; the older nurse never failed to save Gail from herself or from other hostile forces. Nearly every episode showed motherly Liz leading Gail from a new debacle, arm around the student's waist, comforting her with words of wisdom.

Liz enjoyed other friendships with nurses and also intervened to help save troubled R.N.s, although not with the same regularity as she rescued Gail. In "A Private Room," Verna Ayres appeared very concerned about Liz's growing involvement with the still married Anson Kiley, and she tried to keep Liz from making a big mistake. In "The Thunder of Ernie Bass," Verna recognized Liz's loss of objectivity with regard to a patient and warned her away from dangerous complications by urging her to take a needed vacation. Liz also stepped in to save Grace Milo's career ("Fly, Shadow") and Margaret's unborn baby ("The Life").

In addition to personal friendships and affection, the nursing staff at Alden apparently had an administrative support system run by nurses. Only two episodes indicated that nurses were subject to discipline directly from hospital administrators rather than through nursing channels. For example, in "Show Just Cause," Gail faced dismissal or resignation from school on the insistence of the hospital's administrator, and no nursing supervisor was involved. Usually, nurses handled nursing problems. Mrs. Lavan, the director of nurses, appeared in a few episodes or was referred to by other nurses. A Mrs. Willan, in "The Imperfect Prodigy," provided support to staff nurse and clinical instructor Ollie Sutton who had been verbally abused by a tyrannical young resident. It appeared that nurses would not tolerate being treated like serfs and that they insisted upon the respect due them in their professional status. In "For the Mice and the Rabbits," nursing administrators decided that Carrie Bruner had to be dismissed because she disobeyed an order and falsified the medical record; although the complaint against her was initiated by a physician, nursing administrators carried out the discipline.

The interactions between nurses and physicians at Alden General Hospital demonstrated friendly but rather formal relationships. More often than not, nurses addressed physicians as "Doctor" or "Doctor X" while the doctors, in turn, spoke to the nurses as "Miss/Mrs. X," including nursing students. Orders were given and taken in a mutually respectful manner; often a physician complimented a nurse or student if her handling of a given situation merited it. Also, physicians thanked nurses for help given, even on such minor tasks as handing over a tongue blade or fetching a piece of equipment. Liz Thorpe stood on a first name basis with several of the physicians due to her many years in the hospital; she especially called the younger physicians by their first names, although they occasionally still referred to her as "Mrs. Thorpe." Physicians listened to nurses' assessments of patient related matters with interest, and Liz in particular contributed to the determination of patient care. For example, in "A Private Room," Anson Kiley asks for Liz's opinion on whether or not to use an experimental drug on the obstreperous Mr. Bell.

Often nurses acted as protectors of the doctors; in "A Strange and Distant Place," Gail took upon herself the responsibility of making a foreign resident at home in the United States; "The Imperfect Prodigy" found Liz as the only champion for a brilliant but rude resident who faced expulsion. Gail also defended "Dr. Lillian"—in one of the two episodes featuring female physicians—who faced great hostility from a male colleague and suffered from her own emotional problems.

In conclusion, *The Nurses* provided an image of nursing in a big city hospital which could not fail to impress the viewer with the heroism, idealism, and dedication of the leading nurse characters. Even troubled nurses found solutions to their problems, usually due to the intervention of another nurse. Despite the obvious distortion predicated by the search for dramatic material, the producers presented balanced portraits of the nursing profession. Perhaps the most important contribution of the series was that it did present nurses as a group of "professionals" who had their own standards and who solved their own problems.

Far removed from *The Nurses* in its presentation of the profession was NBC's situation comedy about a registered nurse, *Julia* (1968–1971). This show was important primarily because its leading lady was Diahann Carroll, the first black woman to star in a regular network show since the days of *Amos 'n Andy*. The series concerned the domestic and personal events in the life of a young, black, Vietnam War widow, Julia Baker (Diahann Carroll) who was raising her six-year-old son Corey (Marc Copage) alone. A registered nurse, Julia worked at the Astrospace Industries health office under the supervision of head nurse Hannah Yarby (Lurene Tuttle), a fiftyish attractive woman, and Doctor Morton Chegley (Lloyd Nolan), a sixtyish, gruff but kindly physician who in his spare time operated a free-clinic for the poor. The series also featured Julia's neighbors and friends—the white Waggedorns, a landlord, and, at the end of the second season, Julia's romantic interest, Steve Bruce.

Julia's family and professional lives often overlapped when kindhearted Dr. Chegley or motherly Hannah Yarby intervened in Julia's affairs; for example, when Dr. Chegley tried to get Julia a good deal on a new car, or when Hannah and Chegley both attempted matchmaking for Julia. Julia's domestic crises dominated the development of the storyline, and her friendship with Marie Waggedorn appeared to be the most frequent relationship highlighted, other than her interaction with her son and his usual elementary school traumas.

Supposedly *Julia* represented the hardships of a young, black woman trying to raise a child alone, but in fact the series rarely touched upon realistic situations. For example, Julia never seemed pinched for money; she wore beautiful clothes, lived in a nice apartment, and throughout the three year series, she hired and fired a succession of housekeepers, mother's helpers, and babysitters. Occasionally the series did focus upon racial questions; Marie and Leonard's relative, Wanda, found the Baker family a real novelty; a nasty lady tenant of the building revealed her hatred so that Julia had to explain prejudice to Corey; and as in the first episode Julia had to overcome the prejudices of a hostile personnel manager. However, these episodes all appeared during the first season; thereafter the Baker family apparently suffered no discrimination so they could freely pursue traditional sit-com patterns.

One of the most controversial issues surrounding the show was the air of unreality about black life in the United States. Producer Hal Hanter defended his low-keyed approach to the subject: ". . . I feel that if we had starred Hope Lange in *Julia* and Diahann Carroll in *The Ghost and Mrs. Muir*, the results would have been about the same. I also feel that if we made social comment within our context our show would have been a failure. On the other hand, there is a fallout of social comment. Every week we see a black child playing with a white child with complete acceptance and without incident" (*TV Times*, May 6, 1968, p. 5). Perhaps the best evaluation of the show appeared in the *Los Angeles Times:* "*Julia* might not tell it like it is to the satisfaction of some, but at least it's a start." (November 21, 1968, part IV, p. 30).

Although Julia was clearly identified as a nurse and appeared in uniform and at work, absolutely no attention was paid to her professional role or skills. Occasionally she dealt with job-oriented problems: helping her boss in a charity project, dealing with an efficiency expert, coping with a loquacious maintenance man. But she never had nursing problems or became involved with a patient's outcome. This held true for the two other health care givers, Hannah Yarby and Dr. Chegley. In a typical episode, the nursing tasks included such jobs as fetching an X-ray, putting a patient in a treatment room, and daubing something on a man's arm. The only interesting nurse-related issue raised by this series was: Why did the creator choose to make Julia a nurse and not a secretary, schoolteacher, or saleslady? In the absence of any information on this point, the viewer might speculate on some possible reasons. First of all, Diahann Carroll looked spectacular as a nurse. Perhaps too, in the altruistic motives of the creator, it seemed a good idea to give a black woman a very obvious professional identity rather than a less identifiable or less respectable job. One might wonder if nursing was intended to be considered a more open, less hidebound profession, or if nurses were, due to their experience in dealing with all types of people, less racist than other women?

Being a nurse did allow the writer to include the stock character Dr. Chegley, the older, kindly physician, crotchety on the outside, but a softie within. The nurse–physician relationship was close, but on a personal and not a professional basis. In the office Chegley called the nurses by their last names, and they referred to him as "Doctor." Hannah, in a phone conversation, employed a rather old-fashioned mode of reference, "I'll remind Doctor when he returns from lunch" as if Chegley's identity and profession were totally united. The relation between Hannah and Chegley was one of those doctor–nurse partnerships based on years of working together; he spoke to her gruffly, but liked her a lot.

Perhaps it was significant that this ground breaking series did feature a leading black woman as a professional nurse, but one doubts that viewers of this series gained any insight into the nursing profession, other than that the two nurse characters were attractive, nice, motherly ladies. In addition, the show clearly predated the *All in the Family* sit-com format; *Julia* relied on homespun, gentle clichés about domestic and romantic situations.

One very memorable presentation of nursing in the 1960s was *Hallmark Hall of Fame's* production of James Lee's screenplay based on the life of Florence Nightingale. "The Holy Terror" aired April 7, 1965. The ninety-minute drama touched only certain high points in Miss Nightingale's long career and yet delivered a convincing and consistent portrayal of her personality and special powers. The play, in three acts, developed Florence (Julie Harris) from age seventeen to a mature woman in her forties or fifties. The focal point of the play concerned her struggles in the military hospital at Scutari and her eventual triumph over the forces opposed to her interventions. The theme of the play concerned Miss Nightingale's early call to do God's work and her increasing militancy in pursuit of this divine calling.

In the opening scene of the play Florence announces that she heard God's voice and that God has ordered her to help Him. Florence's remarks sound ominously sinful and frightening to her father, and he orders his daughter to deny her statement. He reasons with her that the Angel of God could not have spoken with her because "Angels are Angels, and . . . Angels cannot talk to human beings." Aunt Mai, however, has been moved by Florence's sincere insistence upon her calling and she clearly does not agree with William's attempt to ignore the event. Some years later, Florence's meeting with Sidney Herbert brings her into the world of hospital administration and reform. Her work on a London committee to establish a hospital for elderly gentlewomen in distressed circumstances introduces her to exciting discoveries about the reduction in mortality given proper sanitation. Although Miss Nightingale had been strictly forbidden by her parents to enter an actual hospital, she finally visits one where she immediately decides to become a nurse after she sees the current weaknesses and faults in hospital care, especially the lack of decent civilian nurses and experiences her first encounter with a sick patient as well as her first opportunity to actively and directly help someone.

With Sidney Herbert's help and against the strong opposition of her family, Florence follows through on her decision. The mounting death toll among British soldiers in the Crimea is the catalyst that places Florence in the public's eye. With Sidney Herbert in the War Ministry, Florence is asked to organize a group of female nurses to attend the sick and wounded at Scutari. The London *Times,* which has publicized the horrid conditions, has raised a fund to finance her work, but when the group arrives in Scutari, Florence and her nurses are denied the opportunity to nurse the wounded because the military medical establishment did not ask for help and refuses to accept it from the women. Yet Miss Nightingale and her nurses remain, despite the strain and privation, and wait for the opportunity to prove themselves.

The opportunity comes during an especially severe epidemic when even the medical staff is stricken. Florence and her nurses move into the wards, cleaning and scrubbing them, changing bed linens and soiled bandages, bathing the patients, and comforting them. The famous "lady with the lamp" image emerges as Florence walks the wards at all hours, offering words of hope. The men revere her, and soon her fame spreads to England. The turning point in Florence's life comes upon her own recovery from the fever. Close to death, she realizes that she has wasted too much time being patient with the military staff and vows never to be obstructed in her work again.

In a dramatic scene, Florence has journeyed to Constantinople to regain control of the *Times* fund, which has been entrusted to the Ambassador during her illness and which he has decided to use to build an English Church in Constantinople. Florence proceeds to appall the overly civilized ladies and gentlemen with her tales of the blood, gore, offal, and dysentery encountered at Scutari. She wins her point, and the Ambassador returns control of the fund to her but refuses to take her to dinner.

After returning to England, Florence avoids publicity and adulation unless she needs public support to force through her reforms. She claims invalid status and uses her physical weakness to pressure others into complying with her wishes. She works constantly and probes into diverse topics touching on military administration and public health throughout the world. The last scene shows her old and aged friend Sidney Herbert taking his leave of her; he tells Florence's Aunt Mai, "I must confess that even now there are moments when her behavior could convince me that she is less a saint than a devout charlatan." But Aunt Mai, the only witness to Florence's youthful vision, recalls William's argument that "Angels cannot talk to human beings" and adds, "but no one denies that Angels can talk to one another."

The image of nursing in "The Holy Terror" has to be judged positive because the entire film sought to present the life and contribution of Florence Nightingale in very laudatory terms. The story of the birth of modern nursing, with emphasis upon the contributions made by the nurses in the hospital at Scutari, underlined the heroic dimensions of the profession as well as the role of the nurse as the defender of the downtrodden and weak. A great deal of importance was attached to nursing, but it must be mentioned that of even greater importance than nursing per se was the personality and personal development of Florence Nightingale. Several nurse characters appeared in the course of the narrative. The group of thirty-eight nurses, both religious and civilians, who Florence took with her to Scutari, are shown following Florence's orders and caring for the patients; however, none of these nurse characters was developed nor allowed to express her attitudes toward her nursing work. Thus, Florence Nightingale was the only nurse character who received any attention from the playwright, and thus she projected the only well developed image of nursing.

Personal qualities associated with the nurse characters must be divided into the pre-Nightingale era and the post-Nightingale era. On more than one occasion before Florence decided to become a nurse, civilian nurses were described as being drunks and prostitutes. The nurses brought together by Florence for work in Scutari contrasted greatly with the earlier presentation of nurses. Without specific attention to any one nurse, they all seemed to be brave, obedient, compassionate and self-sacrificing. The conditions at the Barrack Hospital were hideous, and each of the nurses risked contracting cholera or some other contagious disease. Each sacrificed her own safety in order to put her nursing services to the aid of needy patients. All the nurses obeyed Florence immediately, and her discipline over them seemed complete. They wordlessly accepted her instructions and followed her example in approaching the dirtiest and most menial tasks, such as scrubbing the unspeakably dirty floors. Although all the nurse characters did not seem to possess Miss Nightingale's strength of character and her firm self-control, they did all appear to be motivated by compassion and a desire to work.

Of course Florence's own personal characteristics and qualities have come to be equated with the best attributes of the nursing profession. In addition to the qualities of heroism, bravery, leadership, and humanitarian efforts, she displayed other, less attractive traits. Miss Nightingale became, through the course of her life, a demanding, manipulative, impatient, and autocratic woman. In her struggle to achieve her goals, she purposefully put aside the more tender virtues of simple friendship and politeness and concern for those around her. Florence worked for mankind but forgot individuals. She demanded energetic service from her two closest allies, her aunt and Sidney Herbert, and she used them to help with her reforms. When Herbert intended to retire because of his poor health, she spared not a word of sympathy or concern for him but urged him to remain at his post because she needed him.

Miss Nightingale saw the work of a nurse as important. Through her work on hospital planning committees she learned the significance of hygiene and sanitation; perhaps she saw the trained nurse as the person best able to oversee these sanitary procedures. Certainly her deployment of nurses at Scutari indicated her appreciation of the nurse's value in achieving sanitary standards. The hands-on role of the nurse also impressed Florence; her own decision to become a nurse followed her experience in a hospital ward when she calmed down an hysterical patient by simply and gently easing her into her bed. Above all, Florence saw the profession of nursing, at least for herself, as an opportunity to serve God. Florence became a nurse at the express order of God, and all of her life she considered her work to be divinely ordained. The other nurse characters never expressed any attitudes about their work; the viewer could only assume that they felt deeply committed to proving to the world that their work did make a difference to the health and survival of patients.

Non-nurse characters showed mixed feelings about the nursing profession. Before Florence proved the value of nursing at Scutari, the general public held that nurses were drunks and prostitutes; and apparently they were. Florence's family was horrified by her decision to become a nurse because of the scandal it would cause. Even Sidney Herbert, Miss Nightingale's friend and ally, worked to keep Florence away from association with civilian nurses. The image of the profession, despite Florence's success, did not change overnight. The Nightingale family, proud of Florence's patriotic and heroic contribution to the British military, did not overcome their opposition to her work. Dr. Poole, who had to recognize her contribution at Scutari, persisted in resisting her other demands for peacetime reform of the British military hospital system. The audience preceived that although the nursing profession achieved a dramatic change in its public image, individual attitudes toward the profession would be more difficult to overcome.

The most successful health care series of the 1960s, *Ben Casey* and *Dr. Kildare,* not only developed the definitive version of the television doctor as hero but also established the hospital nurse as a background prop who occasionally came forward in need of rescue by the physician hero. The nameless and forgettable nurses who populated the nursing stations and corridors of Blair and County General hospitals contributed to the image of their profession in a negative way: the nurse as nonentity. Unlike nurse characters of the 1950s who were credited with providing important spiritual or maternal support and comfort, the typical nurse characters of the 1960s were reduced to wordless factotums and often to mere background scenery. When a nurse character did receive more than a cursory glance in *Ben Casey* and *Dr. Kildare,* she usually came to the attention of the doctor hero because of some personal problem she faced or because her personal problems interfered with her nursing duties. Only when a nurse dared reveal her personality or her individuality did the doctors notice her and then for the express purpose of controlling or erasing the nurse's aberration from the wordless norm expected of the nurses. Miss Wills of *Ben Casey* was the ideal television nurse of the 1960s; she was attractive and professional looking. She admired and respected the doctors, had no first name and no private life, lived at the nursing station for the purpose of delivering messages and taking orders. Never did this nurse intrude with a personal opinion into a conversation with the physician, nor did she expect to be consulted in matters of patient care. Her supreme forgettability constituted her role in the series.

The image of nursing in other dramatic series of the decade did little to improve the image of the profession. Because of their short life and their limited attention to hospital based health care, *The Breaking Point* and *The Eleventh Hour* made little impact upon the audience's view of the nursing profession. The only exception to the prevailing image of the nurse as a nonentity came in the two-year run of *The Nurses,* and to a lesser extent in the series' third year as *The Doctors and The Nurses.* Shirl Conway's portrayal of nurse Liz Thorpe was memorable in its subtlety and credibility. The producers of *The Nurses* did not try to ape the competition by making Liz and Gail superwomen who could have matched Ben Casey and Jim Kildare in terms of omniscience and heroism. They chose a far more believable approach, emphasizing the nurses' constant struggle to find the middle course. In *The Nurses* the TV viewer found a fully developed profession that had its own standards and maintained its own discipline. Nurses supervised nurses and disciplined their own ranks. When nurses had problems, nurses solved them. *Julia,* however, which featured a nurse character in the title role, did little to enhance the image of the nursing profession. Although nursing received more prominence in *Julia* than in *Hennessey* or *Mr. Peepers,* by and large the series remained firmly within the domestic situation-comedy tradition of the 1950s.

In sum, with the major exception of *The Nurses,* the decade of the 1960s did not contribute to the public's appreciation of the nursing profession. In fact, the repeated image of the nursing profession taken from the decade's two biggest successes, *Ben Casey* and *Dr. Kildare,* was that nurses played a very small role in the care of patients in U.S. health care.

3
Close-Up: Major M.D.s and Minor R.N.s in the 1970s

During the 1970s the television networks offered a veritable smorgasbord of programs featuring nurses and doctors, many of them short-lived. The relaxation of censorship as well as the influence of feminism on some television writers have left their mark on health care programming and the image of nursing. More than the previous two decades combined, nurse characters in shows of the 1970s were likely to appear in professional situations outside the general hospital, primarily but not exclusively in military establishments. The only way to begin to digest this vast amount of material is to impose a few obvious categories upon the television series that have aired during the 1970s.

The most important category of the 1970s remained the mainline health care drama, derived from the *Ben Casey/Dr. Kildare* tradition: *Marcus Welby, M.D.; Medical Center;* and *The Bold Ones*. Although these three series dominated the genre because of their long runs, the networks continued to vary the basic format and to offer new versions of the old story to audiences. Most of these short-lived efforts aired as *Marcus Welby* and *Medical Center* were winding up their long runs. However, not until 1979 with the introduction of *Trapper John, M.D.* did these imitative efforts succeed in finding a loyal audience. It would appear that television audiences simply needed a break from doctor shows after the demise of long-running series.

The second major category includes all the network attempts to create situation comedies around nurses, physicians, and hospitals. Only in the 1970s, with the relaxation of censorship and the glorification of irreverence begun with Norman Lear's *All in the Family* was the comic treatment of things medical possible.

In a third category nurses appeared in hour-long action adventure series that focused more on non-physician characters than on events within a general hospital. These shows include: *Emergency!*, *The Rookies*, and *The Black Sheep Squadron*.

A final category consists of two programs that have, more than any other series, developed lives of their own: *The Waltons* and *M*A*S*H*. Despite the obvious dissimilarities between these two shows, they share a solid core of genuine and recognizable human values that are consistently presented; both project a realistic view of certain subjects; both depend for their success on the interrelations among an ensemble of regular characters; and finally, in both series the characters grow, change, and develop like real human beings. Strong and very positive nurse characters have developed from these two shows: Mary Ellen Walton and Major Margaret "Hot Lips" Houlihan.

In 1969 each of the networks introduced hour-long health care dramas. *The Bold Ones, Medical Center,* and *Marcus Welby, M.D.* brought to the television audience a new generation of physician heroes who carried forward the banner of medicine once held by Dr. Kildare and Ben Casey. These two generations of health care shows differed in significant ways. The health care dramas of the 1970s put even greater emphasis on advanced technology than noted in the shows of the 1960s. Furthermore, maturity and success became attributes of the heroes. Surly residents and poor, naive interns gave way to established, confident, and obviously well paid physicians and surgeons. Although the old doctor/young doctor format so popular in the 1960s did not completely disappear, there was less distinction between the responsibilities and duties of the two age groups. Nurse characters appeared with more regularity in the newer series but often in less than admirable roles.

The Bold Ones was heralded by NBC as a new concept in television drama, a show which offered three separate dramatic series on a rotating basis in a single time slot: "The New Doctors," "The Lawyers," and "The Protectors" (replaced in the second season by "The Senator"). By the fourth season, all the other segments had dropped away, leaving the physicians in full sway. Three doctors shared the glory in this series, one older physician and two younger ones. Although the old doctor/young doctor format was familiar from earlier programs, the physicians in *The Bold Ones* did not repeat the familiar mentor/disciple relationship. The relationship among the three physicians on the show was friendly, professional, and, for the most part, egalitarian; together they tackled all the problems that could arise at the frontiers of new medicine.

While many of the plots focused on traditional medical–surgical themes, on the doctors' personal problems, on medical ethics, or on social problems, many also emphasized these new frontiers in medicine. They dealt, for instance, with psychosurgery, with embryo transplants, with the moon mission, with a sight-substitute system for the blind, and with other space-age technology. Highly sophisticated medical gadgetry enhanced the modern and realistic atmosphere of the show, particularly since all the equipment was real and functional.

The sets and equipment were not the only touches of realism in *The Bold Ones*. More important, all of the physicians and nurses shown, except for the stars and supporting actors, were real physicians and nurses. Furthermore, Joel Rogosin, a producer under Chermak, added "We don't use just ordinary surgeons. If we're doing a nerve operation, we use a neurosurgeon" (*TV Guide*, October 25, 1969, p. 42). Moreover, the scripts were cleared with the American Medical Association to insure their accuracy.

The nurses in these bold tales received considerably less attention than did the physicians who were the true heroes of each program. Only one episode featured a nurse as the main character ("A Threatened Species" was about a nurse who does not want her unborn child). Although the nursing image benefited from the intelligent and realistic approach with which the entire series was produced, nurses did not play a very large or visible role in the episodes, and most often they were seen doing basic nursing activities in the emergency room, operating room, intensive care unit, individual patients' rooms, nursery, children's wards, and at the nurses' station.

Nurses appeared only within the hospital setting, and there were no indications of romantic involvements or personal problems. Contrary to the practice in most health care dramas, *Bold Ones* did not depict romantic relationships between nurses and physicians. This exclusion of the nurses' private lives from the plots limited their development as rounded characters somewhat, but it also kept the emphasis on their professional capabilities and contributed to the earnest tone of the series.

The world of *Medical Center,* which existed in the hearts and minds of millions of American viewers for seven years, 1969 to 1976, was populated with a mixture of the seventies' au courant types—drifters and students, rebels and psychopaths, professional athletes and transvestites. To this sociological pot pourri, the creators of the show added a handsome, young hero who managed his patients with sterling, Boy Scout virtues and the laid-back, cultural relativism of the Pepsi generation. The storylines included controversial and front page items, but the plots were predictable. The acting qualities of the series star, Chad Everett, were reduced to smiling understanding, and grim determination, and the supporting cast never advanced beyond routine background appearances.

To give some credit to the producers of the show, *Medical Center* demonstrated slick production qualities that contributed to a sense of realism and superficial credibility. The settings in and around the U.C.L.A. campus and the real hospital footage established a sunny, southern California location and a modern health center atmosphere. Frequent and casual use of esoteric jargon, apparently convincingly pronounced, contributed to the realistic impression of modern hospital routine. Each script was submitted to a medical specialist for approval, although the writers often failed to incorporate the physician's notes and suggestions for improvement, especially if the suggestions altered the personality of the T.V.-doctor in question. For example, on a couple of occasions, real doctors circled production notes in the master script that had Joe Gannon or perhaps a T.V.-psychiatrist comforting his patients with hugs, hand holding, or affectionate grasps; never did subsequent script changes exclude the physical contact. The writers and creators of the show were interested only in surface accuracy and not in the presentation of true professionalism either in the medical or in other health fields. The viewer who regularly watched *Medical Center* thought he was seeing high-powered, sophisticated, big-league medicine in action. The message was, if you were going to be sick, you ought to be sick in a place with the biggest and most expensive machines and with a group of researchers in the background ready to provide a risky cure.

Beneath the polish and promise of the medical efforts shown on *Medical Center,* a phoniness emerged that remained with the viewer long after the sounds of "polyarteritis nodosa" and "endarterectomy" had faded from the memory. In retrospect, much of the show's premise was painfully absurd. Joe Gannon, the roving surgeon, used his position as Director of Student Health to demand carte blanche access into any corner of a student's life. He could close down student housing, demand the student's presence in the infirmary, stop a student from attending classes or from playing football. In no known university in the western world is the student health program considered a professional plum, yet *Medical Center* portrayed the position as enviable and even, in one episode, showed two doctors feuding over the job. Despite the onerous burdens of his job as Director of Student Health, Joe also taught courses in the medical and nursing schools; he participated in a variety of campus administrative committees; he supervised the clinical experience of dozens of interns and residents; he conducted a number of surgical research projects, occasionally perfecting innovative techniques; and still he kept a full schedule of his own patients. Given this remarkable professional load, Joe never rushed through a patient interview, never turned his back on a friend, and frequently spent hours of his own time goading and pestering a reluctant patient into coming into the hospital for a bit of open-heart surgery.

In principle Joe was a cardiovascular surgeon, and most of his surgical cases were in keeping with his specialty, but sometimes he stretched the limits of his special gifts and performed brain surgery and other difficult procedures not directly associated with the cardiovascular system despite the staff of world famous surgeons surrounding him. If there was an underlying problem, the heart for example, the tension would build as Joe first secured permission for a risky diagnostic procedure, probably a cardiac catheterization, and then had to secure permission for the surgical repair. Securing permission from the patient or next of kin often involved Joe in long trips and certainly in emotional confrontations as most of his patients preferred death—at first.

In addition to unspecified internal injuries and cardiac defects and insufficiencies, the writers relied on a few other stand-by, all-purpose diseases. Arterial problems in the form of aortic aneurysms, cerebral aneurysms, or carotid blocks and tumors threatening stroke at any moment, offered the classic time bomb symptom beloved of television writers. The patient's health, to outward observers and to the patient himself, would be perfect, and the statistical prediction of problems would be unconvincing. When Joe would then tell the patient that his aneurysm might blow tomorrow or in twenty years, a lot of the patients would put their money on the twenty year odds (and always lose). Of course cancerous tumors and systematic cancers often afflicted Joe's patients, but tumor resections usually cured them. At least three times Joe resorted to the infamous Whipple procedure (not a cardiovascular operation) and always brought the extensive surgery to a successful conclusion.

The patient population of *Medical Center* had a decided bias toward the young and attractive. More women than men appeared to be patients; of the male patients, a good proportion were under age 12. Thus, mature males appeared with considerable less frequency than did adult females. A good proportion of the adult females were between the ages of 18 and 30, and most were considered attractive. A large number of Joe's patients were drifters, orphans, or young people estranged from their more affluent families. Generational misunderstandings and alienation from the establishment frequently complicated Joe's attempts to straighten out his patients' physical and emotional crises. Most families represented were from the affluent middle class and professional ranks. Very often physicians and their families became patients of Joe Gannon. The working class, blue-collar family was underrepresented. Racially and ethnically the patients were overwhelmingly white, Anglo-Saxon, Protestants, although the show did include episodes featuring black and chicano families on occasion. In addition the show suggested that hospitals were quite romantic places; physicians frequently brought their marital problems into the hospital; patients found true love in the solarium of the hospital or in the waiting area of the radiology department. Modern health problems were distortedly presented. The chronically ill, the poor and aged, rarely appeared on the show because their health problems were not readily curable by the techniques of a crack surgeon.

In addition to these distortions of the hospital world were the distortions of the health care professional. Not surprisingly, male physicians (the majority of whom were surgeons) appeared as dedicated, often heroic practitioners who were able to reverse the odds in favor of their patient's recovery. They were ambitious, impatient, self-confident, and occasionally arrogant. They took decisive action which, even if on occasion the action turned out to be misguided, forced the resolution of the dramatic conflict. Given the series' emphasis on the role of Joe Gannon, none of the other surgeons portrayed ever proved him wrong or successfully competed for the viewer's sympathy. In fact, a good many of the physician characters suffered a variety of personal, emotional, domestic, and physical problems that always gave the edge to Joe Gannon. Despite the fact that the other physicians appeared flawed and human, as doctors they still functioned well and helped their patients. On very rare occasions, a physician acted to the detriment of a patient. In one story, "The Quack" (March 18, 1970) from the first season, a research scientist, eager to test his new serum on a patient with Hodgkin's Disease, ignored the side effects of the drug. The American Medical Association's reviewer of the script felt that the story was awful and should not be filmed. In another show, "Life and Death and Mrs. Armbruster" (February 23, 1976), a chief resident inadvertently caused the death of a patient through an act of poor judgment; although his intervention was not deemed criminally culpable, the Center and Joe Gannon insisted upon his discharge from their hospital. With these two exceptions, none of the other stories ever depicted a physician actually harming a patient. A frequent theme, however, showed a good, capable, often brilliant surgeon displaying poor judgment because of his own intense personal and emotional difficulties. In these instances, Joe always managed to persuade the doctor to come to his senses before any real harm could be done.

Some actually negative portrayals of physicians did occur, but the negative traits only threatened to affect medical judgment. For example, a Vietnam veteran returned to *Medical Center* where he had had Joe's job before he entered the Army; when he came back he was revealed to be an alcoholic. Another well respected surgeon was accused of having massacred a village full of people while in Vietnam, and the charge apparently had validity. More frequently the physicians only appeared to be unsympathetic or suspicious men; usually, the story developed them unsympathetically until the last few scenes in which they were vindicated. For example, an antisocial resident looked like the perpetrator of a series of rape–beatings around campus; of course, in the last minute chase the real rapist turned out to be, more understandably, a hospital orderly. At the end of the show, each of these physicians thanked Joe for his help and admitted that he had been right all along. The idea seemed to be that physicians scrupulously policed their ranks, and when temporary and understandable aberrations in professional conduct did occur, they were promptly identified and straightened around.

Medical Center did present female surgeons many times if not as often as male physicians. At least seventeen female doctors appeared in the seven-year history of the show. (There was not a single female M.D. in the first season, and the only one in the second year was portrayed as an ambitious harridan who psychologically castrated her husband. In subsequent seasons, female physicians appeared with some regularity and with more sympathy. The female surgeons suffered the same types of problems as did their male counterparts, and most were described as being excellent physicians with good reputations. At least three of these women became involved romantically with Joe Gannon, but their careers remained more important to them than their feelings for Joe.

Dr. Jeanne Bartlett (Corinne Comacho), a staff psychiatrist at *Medical Center,* appeared as Joe's semi-regular romantic interest for a couple of seasons.

Although she did have her own work and practice, and occasionally disagreed with Joe about a professional matter, her main role was romantic. (Of interest is the comparison between this character and Dr. Maggie Graham, anesthesiologist on *Ben Casey;* Maggie remained much less active and believable as a physician). Considering the show's generally flat-footed efforts to be controversial and relevant, the depiction of female doctors was well balanced.

If the show's producers and writers carefully nourished the image of female physicians, they did little to enhance the respect due to professional nurses. Featured nurse characters never became involved in professional concerns; their interest to the audience always came as a result of personal difficulties. Regular nurse characters followed the pattern established by Miss Wills of *Ben Casey*. Although three staff nurses appeared recurrently during the seven-year run of the series, only once did personal information about any of these nurse characters appear. Never did the writers indicate that any of these nurses had first names. Their dialogue was interchangeable; not one of the three developed an identifiable personality. In the world of *Medical Center,* they existed only to serve and to obey the physicians. This menial and subservient role became explicit in at least two episodes in which Joe and Paul Lochner discussed the merits and importance of the nursing staff.

In "The Secret Heritage" (February 3, 1971), an episode from the second season, Joe experienced difficulties with a head nurse who felt that he made too many demands upon her nursing staff, whom she always called "my girls." Joe rejected Paul Lochner's advice to explain his ideas and treatment plan to the nurses, "I shouldn't have to spend an hour, . . . or five minutes explaining medical practice to a head nurse. Any time I have to spend in explanations or reminders or criticism, is dead time." In this conversation, Joe and Paul showed their complete agreement about the nursing staff; the nurses were important only insofar as they obeyed the doctor's orders. Furthermore, a physician could not see any possible value to discussing patient care with a nurse; her duty was to follow his orders without question. In addition to these explicitly negative remarks, the storyline of this episode emphasized that nurses were capable of sincere compassion and sympathy for patients, but they were unable to subject their natural sympathies to the best long-range rehabilitative programs for the patient. Calling the nursing staff "girls" also encouraged the audience to think of nurses as immature women who naturally followed the guidance given by stronger personalities, in this case a reactionary head nurse.

Four years later, in a sixth season entry, "The Captives" (January 13, 1975), Joe and Paul once more discussed the nursing staff at the hospital when, to their surprise, one of the head nurses, Phyllis Rank, became a patient in the hospital due to pregnancy. Joe somewhat guiltily said that until that time, as long as Rank functioned efficiently, he wasn't aware of anything human about her. Phyllis Rank had been "as sterile and colorless as a syringe." Furthermore, Paul expressed a little irritation at the new situation, "You can't trust women. You put in all that time training them to be indispensable—which means sterile—and they turn around and go pregnant on you. And on your time yet."

Perhaps even more damaging to the image of nursing in this unit was Nurse Chambers' congratulations to Phyllis Rank on her pregnancy:

> Honey, you don't seem to understand that you're a heroine around here. You've done wonders for the nursing profession! You've made the doctors realize that we're real, living breathing *people*. They look at us now and think: 'Hey she's not an autoclave, she's a *woman!* She can do what Rank did!'

The nursing staff at Medical Center apparently believed that the only way for a nurse to get recognition was not by her professional performance but by becoming pregnant. In order for a nurse to win Gannon's attention, she had to have a health problem or a personal claim on Joe's time, for example being the widow of one of Joe's best friends.

To add insult to injury, according to the storyline of *Medical Center,* the surgical staff had the ultimate authority and responsibility in matters concerning the school of nursing. Nursing education in the series never became very clear; although the school of nursing was purportedly a B.S.N. program, the nursing students seemed to work in a diploma school environment. In one episode, "The Loser" (November 24, 1971), a nursing student, Diana Morton, supposedly an intelligent and gifted young woman with a driving desire to become a nurse, nearly flunked out of school because of her enormous burden of personal responsibilities. Joe Gannon was the only person who tried to help her. He claimed responsibility for getting her enrolled in the program, and for finding her a stipend; when he realized that she was in trouble, he made a special effort to counsel her and to help her with her studies. Furthermore, he was the lecturer in one of her classes. There was not a single hint that the school of nursing had a support system to provide the counselling and financial help clearly indicated for the student. No nursing faculty, supervisor, or even fellow nursing student seemed aware of Diana's difficulties nor did any of them express an interest in her. The future of her stipend depended not upon the nursing school administration but upon the discretion of Paul Lochner.

In another episode, "The Woman in Question" (January 1, 1971), Gannon again found it necessary to counsel a nursing student; Ellen Beeker had a venereal disease, and Joe had to help her through the emotional crises the disease caused. Again, not a single nurse or nursing student appeared capable of helping Ellen, although some of the students did express concern about her. Ellen was described as being nineteen-years-old and in the last year of her nursing school course, which was a bit odd, if she was, in fact, in a B.S.N. program. The other nursing students chatted about only one topic—how to find a man, preferably a doctor.

Nurse characters received extensive treatment in only a handful of episodes of the nearly 170 produced for the series, and the producers paid no attention to an accurate portrayal of modern nursing. The overall impression of these featured nurses left the viewer with the feeling that nurses were a sorry lot, victimized by either their men or by fate. Not a single episode featured a strong-willed, professionally and personally competent nurse character. Nor did any nurse indicate that she valued her professional identity or strove to achieve professional excellence.

Phyllis Rank, the veteran nurse who became pregnant in "The Captives," offered the audience a view of a nurse with a deeply unsatisfactory private life. Although the nurse was supposed to be efficient and competent on the job, she was so emotionally torn that she planned to give up her baby for adoption—a baby that was not illegitimate. This nurse was presented as being less sensitive and less rational than her own ten-year-old daughter, Ivy, who wanted the new baby. Again Joe Gannon referreed the final confrontation of mother and daughter and engineered the happy conclusion of the episode.

The most positive nurse character presented, Jenny Delaney in "Torment" (September 23, 1975), was only a minor character and even though positively portrayed, she also was something of a victim. After an apparently unsatisfactory marriage, Jenny despaired of finding true love until she met Ben; during the episode, she learned within minutes that she was pregnant and that Ben was dying. She bravely handled the news, offering comfort to her love and keeping her own condition a secret. Although this nurse was competent to handle her personal life as well as being respected for her professional contribution to the nursing staff, the predominant emotion elicited for her was pity rather than admiration.

The writers of the episodes featuring nurses intended the viewer to feel sympathy for the nurse in question. The nurse usually suffered from understandable emotional stress arising out of romantic complications in her life. All of the women in question were supposed to be good nurses or promising nursing students. There were no blatant presentations of sadistic, brutal, incompetent nurses who endangered their patients. Nevertheless, the overall attitude toward nurses expressed by the writers of *Medical Center,* through explicit dialogue and character portrayal, suggested that nurses were necessary to the hospital but had little to contribute to patient care or recovery. Nurses were caretakers who absolutely and without question followed a physician's orders. Occasionally nurses appeared to be so guided by their own sympathy and compassion that they could not see the patient's true welfare. The nurses never expressed pride in their profession nor did they indicate that they hoped to achieve some level of professional excellence. Indeed, the series did not indicate that there were standards by which to judge nursing care, other than those engendered by the expectations of physicians. Given the university setting of the medical center, and the series' attempts to appear contemporary and sophisticated, the image of nursing was especially sad. If the writers were sufficiently aware of the emergence of female physicians, they could as easily have been aware of the evolution of the nursing profession. One must conclude that they felt the nurse characters unworthy of their energies.

Marcus Welby, M.D. premiered on ABC on September 23, 1969 and ran a full seven years until May 11, 1976, when Drs. Welby and Kiley closed up shop for good. The show immediately impressed both viewers and critics as the 1969 season's best new entry, garnered all the top Emmy awards for an hour-long drama after its first season, and won awards for Robert Young, James Brolin, as well as for the series itself.

Marcus Welby recounted the professional exploits of an elderly general practitioner who worked in partnership with a young, newly graduated doctor. Unlike most medical dramas which concern feats of surgical prowess and acute, rare, life-threatening illnesses, *Marcus Welby* more often than not focused on chronic medical conditions and the human circumstances surrounding a patient's ability to cope with illness or pain. Although Drs. Welby and Kiley offered first-rate medical care, calling in specialists when necessary, they concentrated their considerable energies on persuading their patients to accommodate their lives to changed physical needs and to reduce emotional or psychological stresses which needlessly complicated their problems.

The show followed standard television drama constraints, attempted little in the way of controversial topics (unlike its counterpart on CBS, *Medical Center*), and used the disease-a-week plot device cherished in medical programs. Somehow out of the very traditional and unassuming premise of the series there emerged a very solid and credible product, a show already familiar to the viewer. Undoubtedly the casting of Robert Young (star of *Father Knows Best*, a successful series of the 1950s) in the title role provided instant recognition and trust for the character Marcus Welby. The supporting cast, James Brolin as Steve Kiley and Elena Verdugo as nurse Conseulo Lopez, looked right in their parts and established a cozy, homey atmosphere for the show. The storylines and dialogues, while not particularly unique or innovative, achieved a consistently high standard of believability and realism. Rarely did the writers contrive situations to make the show more exciting as was often the case on *Medical Center*.

Marcus Welby was a widower in his early sixties with one married daughter who appeared only a few times. He lived and worked in a pleasant, affluent Santa Monica neighborhood; in fact, his offices were conveniently attached to his home. Conseulo Lopez (Elena Verdugo), a dark blond, Mexican–American, worked as his long-time office nurse and dedicated herself to the service of Marcus Welby and his many patients. At the beginning of the first season, Dr. Welby had just taken into partnership a promising young physician, Steve Kiley (apparently Welby had suffered a heart attack and needed to curtail his work), who came from a disadvantaged background. Only sheer determination and hard work allowed Steve to get through medical school. Steve's first interest was in pursuing a specialty in neurology, but financial problems (he wanted to help his young brother in school) forced him to quit his residency and accept Marc's offer. Marc realized Steve's potential to become a skilled and compassionate family practitioner, but the younger doctor was clearly skeptical of the lure of family medicine in the first season. Kiley lived in Marc's home and acted the part of a younger son and neophyte learning from the master. This older/younger physician relationship, apparently de rigueur for any medical show, followed in the tradition of Kildare/ Gillespie, Casey/Zorba, and even Gannon/Lochner. Unlike the others, the young doctor in *Marcus Welby* was very definitely the secondary physician in the series. Marcus Welby, a man of moderate views, measured reactions, and infinite compassion, dominated the action and remained the central character throughout the series' long life. He transcended the role of physician and became family counselor, teacher, and resident sage for all the folks who came into his sphere of activity. Welby drew from his vast experience with people to handle difficult situations that young, brash Steve Kiley could not comprehend. He often lectured Steve on the need to maintain a professional reserve, to be patient, to be practical, and to be cautious. Steve, of course, was always motivated by good intentions and eager to put into practice his recently acquired knowledge and skill, but frequently his enthusiasm jeopardized a patient's recovery and offended the family's sensibilities.

Consuelo Lopez filled out the family circle. Unmarried, in her late thirties, perpetually perky and optimistic, Consuelo domesticated the series. Although she did not live in the Welby home, her working hours often extended into the night, placing her in natural contact with the two doctors at almost any time. She often appeared in Welby's kitchen or living room, where she might fix breakfast or a light lunch for her employers and herself. She believed in Marcus Welby and conveyed her confidence in the physician to the patients. Furthermore, she clucked after Marc's health, worrying about his meals and long hours; she quickly developed a sisterly relationship with handsome Dr. Kiley, teasing him about his romances and sympathizing with his dilemmas. The three cared about each other personally and respected each other professionally. Consuelo rarely contributed to the diagnosis and treatment of the patients, but the viewer was in no doubt that Consuelo was a skilled professional, valued by the physicians and appreciated by the patients.

Throughout the first few seasons, most of the action took place in Welby's home and office or in the homes of his patients, but in the sixth year, Welby and Kiley became the heads of a Family Practice Center located in Lang Hospital and spent considerable professional time working in this public clinic, thus shifting the scenes to hospital and surgical settings. Kiley and Welby, as supervisors of the Family Practice Center, were involved in teaching younger physicians as well as seeing a wider variety of patients in this new setting. Concurrent with the increased use of hospital footage and acute care cases, the series began using more background nurses and a few more R.N.s appeared, almost all in a positive way. The only other important shift in the series' format came in the seventh and last season when additional regular characters were added. In an effort to revitalize the aging show, the producers tried to infuse a little youth, excitement, and sexiness into the stodgy vehicle. Steve Kiley's role grew, especially with the introduction of Pamela Hensley as Janet Blair, public relations director of Lang Hospital, who became his romantic interest and ultimately his wife. Thereafter, their marital adjustments, usually stemming from their conflicting careers, became a routine sub-plot of the show. In addition, Steve began looking around for a residency in neurology, prefiguring the show's imminent demise and the dissolution of his partnership with Welby.

Despite a few cosmetic changes, the format of the show never changed. *Marcus Welby* earnestly and successfully strove to depict the medical profession in positive and frequently glowing images. Few viewers could resist the desire to find a family physician so concerned with their welfare. The medical profession clearly approved of the series: each show carried the imprimatur of the American Academy of Family Physicians; the American Medical Association asked Robert Young to address their numbers; and Young also spoke at medical school graduate ceremonies. Welby became the epitome of American medicine; wise, discrete, compassionate, thorough, patient, and skilled, he was also honest and human enough to admit his limits as well as the limits of modern medicine.

One aspect of the series which made it a critical success was undoubtedly the show's public service contribution. In many ways *Marcus Welby* was an important source of health information. A clear didactic purpose emerged in many of the show's 170 episodes, with Dr. Welby educating the entire viewing public regarding certain common diseases. Perhaps the most public spirited episode involved the danger to women of failing to have regular breast examinations. In addition, a frequent public service theme of the series was found in Welby's referral of his patients to special institutions and centers where they would receive help with their particular problems. *Marcus Welby* also broached a subject rarely mentioned or acknowledged by television's doctor-heroes: the cost of health care. Kiley, Welby, and Lopez were careful to acknowledge such expenses as tests, while CBS's doctor-hero, Joe Gannon, dragged every indigent and transient bum he could find into a high-powered and costly medical center.

Along with these very high-minded goals and valuable services, Marcus Welby did perpetrate some very unrealistic views of the American physician. Perhaps the most amazing aspect of his and Kiley's medical practice was their willingness and even joy in making house calls day or night. The producers and writers of *Welby* felt that only by having their protagonists make house calls could they identify them as having all the qualities of that now legendary figure from the golden age of America, the circuit-riding General Practitioner. Another far-fetched, although not quite so improbable feature of the Welby practice was his 24-hour bedside vigils with seriously ill patients which subtly conveyed the notion that nursing care was not adequate. Often the dramatic nature of the material would lead the viewer to believe that the physician's presence at the bedside somehow emanated healing vibrations that kept critically ill patients just this side of eternity. Another frequent plot would have Welby, Kiley and even Consuelo involved in time-consuming detective efforts in search of mysterious drugs and strands of family histories. These distortions of modern medical practice promoted the notion that a good doctor had an infinite amount of time and energy to spend on each patient.

Another false image of American physicians came from the writers' reluctance to use female physician characters. (Only five or six examples were found). Perhaps the show's producers could not accommodate their image of the ideal physician—an aging wise man—with the notion of women M.D.s.

The type of diseases chosen by the writers of *Marcus Welby* also reflected the producers' family orientation. Unlike *Medical Center* which most often featured acute medical conditions requiring life-saving surgery or emergency treatment, more often than not, *Marcus Welby* featured such chronic diseases as diabetes, asthma, arthritis, hypertension, heart disease, ulcers, and emphysema; such traumatic surgeries as mastectomy and hysterectomy; and such long-term degenerative diseases as hemophilia and sickle cell anemia. These diseases, while responsive to treatment, did not leave their victims totally recovered or returned to their pre-sickness state. Most of the *Welby* diseases demanded that the patient adjust his life so as to control exacerbation or complications of his disease or else make changes required by altered physical capabilities. Many times families had to reconcile their outstanding differences and conflicts in order to handle the demands made upon them when a child or close relative fell ill.

If the writers and producers of *Marcus Welby* created a health care world dominated by sensitive, skilled, and wise physicians, they created a nursing world in which maternal instincts and mother love were the most prized, but not exclusive, nursing virtues. The overall image of the nursing profession in the series would have to be judged positive: Nurses were never exploited as objects of sexual innuendo or jokes; nurses never appeared to be chronic victims; nurses were not portrayed as sadistic, unsophisticated, poorly educated, or insensitive. The fact that the writers did not portray nurses in negative terms must be counted as an important source of the positive image because so many other health care shows have treated nurses in a very stereotypic and simplistic fashion. On the other hand, instances in which nurse characters were shown to be acting in a decisive, professional, and competent manner were decidedly infrequent. During the last three seasons, positive images of nursing characters, albeit minor, did appear with more frequency, perhaps as a result of the series' shift to larger, institutional settings. Not counting Consuelo's role, only seven episodes featured a nurse in a leading role (including one L.P.N.). However, especially in the final season, quite a few nurse characters in minor roles contributed to the storylines.

The major problem with the depiction of nurses in the series rested upon the writers' emphasis upon the physician as primary caregiver and as the major source of compassion and consolation. In the office, Welby and Kiley, rather than a nurse, would routinely take vital signs, administer injections, and take blood samples. (Consuelo would also do any of these tasks, but not as frequently.) In the hospital the physicians were always shown as the main sources of the patients' emotional and psychological comfort. In hospital scenes the nurses served primarily as observers of physicians at work or as messengers. Physicians did all of the bedside education and instruction for patients.

An understanding of the presentation of nurses on *Marcus Welby* must begin with the character of Consuelo Lopez. The obvious criticism of her part stems from her preoccupation with clerical and receptionist duties. The most lasting image of Consuelo in the viewer's mind would be the picture of her standing behind the reception counter, waving to arriving/departing physicians or patients, and arranging some important appointment over the phone. She was busy, efficient, friendly, enormously valued by her employers, skilled and interested in the patients, but essentially she did not perform nursing functions. Interestingly, a few publicity articles about the series mentioned Consuelo as the doctor's secretary, and the A.M.A. gave her an honorary award as medical assistant. Consuelo's Mexican–American identification was important to the development of the role. Aside from her occasional use of Spanish for communication with patients or her tiny explosions of anger in Spanish, she spoke perfectly grammatical and well-articulated English. However, over the years the writers developed for Consuelo a set of values and aspirations that remained constant; many of her values would be consistent with a conservative, religious, Hispanic background. Consuelo had worked for Marcus Welby for many years as the series began. In one episode she admitted that she had first wanted to be a doctor, but, because she could not afford medical school, became a nurse. After working for Marc Welby she realized that she could never be as good a doctor as he was and decided to settle for helping him in his practice. Despite her unmarried status, Consuelo apparently enjoyed a moderately active social life, had many friends, and was always open to new friendships and experiences. Consuelo's most constant personality trait and the source of her greatest personal conflict was her maternal feelings and thwarted desire to become a mother.

The writers devoted about one episode a year to Consuelo. During the third season in "Yellow Bird," (November 23, 1971), Consuelo gained temporary custody of a young, asthmatic child whose divorced mother has just died and whose father has ignored him. Against Marc's judgment, Consuelo thought seriously about adopting the boy and did everything in her power to win his affection. The boy, who already had emotional problems before his mother's death, did not respond to Consuelo's good-hearted but inadequate efforts to help him. When the father did show up, he claimed he did not want his son, and Consuelo's hope to be a mother rose. Although the boy's father had performed poorly in the past, it finally became clear to both him and Consuelo that he alone could fill the boy's needs. Reluctantly Consuelo abandoned her attempts to claim a child.

Most of Consuelo's shows featured her thwarted desire to be a mother. She still cherished the hope that she might one day bear a child—a hope the rather blunt Steve Kiley told her was unlikely to be fulfilled. Suffering from fibroid tumors of the uterus, Consuelo refused to follow the physician's advice to have a hysterectomy. The surgery was done only after a severe hemorrhagic episode. Consuelo's recuperation was retarded by severe depression. She stayed with Sandy and Phil, Welby's daughter and grandson, for several weeks after her surgery. She became increasingly depressed and concluded that her life was over. She angrily resented Sandy whom she accused of using her as a free babysitter; she accused Marc of trying to ease her out of her job. Finally, she turned to a casual boyfriend who had always been interested in her. She encouraged his romantic interest and decided to quit being a nurse and settle down to be cared for by her husband. Welby (and everyone else) saw this as a poor strategy, one which Consuelo would regret when she did finally recover from the surgery, both physically and emotionally. Of course, Consuelo at long last accepted the fact of her hysterectomy and her inability to bear children; furthermore, she realized that she did not want to retire from nursing and would not be happy as the pampered and childless wife.

Consuelo's maternal affections also found release in her relationship with her two employers and in her job. She fussed over Marc's health, worried about Steve's problems, lent a sympathetic ear to both them and their friends. She took a slight motherly concern for Welby's daughter and grandson and seemed to especially love dealing with the children who came into the office. In addition to her efficiency and clerical skills, Consuelo contributed a strong dose of feminine intuition and insight and occasionally found diagnostic answers which eluded the doctors. For example, she was the first to diagnose a case of wife beating.

Many times Consuelo would find patients in need of extra sympathy and support, and she would go out of her way to provide this support. For example, a young man living with his pregnant girlfriend found himself ambivalent about his feelings for the soon to be born baby. He got little sympathy from the doctor and was generally ignored in all the attention given to the pregnant girl. Although Consuelo could not share his hopes that the girl would miscarry, she did listen to him and offer him some understanding and sympathy when he needed it. In her capacity as maternity nurse during the pilot project, one of Marc's private patients came to Consuelo with her problems, being unable to confide in the physician.

Consuelo remained the only regular, continuing nurse character throughout the series' long life. However, occasionally a minor nurse character might appear more than once, and during the last three seasons of the show, the writers more frequently included roles for nurses. Only two other nurse characters had anything approaching recurrent roles in the series. Nurse Donnelly, played by Marcia Ralston, appeared several times as a mature staff nurse at one of the hospitals in which Marc Welby worked. She contributed almost nothing to the plots of any episodes, but she did indicate her respect and admiration for Dr. Welby. In the first season, pretty nurse Anne MacAndrews, who worked as a staff nurse in one of the hospitals, appeared primarily to play a romantic interest for Dr. Kiley. In two of the episodes she merely appeared arranging a date or sitting in a restaurant with Steve. However, one story in which Steve was hospitalized for the chicken pox, featured her as his nurse, and he was made to suffer all the indignities common to any hospitalized patient on Marc Welby's orders. In a final scene in this story, on Steve's last night in the hospital, she dressed up in a cocktail dress and prepared a special meal for her patient, in a mock romantic mood. She dropped out of the story after three appearances.

Almost all the presentations of nurses in small roles gave positive images of the profession. For example, in a fifth season episode, "The Tall Tree" (November 6, 1973), a psychiatric nurse named Sue who lived at a residential center for disturbed children was one of the few loyal supporters of a brilliant but unorthodox therapist. In the seventh season in "The Covenant" (September 30, 1975), an older, emergency room nurse offered to administer a debated blood transfusion to save Marc from a possible malpractice suit. A pediatric nurse in "Double-Edged Razor" (October 7, 1975) appeared in a special children's hospital and obviously contributed to her patients' good attitudes and compliance with therapy.

Very few bit-part nurses exhibited negative characteristics. Sarah, a pretty young scrub nurse with designs on Steve Kiley in "The Comeback" (January 1, 1974), showed a jealous and intolerant attitude toward a female orthopedic surgeon recovering from alcoholism, but by the end of the episode she finally accepted the female surgeon. In a sixth season story, "The Last Rip-Off" (November 26, 1974) about a nursing home which worked in league with a funeral home to fleece unsuspecting relatives of recently deceased patients, a staff nurse at the home was taking bribes for passing on information about the deaths of her patients to the funeral director. Aside from these rare negative characterizations, nurses that received attention were invariably presented as bright, efficient, friendly, compassionate women, but with the exception of the episode in which Consuelo co-directed a maternity pilot project for the training of nurse–midwives and the unit in which a coronary care nurse exhibited obvious professional expertise, none of the nurse characters who appeared in small parts demonstrated evidence of extensive professional involvement or identity. Only about eight nurse characters (one of whom was an L.P.N.) in seven episodes—excluding those episodes concentrating on Consuelo—played a major role in plot development. In keeping with the maternal, caring image of nursing most often apparent in Consuelo's characterization, these nurses more often than not appeared in parts calling for maternal love and concern rather than professional commitment. Unlike featured nurses in other health care dramas, these nurses were not portrayed as the victims of rape, abandonment, bitter disappointments, and loneliness. "To Carry the Sun in a Golden Cup" (December 8, 1970) found Dr. Kiley involved with two sisters who were nurses at the hospital. The older sister, Maggie (Joann Pflug), was an attractive, outgoing, popular staff nurse with several years experience who appeared more as "one of the guys" than as an object of persistent romantic pursuit. Her younger, adopted sister, Paula (Mariette Hartley), a recent graduate of nursing school, was going to begin work at her sister's hospital. Although Maggie doted upon Paula, a certain wistful tension emerged. Paula received the romantic attention of the hospital's favorite bachelor doctor, Steven Kiley. The examination of nursing in the episode stemmed from the personality differences between the two sisters. Although Paula did well at school and knew the technical side of nursing perfectly, she lacked the empathy and ability to put her patients' needs first. Her sister, on the other hand, received nothing but compliments for her nursing work. Marc noted that nurses like Maggie had been making doctors look good for years, and he acknowledged the important role of nursing in the modern hospital, saying, "... it usually isn't the doctor who puts in the long hours through the crisis of a patient—it's the nurse. Her skill can save their life, and has countless times ... I've seen Maggie do that." At the end of the episode Paula indirectly admitted that she never wanted to be a nurse except as a way of competing with her sister; she claimed she would quit nursing and become a researcher or a physician. Thus in this episode, the writers formally referred to the nurses' contributions to patient care; however, the story pointed out that often ambitious and self-centered women were not suited for nursing, while those women who possess the maternal, self-sacrificing instincts (like Maggie) make truly fine nurses.

"House of Mirrors" (October 10, 1972) featured Marilyn (played by Brenda Vaccaro) as a plain, rather dumpy staff nurse engaged to marry an attractive, very successful older research physician who was a widower and father of a young son. No one in the hospital understood the basis of the romance since the physician's late wife had been a very beautiful woman. However, Marilyn attributed it to incredible luck and lavished great love and attention upon the doctor and his son. The boy, injured in the car wreck that killed his mother, had come to rely upon Marilyn's care and love. As the story developed, the doctor turned out to have lung cancer but refused to postpone his wedding until after surgery. Welby and Kiley worried that the afflicted doctor was marrying Marilyn only to find a mother for his son, a probable orphan. Finally they convinced him to be fair to Marilyn, and after he told her the truth, he and Marilyn still decided to marry after the surgery since he really did love his improbable fiancée. Again, the main personality characteristics of this featured nurse were her self-sacrificing tendencies and her maternal instincts.

In all of the episodes featuring nurses, Marc and Steve were appreciative physicians and occasionally acted as providers of care to the nurses themselves, yet never did the writers resort to the device whereby the physician saved the nurse from her own problems. Steve and, more often, Marc offered advice and sympathy, but they did not step in and straighten out the nurses' problems with argument or force in the manner of Joe Gannon or Ben Casey. In most cases, the nurses, who ranged in age from their early twenties to the late fifties, while possibly troubled, appeared more than capable of straightening out their own lives and coping with difficulties. The two main drawbacks to the presentation of nursing in this series are to be found in the limited attention given to nurses and nursing, considering the long life of the series, and to the recurrent presentation of Consuelo as a receptionist–secretary rather than as a professional nurse. Compared to such earlier series as *Ben Casey* and *Dr. Kildare* and even to its contemporary *Medical Center,* the writers and producers of *Marcus Welby, M.D.* avoided demeaning stereotypes of nurses as chronic victims, and they attempted, in a limited fashion, to accord the nursing profession some respect and credit.

As in the earlier series of the 1960s, the image of nursing in *The Bold Ones, Medical Center,* and *Marcus Welby, M.D.* suffered because of the limited attention given to the role of nursing in contemporary health care. As in all of these doctor dominated series, the physician-hero was simply placed in the center of every health treatment, whether or not his presence in such a situation conformed with reality. By allowing physician characters to keep bedside vigils, to administer most drugs and treatments, to take routine vital signs, and to offer psychological support, the producers of these series eliminated the professional nurse from the public eye. When the nurse was brought into the camera's eye, she was almost always placed behind a desk where she answered the phone and did unidentifiable paperwork.

The Bold Ones and *Marcus Welby,* at least, rarely presented nurses as particularly troubled or problem prone women. *Medical Center,* on the other hand, introduced its viewers, over time, to a selection of nurse characters that were pitiful victims of thwarted love of vicious circumstances beyond their control. On more than one occasion, the physician-heroes of this series expressed, in explicit terms, their disregard of the nurses' contribution to patient welfare in the hospital. The regular staff nurse characters of *Medical Center* remained indistinguishable ciphers.

Three medical series dominated the 1970s: *The Bold Ones, Marcus Welby, M.D.,* and *Medical Center.* All of these shows featured nurses to a greater or lesser degree, but only *Marcus Welby* had a regular and major nurse character—Consuelo Lopez, played by Elena Verdugo. These three shows followed in the *Dr. Kildare* and *Ben Casey* traditions. Each series featured old doctor/young doctor teams; almost all the physician-protagonists were unmarried, handsome, white males. In all cases, the doctors were extremely dedicated practitioners who not only cured physical ailments but also straightened out difficult emotional situations. The differences between these three new doctor shows and their predecessors of the early 1960s were minimal. In the 1970s, there appeared to be less difference between the work of the older doctor and that of his younger colleagues; the older doctors took a much more active role in the series. The doctors appeared to be more successful and mature in the shows of the 1970s; gone were the struggling and poor interns and residents, replaced by affluent private practitioners and well-placed hospital staff physicians. The shows of the 1970s placed more emphasis on developments in medical technology and surgical techniques. Basically, all three series ignored the role of the hospital staff nurse and used her as background scenery in the manner of earlier medical drama. The doctor heroes would frequently perform nursing tasks and provide the major source of compassion and comfort for their hospitalized patients. Nurses were left to perform such duties as carrying trays, pushing wheelcarts, and answering the phone.

4
Stock Footage: Nurses and Physicians in Short-lived Medical Dramas, 1970s

Throughout the 1970s television networks attempted to repeat the successes achieved by *Medical Center* and *Marcus Welby, M.D.* by introducing new health care dramas. The settings and premises of these short-lived efforts varied: Colorado doctors in medically equipped campers; ex-military physicians driving beat-up sports cars; teams of young doctors working together; female doctors; and a mixture of medical specialties. Despite surface differences, the underlying assumptions of all were that doctors were true heroes who alone carried the burden of the weak and the sick. These doctors sacrificed all thoughts of personal recompense in their crusade to cure the afflicted and to reform the misguided. The physician characters' excellence made the efforts and contributions of other health care providers, namely nurses, pale in comparison.

Matt Lincoln premiered on September 24, 1970, ran for fifteen episodes, and did not surface again. This short-lived series starred Vince Edwards (of *Ben Casey* fame) as a psychiatrist, assisted by four young aides, at a walk-in clinic in a large hospital. Their motto was "Somebody Cares." The emphasis was consistently on Matt Lincoln's ability to say the right thing to soothe troubled patients. Most often the episodes dealt with young people—drug addicts, unwed mothers, and so on. Sometimes the people with problems were older—a priest who wanted to marry, an alcoholic doctor. Most episodes offered little place for nurses other than in the background.

One episode was, however, atypical. The story took place in a hospital, not Matt's clinic, so a fairly large number of nurses did appear. Unfortunately, the nursing image was both simplistic and sentimental. The show, entitled "Misty" and aired on Dec. 17, 1970, began when a well-dressed, pregnant woman collapsed in a diabetic coma. She was brought to the hospital, but the only clues to her identity were the name "Misty" embroidered on her coat label and a slip of paper clutched in her hand, bearing the name of Matt Lincoln. The other doctors assumed she was one of Matt's patients and called him in to identify her, but Matt declared that he had never seen the woman. Although Misty was nominally declared Matt's patient, he called in his retired father (a distinguished internist), and the rest of the plot spun out as these physicians all struggled to discover her identity, find her husband, deliver her baby alive, and save her life. The nurses' lines were generally limited to "Yes, sir," "Yes, Doctor Lincoln," "Yes, Doctor Hughes." When they had any more extended lines, they were either exaggeratedly maternal or nearly swooning in admiration for the doctor (especially Dr. Lincoln, Sr.). Mrs. Tweed, a plump, motherly person, though clearly more knowledgeable than a young intern, was first seen soothing and coaching him as he examined an emergency patient. Miss Salt, an angular nurse in her forties, though a brisk, efficient person, nonetheless hovered anxiously over the X-ray technician, urging him to hurry because he was dealing with "a mother and a dear little baby—two lives, Carl." Another nurse, Miss Cobb, was a severely lean woman who ruled her realm (the premature nursery) with zealous fervor, but she too was all motherliness in action, lifting a baby with great tenderness and arguing vociferously with the doctor who said the baby could not yet handle food. The overwhelming effect of all the nursing scenes was to present the nurses as having all heart and no brain. Though possessed of the most loving intentions, these nurses had to be constantly reined back to sensibleness by the doctors who were both loving *and* wise about the patients. To be sure, the physicians seemed to feel that this attitude was only proper, as the following bit of dialogue illustrated. Although the older Dr. Lincoln did nothing except wait for the baby to get better by itself, the doctors were unanimous in their acclaim for him:

Dr. Graham: You're an incredible doctor, Dr. Lincoln.
Dr. Hughes: We ask for a miracle, and you delivered!
Dr. Lincoln: Don't give me credit; nature worked that miracle.
Matt: But you had the faith. You *waited* for it!

That such a portrayal was developed at all revealed the show's most basic assumption to be deification of the physician. The viewer was expected to believe this because the characters themselves seemed to believe it.

Another view of young and old physicians working together appeared in *The Interns* which premiered September 18, 1970 on CBS. The twenty-four episodes, many repeated to stretch the season to a full twelve months, concerned the dedication and idealism of five young and uniformly attractive interns at New North Hospital of Los Angeles who worked under the close supervision of the sweetly tyrannical Dr. Peter Goldstone (Broderick Crawford). Ten of the episodes involved all the interns dealing with common problems and activities; fourteen of the episodes featured a particular intern, though a black intern and a female intern were featured in only one episode each. It appears that as far as the writers were concerned, physicians really ought to be white males. In addition, the female physician's "show" found her debating a marriage versus a career rather than solving the problems of patients.

Usually an episode focused upon a patient-related problem, in the midst of which the interns occasionally dealt with their own personal problems. They went to incredible lengths to solve mysterious diseases or to straighten out a patient's life far beyond his health problems. Often these stories were complicated by friendship between the patient and an intern. Professional and ethical problems also kept the interns abreast of the wide ranging issues of their profession: A sub-plot had Lydia Thorpe (female physician) out to convince a misogynist physician that women doctors were all right. Even Dr. Goldstone, the other regular character, served to emphasize the interns' skills, dedication, and idealism. He was a gruff, crusty man who provided welcome contrast to the fresh-scrubbed innocence of the young physicians. Offered a cheery "Good morning," Goldstone growled in reply, "Prove it." With deceptively gentle ferocity, he kept the interns on their mettle by demanding discipline, preparation, excellence, and unstinting effort from them. He assumed that he had authority over any aspect of their lives that met his eye.

Some degree of realism was intended, and realized, in *The Interns,* as it tackled such difficult subjects as rape and its consequences, or an unmaudlin view of the blind. However, the interns' perpetual nobility, courage, and superhuman efforts on behalf of the patients sometimes tended to strain the viewer's credulity. While the set captured the hustle and bustle of a large, metropolitan hospital quite well, the show's writers ignored the reality of health care whenever they pleased. Doctors pushed the drug cart and handed out medications to a ward full of patients; they delivered messages; and major surgery (not emergency) was scheduled without time to prep the patient. In addition, the virtual absence of nurses in anything but decorative appearances did much to undermine any sense of realism otherwise built up in this program about hospital life. *The Interns* was a showcase for the zeal and courage of the medical profession and had no room for the associated talents of nurses or other health care providers. The nurses silently took orders from physicians, acknowledging them with a nod or facial expression. Occasionally a nurse was seen doing some sort of patient care, such as checking an I.V. drip or taking a pulse, but she moved away immediately at the approach of a physician, leaving him the entire field. Even the nursing stations seemed more filled with interns than with nurses. Aside from the prologue of one episode ("Tasha") in which a nurse took some initiative in calming a violent patient, the nurses seen in *The Interns* never so much as suggested anything resembling information or knowledge to a physician. Nothing remotely hinted at the fact that nurses were responsible for a large proportion of patient care or that there was a separate body of nursing knowledge separate from medical knowledge. From this series, the viewer would perceive nursing as a profession secondary to medicine or as peripheral to patient treatment and recovery.

The 1973–1974 season's *Doc Elliot* lasted for only fourteen episodes despite everyone's intentions to make it a quality show. In a way the show was a smorgasbord of proven popular ideas—westerns, doctors, CB radios, and maverick heroes. Ben Elliot, M.D. (James Franciscus) was a handsome, young surgeon who left his successful hospital practice in New York City to become a general practitioner in rural Colorado. There he dressed in plaid shirts, jeans, and boots and made his rounds in a medically-equipped camper, guided to his patients by CB radio calls. "Doc" had a few regulars to offset him in most of the shows: Mags Brimble (Neva Patterson), the woman who managed Doc's home/office and who let him know by radio where he was needed next; Barney (Noah Beery), a combination storekeeper and constable; and a bush pilot, Eldred Mccoy (Bo Hopkins), who was available to fly emergency cases to the nearest hospital. Doc, however, remained as the show's central focus, and in the course of the series he tangled with numerous social, psychological and health care problems.

There was a close resemblance between *Doc Elliot* and *Simon Locke*, a syndicated series released in 1971. In both shows a handsome young doctor left a successful, big city practice to become a general practitioner in a rural area where people often did not understand or trust the young man's skill. Both physicians had to deal with victims of snake bite and car wrecks; both coolly out-talked criminals with guns; both tracked down fugitive typhoid carriers; both persuaded reluctant patients and/or family members to let them administer lifesaving medical treatment; and both performed emergency surgery on kitchen tables, or at the scene where a victim was trapped or pinned down. In all episodes of *Doc Elliot*, Doc solved the problem.

Surface characteristics gave the *Doc Elliot* series a rather modern, updated appearance: The physician was young, handsome, and casually dressed rather than old, venerable, and conservative in appearance; he got his calls on a CB radio, drove to them in a camper, and had a pilot to fly his emergency patients to a hospital; and he dealt with such modern concerns as cosmetic surgery, hijackers, plane crashes, and draft dodgers. However, a closer examination revealed that the real appeal of the show lay in the old-time pioneering feel that pervaded every episode—everyone knew everyone else by name; "everyone in the state" knew Doc's camper by sight; and Doc knew not only the names of his patients but their personalities, problems, and private lives besides; ranch wives bravely assisted him in emergency surgery performed on kitchen tables. Most of all, however, the traditional virtues were conveyed by Doc Elliot himself. Doc, despite surface changes, was really another Dr. Christian (the archetypal old country doctor), twenty-five years younger and ever so slightly updated. Like Dr. Christian, Ben was a man of enormous medical skill and knowledge, dedicated, wise, and understanding. Though he always made critical, correct medical decisions, these were minor compared to the judgments he had to make about human character. When a desperate young criminal held him at gunpoint, Doc had to decide when to obey the nervous boy and when to defy him or call his bluff; in the end, his good judgment was responsible for the boy's decision to turn himself in and go straight. Not only could Doc decide that a blind girl could see with the proper surgery; his heart also understood that the husband's opposition to the operation stemmed from his fear that he would lose his lovely wife when she saw that he was an ugly man.

When there was nursing to be done, Doc called upon the sturdy ranch wives and daughters to help him, and they were always willing and adequate to take on the most hair-raising of medical emergencies (such as amputations on the spot and emergency splenectomies on the kitchen table). Professional training was apparently not considered necessary in a nurse. For this series' creator, then, a nurse's virtues were identical to any good woman's, that is, a loving heart, a strong stomach, and a willingness to do whatever the doctor ordered.

In September 1975 NBC introduced two new hour-long health care dramas: *Medical Story* and *Doctors Hospital* to compete with *Marcus Welby* and *Medical Center* on CBS and ABC. Unfortunately for the network, neither of the new series survived the mid-season cuts.

Medical Story, patterned after Police Story and written under the creative guidance of Abby (*Kojak*) Mann, was an anthology series, in which cast and locale changed each week. The format of the show, regardless of setting (invariably a hospital) or cast, concerned the efforts of a young and dedicated resident, intern, medical student, nurse, or staff physician to deal with a topic taken from the headlines of the recent past: abortion controversy; unnecessary hysterectomies; malpractice ethics; the right to die; and wholesale sterilization of welfare mothers. The problem with such an approach to *Medical Story* hinged on the public's overall impression of the health care world: that patients entering hospitals in the United States would, in all likelihood, suffer more from the hands of their physicians than from their physical ailments. Most episodes dealt with acute care of patients, highlighting surgical interventions and surgeons and practically ignoring the work of internists or other specialists. In fact, "The God Syndrome" divided M.D.s into "fleas" (diagnosticians and internists) and "blades," with most esteem and praise going to the "blades." In this story an incompetent although compassionate surgeon sewed a patient's stomach to the wrong piece of intestine, causing predictable difficulties in digestion; the other surgeons decided not to take action if the man would willingly give up surgery and move into the specialty of internal medicine.

In its efforts to achieve a contemporary, mid-1970s look, *Medical Story* featured a large percentage of female and racially and ethnically diverse physicians; at least two of the eleven episodes focused on female physicians, and they were in evidence in all the other stories examined. Possibly the new emphasis on female physicians led to playing down the role of professional nurses.

The level of realism seemed quite high, even hyperrealistic: A young man was seen retching bright red blood from his mouth; patients screamed and moaned; one female stroke victim was given to atavistic cries; the conversations about health problems had a convincing ring using just the right mixture of technical terminology and casual familiarity with the grotesque.

Nurses played limited roles in the episodes of *Medical Story* and, with the exception of one story in which a nurse struggled to defend an older woman's right to die in dignity, the episodes provided for minimal participation of the nursing profession in the development of plot. A brief review of episodes highlights the presentations of nurses in *Medical Story*.

"The God Syndrome," appearing October 18, 1975, studied the psychological and emotional growth of an extremely talented but often intolerant and insensitive surgical resident, Dr. Paul Brandon (Tony Musante). Within a time span of several days, Dr. Brandon faced more than one crisis that forced him to examine the generally intolerant attitude he took toward people; the show's conclusion found him, at last, confiding his fears and pains with his live-in girlfriend who had threatened to leave him because of the emotional wall around his feelings. There was no important nurse character in this story; a charge nurse named Ann Harris who assisted Brandon in the operating room apparently worked well with him and once, when the doctor was in trouble with a heavy bleeder, prompted the call for a hematological specialist; beyond this minor exchange, the nurses appeared only in the background of the story. However, Dr. Alice Heverly, a female intern who had a crush on Paul Brandon, worked up a couple of Brandon's patients and in many ways played the part of a nurse. The patients clearly liked the young intern, but only really listened to Dr. Brandon. To a certain extent then, Alice Heverly fulfilled two functions for the screenwriters: She provided a contemporary, 1970s image of medicine—the lady doctor, and she allowed the writer to use the old chestnut, adoring female helper to the busy doctor, now changed from nurse to female intern.

"Million Dollar Baby" (October 23, 1975) starred John Forsythe as Dr. Amos Winkler, a well-known, compassionate, caring, and respected pediatrician in a busy teaching hospital. A patient he had treated twenty-three years earlier charged him with malpractice for the use of highly concentrated oxygen after her birth which resulted in blindness. Despite the advice of hospital administrators and insurance companies, he decided to fight in court, contending that the best medical minds twenty-three years before did not know the correlation between high concentrations of oxygen and retrolental fibroplasia. However he discovered, in reviewing his records, an article annotated in his own hand which indicated that several months prior to the treatment of the patient in question, he did know of the strong likelihood of oxygen causing blindness. He admitted this knowledge to the prosecuting attorney, but still he saw himself as innocent of malpractice. The many ethical, moral, and legal definitions of malpractice were bandied about amidst the greedy lawyers and outraged physicians shown in this episode. No nurse characters participated in the development of Winkler's problems nor played an important role in scenes of treatment though a large number of female physicians were presented. One incident showing Winkler's fairness and good medical sense did shed some light on nursing. He came across a pediatric resident chewing out a nurse for questioning a written order; upon examination the resident's order called for ten times too much of a certain medication, and Winkler informed him that the nurses were instructed to question such orders.

Doctors Hospital, which premiered the same month as *Medical Story,* followed the *Ben Casey–Medical Center* school of doctor-heroes in which the more aggressive and impatient the hero, the more appealing he was. This series focused upon the professional exploits of Jake Goodwin, M.D. (George Peppard), forty-five year old, handsome chief of the neurosurgical wing of Doctors Hospital. By choosing a neurosurgical specialty for the hero, the show's creators guaranteed the performance of the always-exotic brain surgery. Jake Goodwin had dedicated his life to the practice of medicine; a divorced father of one he occasionally worried about spending too little time with his son, but nothing deflected his concern for patient welfare, and when a patient's well-being was at stake, Jake forwent rules and regulations. His aggressive, impatient, and demanding behavior saved lives but won him few friends in the medical establishment. For example, when he believed that a Beverly Hills society physician ordered the wrong surgery for a man, Jake conspired with a nurse to lose the patient for a few hours, until Jake could get authorization to proceed with his own surgical plans for the man. Janos Varga (Albert Paulson), the hospital administrator, was responsible for hiring Jake and thus became responsible for defending or covering Jake's unorthodox behavior to hospital boards and offended physicians.

In addition to patient care, Jake had an abiding interest in the promotion of promising young neurosurgeons. His protégés Felipe Ortega (Victor Campos), a chicano chief resident, and Norah Purcell (Zohra Lampert), one of the eight female neurosurgical residents in the country, proved Jake to be an affirmative action employer, and they followed in their mentor's footsteps, spending every waking hour rushing emergency room patients to surgery. Other regular, minor characters added continuity, but they never developed distinct personalities. For example, Scotty, Goodwin's secretary, who had last-name-only identification, Peggy Stuart who often assisted in the operating room, and Doherty, the emergency room nurse, who transported redblanket patients and delivered brief summaries to the physicians.

The episodes revealed mediocre dialogue and hackneyed storylines. Instead of building a sense of drama by careful character development, the writers resorted to dramatic but unconvincing speeches. Frequently, the writers crammed numerous subplots into one episode to disguise the absence of a dramatic theme. For example, the pilot for the series covered the following components: A transplant specialist, guilt-ridden over the death of his son, has a serious car accident; Jake has to fight the man's private physician over proper treatment; Jake also has to discover why the specialist's son died; Norah must find the courage to tell the truth to a dying man; an intelligent but insensitive intern treats a chronic alcoholic as if he weren't worth the effort; an intelligent but sensitive intern recommends neurosurgery for a promising 16-year-old tennis player and feels guilty when the girl's father refuses the surgery and she later dies.

Summaries of two episodes which featured nurse characters will give a better idea of plot development. "Watchman, Who Will Guard Thy Sleep" (telecast on October 20, 1975) found the influx of neurosurgical candidates to be at the normal, near saturation level common to Doctors Hospital. Against the background of the physicians' hectic schedules and the intrusion of frequent emergencies, two main subplots were featured. The most important strand of the story featured Maggie Steven, the attractive, 38-year-old nurse who masterfully and efficiently supervised the operating rooms. However, she began to make careless mistakes one after another, disrupting the usually well managed surgical wing. At last, Jake fired her. Both Norah and Jake attempted to find the cause of her unprecedented behavior; she refused to talk to them. At last Norah learned that Maggie had a breast mass and a strong family history of breast cancer; she refused to consider surgery because she feared it would ruin her romantic life. Both she and Norah shared their fears and complaints about being single, working women. Then Norah insisted that Maggie return to the hospital for tests, and the viewer knew that all would turn out well.

The second strand of the story featured the efforts of hospital orderly Johnny Almo, a homosexual, to smooth the hospitalization of a business tycoon who turned out to have a metastatic brain tumor. There was considerable conflict between patient and orderly when the tycoon learned that his orderly was a homosexual. But the interesting feature of this plot was that the orderly performed so many nursing tasks. The orderly seemed the only member of the hospital staff who cared about the patients' feelings; everyone else was too busy to notice the fear or confusion in the patients' eyes. Johnny explained consent forms to bewildered patients; came up with a blood donor when everyone else had failed; diagnosed a seizure in a patient; straightened out a patient's marital problems; and finally helped his patient to accept the fact of his impending death.

"Come at Last to Love" (September 17, 1975) had Jake involved in the tragic romance of his long-time, skilled and invaluable scrub nurse, Bobbie Marks. Bobbie was in love with a young research scientist, Dr. David Stone who had been developing a serum against virulent neurotropic viruses. Stone was upset because Jake had been hesitant to find him a human subject on whom to test his serum. Bobbie, however, went to David's lab and injected herself with the virus. Soon Bobbie was making careless mistakes in surgery but she told David and convinced him to give her the injection of the serum and to take notes of her behavior and symptoms. He began to worry when she failed to respond to the drug. The next day, in surgery, Bobbie was ordered out of the operating room when she dropped a couple of instruments and handed Jake the wrong equipment; soon she returned to David's where she collapsed. At last Jake figured out what had happened and rushed to put Bobbie in the neurointensive care unit. All his efforts failed, and Bobbie died.

Doctors Hospital presented nurses as generally good people despite the fact that there were occasional indications of their having less than admirable traits. None of the nurse characters emerged as evil, incompetent, or unsympathetic. The featured nurse characters had a variety of positive traits such as the compassion, respect for life, and self-sacrifice shown by Bobbie Marks. Another nurse lavished warmth and love on a possibly dying patient. Even Maggie Stevens was reputedly a valuable asset to the hospital because of her efficiency, decisiveness, and intelligence; the personality changes which made her irritable, irrational, and argumentative were temporary and forgiveable given their cause. Perhaps the most positive fact of the series with respect to nursing was that nurses appeared all over the hospital performing nursing care. As has been noted, many health care series virtually eliminated nurse characters. The operating room nurses especially seemed to be highly qualified professionals who worked as members of a surgical team composed of physicians, nurses, and technicians. The staff nurses most often appeared at the nursing station doing general paperwork, but they were frequently noted to be good at their work and appreciated by the staff.

The nurse–physician relationships portrayed in *Doctors Hospital* underlined the traditional notions that nurses work for physicians, and that nurses are handmaidens to M.D.s. Probably because so many physician–nurse interactions occurred in the operating room, a great emphasis was placed on teamwork. Jake complimented Bobbie Marks on her help to him and noted that she was more than a scrub nurse. However, implicit in this acknowledgment is that just being a scrub nurse is of lesser importance and lower status.

Jake in particular emerged as a defender of the nursing profession. An intern once complained to him that nurse Stanton ran the floor like "a batallion," that he could not get nurses, supplies, or a therapist without appealing to her first. Jake immediately informed the young doctor that not only was she highly skilled, but "in her category" she was underpaid. "In her category" clearly indicated that physicians were at a higher level than were nurses, but at least recognition and appreciation of the nursing role were in evidence in his statement. In another show during a phone conversation with the hospital administrator, Jake argued that the hospital should grant its nurses a raise because of their skill. In another episode a staff doctor who habitually avoided decisions, ordered a young nurse to use her judgment about the use and quantity of carbogen for a patient; she followed his order and nearly killed a patient. Later Jake defended the rookie nurse as being a victim of the staff doctor's own negligence and error.

The other physicians also worked well with the nurses, even if they were not as vociferous in championing nurses' rights as was Jake. Felipe Ortega, the chief resident, never criticized a nurse, but he perhaps wished to turn back the clock. He complained to Norah that he used to dream about his future as a doctor, "Now I'm in the *future*: This morning I ask a nurse to get me a tunafish sandwich before surgery and she tells me: 'A nurse is a professional, not a handmaiden of the doctor.' " ("But Who Will Bless Thy Daughter, Norah?" Nov. 19, 1975) On another occasion, miffed at having to continue a 10-minute pre-surgical scrub at the order of a nurse, he remarked that she was possibly going through the change of life. However, Felipe's occasional nasty comments only emphasized the independent and collegial role assumed by the nurses in Doctors Hospital.

Norah Purcell, the female neurosurgical resident, represented a nice contrast for the image of nursing in this series. Fiercely dedicated to her profession, intelligent, skilled, compassionate, Norah emerged as a major character in the series. Because more attention was paid to her character, the viewer would assess her as being more intelligent, compassionate and dedicated than the nurse characters, but this seemed only a function of the attention given her part, and Norah stressed collegial relationships with nurses. One caveat about this collegial atmosphere concerned the terms of address employed between nurses and doctors. The physicians were routinely called "doctor"—even Norah's friend Maggie called her "doctor"—while the nurses were referred to by last name or by first name.

Four incidents of romantic activity by nurse characters appeared in the entire twelve-episode series. Three of these four interludes were between a nurse and a physician. With one exception, the nurse characters did not seem to be more sexually experienced than most women. In conclusion, the melodramatic anthology *Doctors Hospital* presented a somewhat positive image of nurses and even promoted the notion that nurses were professionals who work in collaborative if not equal roles with physicians.

In January 1977 NBC put a new television doctor into their second season lineup, *Quincy, M.E.*, starring Jack Klugman as the forensic pathologist who takes an active role in solving crimes. Despite some misgivings about the potential for success of a series about a coroner, the show has done quite well and entered its fourth season in the 1980–1981 season. Quincy's habits and personality make him a very sympathetic physician. He scorns the lure of big money and remains with his great love, pathology, working for the Los Angeles County Coroner's Office. At work, he relies upon the assistance of his technologist and right-hand man, Sam, a Japanese–American. Quincy's chief obstacle is the administrator of the Coroner's Office, Dr. Astin; Astin is forced to be concerned with budgets and efficiency and wishes that Quincy would not always assume foul play whenever a slight doubt as to the cause of death occurs. Despite his frustration with the detective–pathologist, Astin really appreciates Quincy's skills and always backs him up when others would have Quincy the sleuth called off. Lieutenant Monahan, of the Los Angeles Police Department, is one of Quincy's good friends, and frequently they find themselves working on homicide cases together. Quincy's philosophy about forensic medicine is not that the specialty is concerned with death but that it is concerned with helping the living.

Although the most frequent settings for the show are in the pathology laboratory, Quincy's boat, or Danny's, often his investigative work takes him into private homes or to the scenes of possible crimes. Because some of his victims or their associates are taken to hospitals, hospital settings and the attendant background personnel are often seen in the series. On rare occasions, Quincy practices medicine among the living, which brings him into professional contact with nurses and other doctors. For the most part the nurses in these background sequences or in minor speaking roles appear to be effective, busy professionals, and the series makes no point of emphasizing their presence.

A 1980 episode of *Quincy*, "A Deadly Silence," (February 7, 1980), featured a nurse character in an interesting role. Margaret Aldred, an attractive young woman in her mid-twenties, the daughter of Quincy's friend, worked as a nurse in the emergency room of a privately owned hospital. The opening scene of the story had Margaret and her father asking Quincy to write a letter of recommendation for Margaret to their medical school. Quincy, of course, was delighted to do the favor but asked the nurse why she wanted to become a physician. She answered that nursing was a limited profession and she wanted the better challenge and opportunity afforded by medicine. That evening at the emergency room where Margaret worked, the regular physician had a friend, a Dr. Drew who was not trained in emergency medicine, stand in for him. Drew became very nervous when a cardiac case came in, and both the nurse and the paramedics realized that he did not know what he was doing. When the patient died, Margaret took her story to Dr. Quincy and in a series of incidents helped to affix the responsibility for the death to the proper man. Although the nurse character in this episode was beautiful, brave, concerned, and ambitious, the profession of nursing received little credit because the character had made it clear that she wanted to be a doctor rather than a nurse.

All in all there is no particular image of nursing characteristics in *Quincy*. As in all doctor shows, the physician-protagonist receives such an inordinate amount of attention that all other members of the health care team appear to be less important. At least in *Quincy* the protagonist frequently clashes with other physicians, making them cooperate in cases where they would prefer to not know the true cause of death. Quincy himself represents the paragon of medical science and dedication, but many of his colleagues do appear to be humans, if humans with feet of clay.

Westside Medical appeared as a late, third-season replacement series on ABC and lasted for five weeks: March 15, 1977 to April 14, 1977. The sixty-minute episodes portrayed the busy lives of three young doctors in group practice—Dr. Janet Cottrell (Linda Carlson), Dr. Phil Parker (Ernest Thompson), and Dr. Sam

Lanagan (James Sloyan)—whose office, Westside Medical Clinic, was located across the street from the Westside Memorial Hospital, allowing them to move freely from hospital to examining room. The doctors of *Westside Medical* practiced a wide range of medicine, were seemingly skilled in all fields, and drew from a heterogeneous patient population. Since the group members routinely exchanged information and consulted each other on their cases, any one of the Westside Medical physicians seemed capable of handling anything from brain surgery to the common cold.

"The Covenant" (March 24, 1977) was an episode which found the three doctors up to their ears in personal and medical crises. An old friend from Phil's childhood, Sister Mary Dolores, turned up at Westside Medical needing surgical repair of a heart valve; she had undergone a horrible experience while a missionary in Africa by being kidnapped by guerrilla terrorists. Semi-conscious and close to death because she lacked the will to live, Sister Mary Dolores called out the name of a mysterious person, "Kurt," and reacted fitfully whenever approached by the well meaning but sinister priest and nun who hovered around trying to administer the last rites. Janet Cottrell (who in the previous episode discovered that she had a breast lump) had postponed her biopsy in order to tend to her patient Laura Donnell, a pregnant woman in the hospital after an auto crash that killed her husband. Phil convinced the hospital administration to place Sister Mary Dolores in Laura Donnell's room in the hope that some of Laura's determination to survive would rub off on the nun (which it did after a couple of critical complications). Laura Donnell went into premature labor, and Sam and Janet had to assist the obstetrical specialist at the C-section, although Janet doubted her own competence as a result of her distraction over her breast lump. Needless to say the delivery went well, the baby was fine, and Janet proved that she was a good doctor after all. Next, Phil and Sam decided to perform Janet's breast biopsy themselves, since the specialist could not do it for another week; of course they realized the limits of their experience in this field, but risk it for the sake of a quicker diagnosis. Predictably the path report came out benign so that they did not have to proceed with the radical mastectomy. Sister Mary Dolores began to resolve her problems after deciding to live; Kurt, a Belgian doctor with whom she had fallen in love, survived the kidnapping too, and she must decide between the convent and her lover; either way, she told Phil, she could be happy.

As seen in the brief summary above, nurses played no important roles in the development of the storyline in *Westside Medical*. The nurse characters presented seemed competent, skilled, and even decisive within a very narrow range of discretion. For example, the obstetrical nurse in "The Covenant" checked the patient first, before deciding that the physician needed to be called. The examples were few and limited since the series focused upon the efforts of the physician to the exclusion of other health care providers.

The female physician, Dr. Janet Cottrell, treated the nursing personnel and was treated by them in the same way as male physicians. Interestingly, Janet's practice never included surgery, thereby confining her to less aggressive, more supportive and comforting medical interventions. When she wanted to back out of assisting at the delivery of Laura's baby, Sam told her the patient needed that to be there even though two other physicians were in attendance. Sam or Phil performed the dramatic, lifesaving medical actions either in surgery or the intensive care unit; in fact, while visiting one of Phil's patients, Janet noticed some breathing difficulties; although she instituted the proper measures, her first order was for Phil to be called. Perhaps some of the characteristics of a feminine-type health care usually associated with nursing, that is, supportive and comforting measures, were transferred in this series to the female physician.

Rafferty appeared on CBS in September 1977 and lasted nine, sixty-minute episodes ending November 1977. The only new health care series of the fall line-up, *Rafferty* starred Patrick McGoohan as Dr. Sidney Rafferty, a blunt physician who operated as a general surgeon, and general gadfly, at City General Hospital (in Los Angeles). He also maintained a practice as a family doctor in partnership with young Dr. Dan Gentry (John Getz). This left him little time for anything except meddling in the private lives of his patients and antagonizing colleagues who did not measure up to his exacting standards. A widower, Rafferty lived alone, a condition his ardently devoted nurse–receptionist Vera Wales (Millie Slavin) would have liked to remedy. An aggressive nonconformist, Sid drove a beat-up Mustang and forewent the usual bedside charm expected of physician television characters. He projected a tough-guy image, yet his actions revealed him to be a great humanitarian and concerned human being—in other words, a softie. Dr. Rafferty particularly prided himself on his diagnostic abilities; once he pushed his way backstage to inform a violinist that he had noticed a missing octave in the First Movement and therefore suspected muscle weakness; he advised the man to enter the hospital for further tests. A nurse dropped an instrument during surgery, and a day later Sid gave her neurological tests which revealed a serious illness. Conveniently, Rafferty practiced family medicine and general surgery which gave him license to enter into any medical field from neurosurgery to epidemiology.

Rafferty's faithful nurse, Vera Wales, assisted him in many ways. In the office she answered the phone, greeted patients, and made appointments. In one episode another nurse accused Rafferty of wasting Vera's talents, but he defended the importance of her work to him. Vera, in her mid-thirties, attractive, unmarried, lived alone and often accompanied Sid to dinner or to social functions. Clearly she was more interested in a romantic involvement than he, but she was not blatantly pursuing him. Dan Gentry, Sid's young office partner, seemed mainly to ask Rafferty's advice and to appear naive and untested next to Rafferty's obvious experience.

The fifth floor of City General was home for Sid's patients, and the staff nurses on that floor, Beryl Keynes, a black nurse in her late twenties who appeared efficient and trim, and Doris Koscinski, a pretty young person who commanded the nursing station and relayed a constant stream of messages to Sid from his nurse Vera or from patients needing his help. These nurses played no role in the development of any plot, but served as familiar background to the hospital scenery. They usually appeared at the nurses' station doing paperwork or answering the phone; only once was one of them seen delivering patient care when she brought medication to a patient.

Every plot, sub-plot, scene, or important bit of dialogue involved Rafferty, and the entire show rested upon his participation with miniscule depth involved in the material. The regular cast members remained undeveloped and stunted into positions of yes-men or familiar background characters. The storyline for any one episode usually found Sid dealing with two big problems (for example, finding a kidney donor for a sixteen year old and finding the amnesiac mother of five children living alone). At times he handled only one major crisis along with a sideline problem partially tended by a colleague (for example, convincing a child's parents that their boy is not possessed by the devil, while advising Dan, long-distance, on the treatment of an appendectomy case). The show sank to absurd measures to bring interesting cases Sid's way. Only a handful of patients came to him through the front door of his office.

A summary of one episode demonstrates the range of Sid's skills and the portrayal of nursing in the series. In "Will to Live" (November 11, 1977), Vera failed to show up at work one morning, and Sid was ignorant of her whereabouts until Vera's friend and fellow nurse, Dee Grogan, called to report that Vera was in the hospital, barely conscious. Rushing to the hospital, Sid discussed Vera's case with the current attending physician, Dr. Tait, who suspected a viral neuritis but didn't recommend prolonged testing or active therapy against the progressive paralysis. His wait and see attitude and advice that strong narcotics be used appalled Sid Rafferty who insisted that Vera would not only live but would also recover full use of her extremities. Dee and Vera secretly reviewed the chart and drew dire conclusions about the significance of a sed. rate of 118. Nurse Keynes, who discovered them with the chart, advised Dee to return it but didn't report the infraction of the hospital rule forbidding patients to see their records. When Sid discovered that Tait had prescribed a heavy painkiller, he decided to take Vera home and let her heal herself. Sid encouraged Vera to think positively about her recovery; he spent the night and answered her call of pain with only an ice pack. Dee relieved him of daytime duty so that he could return to work, but he could not understand why Vera was not improving; her sed. rate had dropped and no physiological reason accounted for her paralysis. Finally Dee, in an angry outburst accusing Rafferty of wasting Vera's skills as a nurse by letting her work as his receptionist, admitted that she and Vera knew the truth about Vera's prognosis. At this Sid stormed into Vera's bedroom and claimed that she had humored him throughout his efforts to help her. She insisted that she did want to live, but Sid left her alone to consider her attitude. When he returned, he ordered her to move an arm or a finger, to no avail. He went into the kitchen and made a fire in a wastebasket and fanned the smoke into Vera's room. Secretly he observed her push the covers aside when he shouted for a fire extinguisher; he gleefully confronted her with the evidence of her cure.

Vera Wales, the nurse–receptionist in Rafferty's office, managed the daily routine of a medical practice. With few exceptions, she answered the phone, relayed messages, or tracked down clues and information by telephoning all over the country. In one episode ("Death Out of the Clear Blue Sky"), Vera admitted that as an adolescent she had suffered anorexia nervosa, and Sid took her along to visit an anorexic teenage daughter of a prominent family. Although Vera's interaction with the child was not shown, later comments indicated that she successfully communicated with the teenager and contributed to the girl's eventual recovery. Aside from this instance of patient care (and this based on her personal experience with the illness instead of on her skill as a nurse) Vera remained tied to her phone. In "Will to Live," Sid insisted that Vera's function was to provide the niceties and handle the "psychology department" of a busy practice, since he was too pressed by the demands of his patients to give them all the attention they might need.

Another nurse character who received more than passing attention was the doomed nurse Ellen McKay ("The Cutting Edge") who fatefully dropped an instrument in Sid's presence. Sid had to remind her that she was a nurse, a medical professional, and that she could not return to the operating room until she had a complete physical exam. After the truth of her condition emerged—she had metachromatic leukodystrophy—she bravely handled the depressing diagnosis. She demanded that Sid admit to the hopelessness of her case, and she thanked him for his honesty. She then acquiesced to Dr. Gentry's marriage proposal only to throw him off her track while she prepared her escape to a nursing home.

The relationship between Sid and Vera deserves some attention; Vera gave up a challenging position as an operating room nurse to work as Sid's nurse–receptionist. They appeared in several episodes at dinner, lunch, or a concert, leading the audience to understand that they were more than working colleagues. Vera accompanied him anywhere and admitted having tried to get him to her apartment. However, no sexual involvement occurred or was suggested, and Vera did not blatantly or monomaniacally pursue Sid. He seemed satisfied with having a devoted nurse and an available dinner companion, but his true passion remained his job—helping people in trouble.

Thus, aside from the "Will to Live" episode, the nurses took little part in the action and, therefore, never exposed themselves to criticism or compliments. They seemed a bright, attractive, brave, and efficient group, but remained undeveloped as characters. With Patrick McGoohan's portrayal of a super doctor, all the other characters seemed prosaic, indecisive, conservative, and competent but boring deliverers of health care.

NBC harked back to the days of *Medical Horizons* when it introduced an hour-long documentary *Lifeline* into its fall, 1978 lineup. Each episode focused on a real physician, usually a surgeon, and featured the doctor in all his roles—in his family and leisure time pursuits as well as in his consultations with other physicians and his treatment of patients. Several of his cases were presented throughout the hour, and the viewer was led through the diagnostic and treatment processes with each patient; at the end of the hour, the fate of each patient was told. The editing of the film and the selection of patients contributed to the making of a real drama. The contrast between the drama of *Lifeline* and the typical dramatic situations of fictional medical shows was startling. Conspicuously absent in *Lifeline* were obstructionist administrators, sexually provocative nurses, belligerent or emotionally warped patients. The producers found sufficient dramatic interest in the reactions of real people—not glamorous actors—to often heartbreaking and frightening news.

Because the focus remained consistently on the physicians, the role of nurses received little attention. When nurses did appear they received treatment as reliable assistants to physicians. Generally the R.N.s shown were quietly assured and professionally deft. Physicians did not yell at them or imperiously issue orders to them. The nurses did not flirt with every man that came along. Surgical procedures at which nurses were often in evidence, were quiet, concentrated affairs with none of the inane chatter characteristic of fictional shows. There was no sexual double talk nor were references made to personal relationships. Surgeons worked and nurses quietly assisted; they had no time for extraneous conversation. However, the subordinate position of the nurse to the doctor was consistently emphasized in *Lifeline;* all glory was granted to the physician.

During the late 1970s networks invented a new form of programming—the mini-series, each of which usually lasted from four to eight weeks; the main purpose of such a short-term series was the opportunity of trying out new program ideas before a commitment was made to place the series in the fall lineup. In March and April 1978, ABC presented the show *Having Babies* for six weeks. In February 1979 NBC aired the three-part series *Women in White,* and in April 1979 ABC broadcast the three-part *Doctors' Private Lives*. None of these series presented the image of the nursing profession in a particularly positive way.

Having Babies began its television life as a series of unrelated made-for-TV movies that aired in 1976, 1977, and 1978, the third of which was the immediate predecessor of the mini-series by the same name which began the following week. After the first four episodes, the series became *Julie Farr, M.D.* and acquired a different introductory format that emphasized the role of the female protagonist. Julie Farr, an attractive, sensitive, thoughtful, and aggressive woman in her early thirties with a private practice in obstetrics and gynecology, was associated with

Lake General Hospital and devoted an unspecified amount of her time to working at a free clinic. This last position earmarked her as an idealist in the sixties' sense of that word. Julie's liberal attitude toward sex (she was living with a man in one episode) was also an attempt to make her appealing to young viewers. During the course of the series Julie dated other men, but the demands of her practice prevented her from starting any serious relationships. In almost every episode Dr. Farr was commended as warm and attentive by at least one of her patients; woman after woman recommended her to friends.

Among the physicians at Lake General Hospital, Julie emerged as a confident professional, well respected by her colleagues. Dr. Blake Simmons, head of surgery, regarded her as an intelligent physician, though he frequently disagreed with her on certain issues. A second physician in the series, Ron Danvers, was an intern in obstetrics. In many ways Dr. Farr acted as his mentor, and their relationship was friendly. Neither Dr. Simmons nor Dr. Danvers had any trouble accepting Dr. Farr as a woman *and* a colleague.

A brief narrative summary of one episode will give a better idea of the format and theme of this series. The plot explored the theme of personal failure and jealousy among professional women. Julie Farr met an old college friend of hers, Lucy Reynolds, at a party. Lucy, a jet-setting editor whose life was characterized by glamor and adventure, envied Julie's stability and the respect that she has earned as a physician, while Julie envied Lucy's energetic personality. Lucy gave in to her disappointment and failure by trying to commit suicide. In the hospital Julie Farr became a stalwart support and source of advice to her friend.

Generally, the dramatic focus of the series remained firmly on Julie Farr's obstetrical patients and less frequently focused on Julie's private life. Nursing never received much attention from the writers who concentrated their feminist inclinations in the presentation of Julie Farr as an admirable character. There were two main categories of nurses presented: those in background sequences and the office nurse who worked for Julie. The background nurses (those seen in the hospital talking on the phone or charting) were all plain and ordinary looking, and they were always wearing the traditional white uniform. Nurses were also present in the operating room and in the delivery room, moving about the bassinets in the nursery, in the corridors pushing a patient in a wheelchair, or hurrying to deliver some medication which a physician had ordered. The nurses took orders from physicians, saw to it that hospital rules were enforced, and went about their day-to-day business with little regard for the life and death dramas surrounding them. In contrast to these white clad, unobtrusive nurses in the hospital was Kelly Williams (played by Beverly Todd), Dr. Farr's office nurse; she was an attractive black woman who wore bright and fashionable clothes rather than a uniform to the office. The average viewer might have been somewhat confused as to whether Kelly was actually a nurse or simply a secretary. Her duties consisted mainly of answering the phone, greeting patients, and taking care of the paperwork. In one episode Julie asked an acquaintance to leave a message with her secretary. Nevertheless, several isolated comments supported the conclusion that Kelly was indeed a nurse. Kelly herself said, in *Having Babies III* (March 7, 1978), "I don't mind being a nurse, handling the patients . . . doing the bookkeeping . . .," and in a later episode (March 28, 1978) she lamented, "I went to nursing school for this?" In many ways Kelly held a position similar to that of Consuelo on *Marcus Welby*.

A subplot of the first episode of the mini-series dealt with the problem of finding a second maternity nurse for Julie's office, and the interviewees all contributed to a negative image of nursing. Nurse Miller, the first candidate, was an officious older nurse who pooh poohed such modern ideas as natural childbirth, Lamaze and other "holistic stuff" because they were inefficient and more time consuming than deliveries at which the physician and nurse worked alone. Nurse Miller was also coarse and opinionated; she complained that she had had to change jobs so often because the physicians made passes at her when she worked overtime. The second candidate interviewed was a male nurse, a six-foot-plus, handsome devil who looked as if he had just stepped out of a *Playgirl* foldout; and he sounded like it. The third candidate proved to be the most ideally suited to the position for she was young, bright, and friendly, but she eventually turned down the job in order to return to Oregon and marry her boyfriend. Finding a nurse was thus left an unresolved problem.

The only episode which had a major nurse character in it was the final one in which Jo-Anne Strauss guest starred as Mrs. Walker, an extremely poised and professional woman who wore soft, but sophisticated street clothes rather than a uniform; the episode was entitled "Captive." Though her professional role was not specified, Mrs. Walker appeared to be in charge of the dispensary at the Hutton Home for the Developmentally Disabled, performing technical tasks such as blood tests, but more often offering psychological support and encouragement to the retarded residents of the home. She seemed to be sincerely dedicated to working with the retarded, and they responded to her with love and trust. She was able to simplify information and to communicate with the retarded on their level, but she never showed any signs of condescension. Mrs. Walker related to Dr. Farr as an equal, discussing the course of treatment for a patient and the emotional problems which would arise when two patients were separated. Mrs. Walker was the only nurse in the series who unquestionably contributed to a positive image of the nursing profession.

In February 1979, NBC serialized the Frank Slaughter novel *Women in White* into a four-hour drama that concerned the professional and personal problems of female physicians and nurses. Set in the fictional Biscayne Hospital in Miami, the series presented and resolved a variety of subplots during its three weeks on the air. As the story opened Dr. Rebecca Dalton (Susan Flannery) had just been named Chief of Staff while her marriage to Dr. Ken Dalton, who like herself was a cardiovascular surgeon, suffered because his career had taken a downward slide since the death of several of his transplant patients. By the end of the series Ken had regained his perspective and self-confidence, and Rebecca knew that she must continue in her role as Chief of Staff. They decided not to divorce. Throughout the series, Rebecca served as mentor to two new interns, each of whom had personal problems that affected his or her career. Dr. Jill Bates (Kathryn Harrold), a beautiful young woman, fell in love, almost at first sight, with the handsome resident Dr. Mike Rayburn. When she learned that he was a married man she dropped the affair, but she remained upset at the incident and still attracted to him. Rebecca often advised young Jill on the need to remain a compassionate physician while not allowing personal matters to intrude. A second young intern, Frank Ebanhauer, began his training with confidence. However, he met and fell in love with a terminally ill young woman who introduced him to a new concept of freedom and life. After her death he seriously considered leaving medicine until Rebecca Dalton convinced him to continue. Nurse Cathy Payson (Patty Duke Astin) worked as a staff nurse at the hospital. At the beginning of the series she met her father who was going to be admitted; he was in the final stages of Huntington's Chorea, a degenerative disease. Cathy petitioned the Moritorus Committee to end her father's life; she insisted to the committee that the request was his. When the committee turned down her request because her father was suffering no pain, she proceeded to end her father's life by injecting air into his I.V. tubing. She promptly fled the country, leaving her best friend, nurse Lisa Gordon (Sheree North), to cope with her own guilty knowledge of Cathy's role in the death. Lisa, who had also become Jill's friend, took her troubles to the local bar where she pondered the meaning of life. The final subplot concerned the ambitious and beautiful pathologist, Karen Fletcher, who used her romantic relationship with the state's attorney to promote her career. She used her knowledge of the cause of Mr. Payson's death to bargain with the attorney for an important promotion.

The presentation of nursing in this mini-series was quite negative, especially when compared with the portrayal of the female physicians. First, all three female doctors had long blond hair, finely chiseled facial features, exceptional figures, and wore beautiful clothes, while the nurses were older, blowsy, and even dowdy. Second, the female M.D.s articulated positive attitudes about their profession, the problems of emotional involvement with patients, the need to sustain empathy and concern, and the strains placed on personal lives by the demands of a career. Karen and Rebecca, the doctors, were ambitious women who expected to advance in their chosen careers. Neither Cathy nor Lisa, the nurses, expressed any interest in advancing her knowledge or in pursuing a career goal. Third, neither of the two nurses seemed able to cope with emotional stress. Lisa Gordon turned to liquor for comfort and strength. Cathy could not accept her father's lingering death. Rebecca Dalton, on the other hand, always managed to retain her professional calm and even to counsel younger physicians in the lessons of keeping emotions out of medical practice, and Jill Bates was always active in her professional work and never lost her professional composure or passed up a professional opportunity. Finally, the moral standards of the nurse characters seemed lower than those of the female physicians. Jill Bates, M.D. fretted and worried about her affair with a married man, but Lisa Gordon, R.N. tried to convince her to shrug it off and chalk it up to experience. The nurse who propositioned Mike Rayburn in the scrub room and the nurse who danced on a table top and prepared to strip for the crowd presented a promiscuous, exhibitionist view of nurses. The female physicians behaved in a more restrained, ladylike fashion at the poolside party, and in general they appeared more selective about their sexual activity.

The average viewer would find the female physicians superior to the nurses in every way. While the nurses were friendly and sympathetic, the female physicians were not only friendly and sympathetic, but intelligent, beautiful, and ambitious as well. The show suggested that exceptional women would choose a career in medicine rather than in nursing.

Two months after NBC broadcast *Women in White,* ABC offered the television audience *Doctors' Private Lives* which featured four major physician characters. Two nurse characters, Kitty (Kim Hamilton) and Diane (Eddie Denton), appeared with some frequency in the story, but they did not play leading roles. In addition, Dr. Wise's son Kenny, a pre-med student, and his girlfriend Sheila, another pre-med student, participated in the storyline.

This series sought mainly to expose the private lives of wealthy and successful physicians, each of whom dallied in some pre- or extra-marital affair. The two nurses, while attractive and interested in romance, did not demonstrate any sexual/romantic liaisons with the medical staff. The story, in a nutshell, followed each of the doctors in his illicit and involved pursuits. The climax of the film came when Dr. Frances Latimer and a plane load of Korean orphans crashed at a nearby airport and thus rallied the hospital staff into a fantastic team effort to save the children and other passengers.

The nurse characters, although minor, did receive considerable exposure in their professional roles. The physicians and nurses generally treated each other as professional colleagues, discussing the patients together rather than simply giving and receiving orders. Kitty was acknowledged to be an essential member of the surgical team, and she performed many of the needed preparations with the same confidence as that of the surgeons. Although the film was heavily spiced with sexual encounters, the nurses remained free from such entanglements. Sex, however, was a favorite topic among and about the nurses. One physician referred to a nurse's gorgeous chest; a nurse humored an elderly male patient, while prepping him for surgery, by playing along with his suggestive remarks. Both these nurses and those in the background appeared to be dedicated nurses who substantially contributed to the care of patients in the hospital.

In the subsequent episodes of the mini-series only the three male physicians returned as regular characters. Diane and Kitty appeared in the first entry but not in the remaining two. The role of nursing generally diminished in the later shows, as the producers continued to explore the professional and romantic lives of physicians and medical students. As in *Women in White,* the producers of *Doctors' Private Lives* made full use of the romantic possibilities inherent in attractive female physicians. The nurses paled beside the glamorous and sometimes threatening female M.D.s. Although the comparison between the two groups of female professionals was not as devastating to nurses in *Doctors' Private Lives* as it was in *Women in White,* the typical viewer would be likely to judge nursing as a far less attractive profession than medicine. The nurses did not become involved in professional problems to the same extent as did the female doctors; the nurses did not appear as ambitious or as eager to learn as the female doctors; and they did not seem to be as sexually attractive to leading male characters as the female physicians were.

As in the successful series on which they were patterned, these short-lived efforts in health care drama downplayed the role of the nurse in modern hospital routine in order to emphasize the role of the physician. Beyond this typical under-representation, a rather unflattering image of the nurse emerged vis-a-vis female physicians. Many of these series attempted to appear innovative and avant garde by using female physicians as colleagues to the male doctor-heroes; in a few cases, female doctors took the leading roles. In all the series in which a regular female physician appeared, the nurses were presented with negative features or were more ignored than usual. Often the female physician assumed duties normally done by nurses, while her male colleagues performed functions typically reserved for the physician-heroes.

The nurses routinely looked less attractive, less intelligent, and less serious than the female physicians. The worst example of this occurred in the mini-series *Women in White,* but the episode on *Doctors' Hospital* in which a former nurse became a physician showed the nursing staff to be a vindictive and jealous group of women. In the series *Medical Story* many female physicians appeared, but they received little attention; the nurse characters that did receive attention were almost always presented as battle scarred veterans who were immune to human suffering.

5
Sounds of Laughter: Nurses in Situation Comedies of the 1970s

In the 1970s, after years of serious adulation of physicians and allegedly realistic depictions of professionals at work, television writers introduced a new approach to doctor shows—hospital comedy. One of these was *Temperatures Rising,* and perhaps the best indication of its intellectual intentions was the *TV Guide* description, that promised the viewers they would be meeting "real fun doctors and crazy mixed-up nurses, frolicking among the scalpels, X-ray machines and bedpans. The merry band of cutups is led by Dr. Jerry Noland (Cleavon Little), 'your friendly intern,' who runs bingo games and off-track betting parlors in the hospital" (Sept. 9, 1972, p. 46). *Temperatures Rising* premiered in September 1972, with Capitol General Hospital under the thumb of Dr. Vincent Campanelli (James Whitmore), a gruff but kindly chief of surgery. He was constantly on the lookout for trouble which usually came by way of Dr. Noland's harebrained schemes. Dr. Noland, a fast talking, streetwise black intern, livened up the hospital with his ubiquitous money making activities and his genius for improbable and successful solutions to dubious problems. As the Robin Hood of Capitol General, Noland always counted on the loyal support and help of his little band of accomplices, the third floor nursing staff: a blond and comely head nurse (Joan Van Ark); a less comely, mischievous staff nurse, Millie MacInerney (Reva Rose); and an eager, clumsy, dumb but cute, young student nurse, Ellen Turner (Nancy Fox).

The plots of the first year's episodes quickly reduced themselves to a few broad categories that invariably provided an unlikely crisis for Noland to mastermind. The largest category (ten of twenty-six) concerned unusual patients who came to Capitol General and their improbable situations, among them a famous baseball player who went to the maternity ward for a secret operation; a mafia type gangster who made Noland an offer he could not refuse; and a lovelorn Chinese ping-pong player who wanted to defect and to marry Ellen. Perhaps the most ridiculous stories dealt with Noland's money-making for worthy causes ploys, including: a bingo game among the patients to save a resident's father's business and Noland's medical commercials to raise money for a nurse's nose job. In addition to these plots where money-making was central, all the other scripts referred to Noland's offbeat concessions run for personal profit. Some of the plots found nurses or other staff members the object of attention. For example, one episode portrayed a hypnotized R.N. who made a play for every doctor in sight. Other storylines included such chestnuts as the let's save the boss variety whereby, for example, Noland and Co. thought up ways to keep Campanelli from quitting. The Noland in the soup genre found the hero having to expose a fraudulent malpractice claimant injured in an ambulance accident, or having to reform his manners for the benefit of a nurse he admired.

Season two of *Temperatures Rising* took place in Washington's Capitol General, but aside from Capitol General and Cleavon Little, only the level of plot and dialogue remained the same. The first eleven episodes found Capitol General transformed into a privately owned institution, administered by a non-practicing physician, Dr. Paul Mercy (Paul Lynde), whose mother owned and resided in the place. Mrs. Mercy (Sudie Bond) seemed to live for the pleasure of berating her son's capabilities. The fun-loving staff included: Dr. Jerry Noland, now a resident; Dr. Axton (Jeff Morrow), who appeared in only two episodes; Miss Tillis of the business office (Barbara Cason); Wendy Winchester, R.N. (Jennifer Darling); Dr. Claver (John Dehner); and Haskell, the orderly (Jerry Hauser). The tempo and focus of the series remained infantile and followed the broad categories as described for the first season. Paul Lynde as Dr. Mercy with his mincing, nervous, and sarcastic attitudes provided a major new source of humor. A number of these episodes featured Dr. Mercy and family. For example, in one episode Noland's mother persuaded Mrs. Mercy to remain at the hospital to the chagrin of Dr. Mercy; Dr. Mercy contracted venereal disease but wanted the treatment kept secret. A recurrent minor theme of the revised series was Dr. Mercy's stinginess. The nurses did not figure centrally in the plots of these eleven episodes, but they continued to aid and abet the genius of Dr. Noland. In fact the new format included only one R.N., Wendy Winchester, in the cast of regulars.

The series revived briefly in the late summer of 1974 with yet another renovation; Capitol General reverted to public or corporate ownership, though Dr. Mercy continued as the administrator, slightly less incompetent, but still contending with the efforts of his fun-loving and wacky staff. Jerry Noland served as the only other physician, and the nursing staff again counted three nurses: Amanda Kelly, an attractive and sexually active head nurse (Barbara Rucker); Edwina Moffitt, a prissy and spinsterish nurse who headed the admitting office (Alice Ghostely); and the returned student nurse, cute but dim-witted Ellen Turner (Nancy Fox).

The six episodes from the terminal stage of *Temperatures Rising* ran the gamut of such typical plot lines as Dr. Mercy needing minor surgery but proving to be a cowardly patient; Mercy saving the life of a country music star, but getting in trouble with hospital trustees about all the publicity.

Despite the changes in format and cast and the discontinuity in the writing staff, the thirty-one episodes shared a common banality unrelieved by realism, witty dialogue, or character development. There was scarcely a nod of recognition toward what really goes on in a hospital. Very little sickness was shown or mentioned; most patients seemed to come in for observation, unspecified tests, or rest. It was just as well, however, that the patients didn't seem to need much nursing or medical care, for there was equally little recognition of what nurses and doctors really do.

The roles of the nurses in *Temperatures Rising* were as fluffy as the series itself. It is difficult to take any of the nurses seriously as characters, even aside from their silly antics, because they were never developed beyond a thumbnail sketch description. Nurse Annie Carlisle was described in the first episode as a gorgeous head nurse who was bright, witty, and a first-rate nurse, but no indications of her rank, her intelligence, or her personality were apparent, and she was mainly distinguishable from the other nurses because of her hairstyle (blonde and coiffured). Millie MacInerney, Annie's right hand, was dubbed attractive, efficient, and very mischievous, but aside from the fact that she occasionally complained about her lack of success with men, her lines were indistinguishable from Annie's, and her personality remained a blank. Student nurse Ellen Turner's dialogue was distinct from the others' only because of its stupidity. Ellen was a one joke character: She was a cute, eager, dim-witted girl who wore looped pigtails and who frequently dropped things. Even discounting the general silliness of the series, the nurses had a poor image. That they knew how to be good nurses was mentioned in at least one episode, "Mercy Beaucoup," (August 29, 1974), in which the staff tried to convince Dr. Mercy of their perfection so that he would feel free to leave them and accept a promotion. Ellen breathlessly reported that she had "given 304 his injection, 302 her sponge bath, 307 his physical therapy, 301 her anti-coagulant, 305 her lunch . . ."; another nurse hastened to replace warm water with hot water in the patient's hot water bottle; and Amanda studied a text on mitral valve procedure in her spare time. However, any possible good effect that this litany of virtues might have had was immediately overwhelmed by the obvious suggestion that this was an abnormal state for the nurses, and by the end of the episode they again took too-frequent coffee breaks, worked crossword puzzles at the desk, and spent most of their time gabbing, trying to look suddenly busy if the chief of staff should appear.

The most salient characteristic of the nurses in both seasons of *Temperatures Rising* was that they were blithe and blind followers. When Mercy seemed to be changing his mind for the second time about leaving the hospital, Ellen said, "Well, he must know what he's doing. Men are smarter than women. You never see a man buy a shirt that buttons up the back" ("Mercy Beaucoup," Aug. 29, 1974). Never did a nurse character suggest an idea to solve a problem. Often they were incapable of solving their own problems, as in "The Godfather" when it took two doctors to rescue Ellen from a hoodlum named Nails. The nurses appeared as loyal friends and comrades, dedicated to worthy causes: saving Amhearst's residency; buying toys for tykes; protecting Campanelli; protecting Mercy. They covered for Noland and participated in his private money-making ventures.

In both formats the professional identities of the nurses remained cloudy: A head nurse sort of stood at the nursing station and answered phones; a staff nurse did such things in hallways as delivering meals and running errands; and the student nurse did a little typing, a little patient care, and a lot of dropping things. No hierarchical pattern appeared among the nurses, and no administrative, nursing-only matters arose. Again, nurses not only failed to provide leadership within the general framework of the plot but also within their own group.

The episodes also demeaned the image of physicians; however, they still emerged as the problem solvers and natural leaders in whatever actions did occur. Noland figured in almost all the successful resolutions of problems presented in the series. The nurses enjoyed a friendly relationship with the doctors, but because the doctors did not command respect, that good relationship did not add much to the nurses' image.

NBC—in its usual imitative fashion—offered a similar show to ABC's 1972 show called *Little People*. Like *Temperatures Rising,* this show seemed to operate on the central premise that dumb is cute. *Little People* starred Brian Keith as Dr. Sean Jamison and Shelley Fabares as Dr. Anne Jamison, his daughter. Both shared a pediatric practice in Hawaii, assisted by nurse Puni (Victoria Young) and Ronnie Collins (Michael Gray), a teenager variously described as handyman and student doctor. The episodes were enlivened by the appearance of a good many cute (sometimes overly cute) Hawaiian kids who were patients and friends of the good doctors Jamison. In the second (and final) season, the name was changed to *The Brian Keith Show,* and two new regular characters—Dr. Spencer Chaffey (Roger Bowen), a prim allergist in the adjoining office and Mrs. Millar Gruber (Nancy Culp), the owner of Sean's clinic—were added. The changes were not enough to save the show, and it was cancelled.

A review of two typical episodes indicates the nature of this series. The first, "Honest Sean Drives Again" (January 12, 1973), was an embarrassingly silly portrayal in which Puni rushed into the office upset because she had forgotten to remind Sean that his driver's license had expired, and she feared that the doctor would be furious. Immediately the viewer began to wonder about the intelligence of both characters. Meanwhile, Sean was out driving, unaware of his expired license, and he picked up two of the show's regular kids—Alfred and Stewart— and lectured them on hitchhiking. As he scolded them about breaking the law, he inadvertently ran a stop sign, made a turn without signaling and backed over a policeman's motorcycle when stopped. The kids gleefully teased Sean and told on him back at the office where Puni and Ronnie also teased him unmercifully. Sean was told that he had to take his licensing test again, so he went in with Ronnie, who was also taking his test and who kept telling him his answers were wrong; Sean changed them. As a result, he very nearly flunked. Sean also had to renew his road test with a prim Miss Gormley as examiner. She treated him like a child, chiding him for slouching, taking points off his score for talking unnecessarily. He failed the test. In a series of misadventures, including an illegal drive to date a "dynamite stewardess," Sean reenacted all this idiocy except that he finally performed a delivery of a baby with perfect skill. The show's writers were obviously convinced that dumb was indeed cute, and that the viewers would find this repetitious display of the good doctor's bumbling idiocy in every area except medicine endearing.

The episode "TV or not TV" (April 6, 1973) opened with two physicians discussing an invitation to announce free pediatric examinations for all the island children on a popular children's television show. The doctors agreed that "The Sunrise Sailor Show" would be an effective way of advertising the free examinations, but refused to do it themselves, saying that the show's effectiveness to kids lay in "that maniac host blasting you with chocolate cream pies." Eventually Sean was tricked by his daughter, nurse, and children into appearing on the show. Once on the air, he hardly had a chance to make his announcement about the free examinations because he was caught up in the silly costumes and makeup and slapstick routines. Sean blasted the star of the show for being in a position to do some good for children and then wasting that opportunity, and the final scene showed Sean's triumph when Bud (the star) came up the walk leading a large group of kids in for their free examinations.

In general, a highly unprofessional image of nursing emerged from this series, however camouflaged it may have been in comedy situations and general friendship between physicians and nurse. The writers did apparently intend to create a good image for Puni, for she was definitely the friend and ally of both doctors, the real heroes. Since none of the characters generated any real sense of respect from the viewer, however, the writers' general intentions did not count for much. There was almost nothing to indicate the measure of Puni's professional skills. She seemed to fit into the traditional mold of the nurse as handmaiden of the physician. Use of names also seemed to confirm this inferior position. Sean always called her "Puni" (in fact, her last name was never mentioned), but she called him "Doctor," "Dr. Jamison," or occasionally the children's nickname for him, "Dr. Jamie."

Although neither *Temperatures Rising* nor *Brian Keith/Little People* succeeded in finding a loyal audience, the networks persisted in their belief that health care themes offered great potential for situation comedy. In a late second season move, NBC introduced *The Bob Crane Show* in March 1975; the series was cancelled after thirteen weeks. The series only skirted the edges of the hospital environment, as it concerned the domestic and personal complications arising from a middle-aged man's (Bob Crane) decision to start a new life as a medical student, giving up suburbia and financial stability. The quasi-medical atmosphere, with an unending supply of cadaver and specimen jokes, was intended to make the show irresistible. The focus of the show was on student hijinks and domestic role reversal; nursing or physician roles were not examined in any sustained way, not even comically.

During the 1975–1976 season NBC and CBS each introduced new health care sit-coms, and both of these shows, *Doc* and *The Practice,* followed very similar formats. Neither achieved great success, although they both spanned two network seasons. *Doc* premiered on CBS in the fall season of 1975 and lasted for about 28 episodes until cancellation early in the following fall season. Produced by MTM and aired in an enormously successful Saturday night comedy lineup, *Doc* failed to find a permanent slot despite its impregnable position and its format change in the second season.

In the first season Doctor Joe Bogert (Barnard Hughes) was depicted with his family, his loyal nurse Tully, and an assortment of oddball patients who filtered in and out of his old-fashioned medical office located on Manhattan's west side. By having Doc and family live in apartments above the office, the writers were able to intermingle family and professional activities in often touching and funny ways; for example, Doc's wife Annie's return to nursing as a temporary replacement for Tully. Barnard Hughes portrayed the sixtyish general practitioner in the typical gruff but loveable tradition expected of gray-haired physicians; however, Doc was also witty and surrounded by an appealing company of friends and relatives.

Annie Bogert (Elizabeth Wilson), Doc's wife of thirty years who had raised a family of eight children, devoted herself to the joys of being a grandmother, but more often to the spiritual and physical welfare of Joe and, indeed, to everyone else. Doc's family included his son Chuck, a physician who wanted to be a writer, son Brian, a priest who wanted to be a stand-up comic, and assorted other characters. The only members to be regularly featured were clutzy, accident prone Laurie Bogert Fenner (Judy Kahn), Doc's youngest and favorite; her husband Fred (John Harkins), a pompous, dim-witted, overconfident paint salesman whom Doc could barely tolerate; and their several children. Downstairs in the office, Nurse Beatrice Tully (Mary Wickes) presided with a military flair. Having worked for Doc for fifteen years, she complemented his crustiness with her own brand of sarcasm and mastery.

The cast and stories of *Doc*'s first season exhibited subtle, biting humor and a proper balance of the credible with the ridiculous, traits expected of an MTM production. Doc and Annie's loving, tender, but often humorously conflictive marriage set the tone for the entire show, while the Doc/Fred dialogues and Tully's repartee provided the right touch of sarcasm and slapstick. Doc's tendency to criticize, complain, and attack the obviously inept Fred was always tempered by his love of wife, daughter, or grandchildren.

In the second season opener, the viewer learned that Doc's wife Annie had died, his daughter and her family inexplicably disappeared; he worked as the medical director of the Westside Free Clinic, and Nurse Tully appeared in the first episode only and was replaced by new nurse character Scotty played by Audra Linley. Scotty was less acerbic than Tully, but otherwise played a good humored R.N. who devotedly concerned herself with Doc's personal and professional life. Other regular characters included: Teresa Ortega (Lisa Mordente), the Puerto Rican receptionist who wanted to become an actress; Woody (Ray Vitte), a jive-talking, black lab technician; and Stanley Moss (David Ogden Stiers), the bureaucratic aficionado of red tape who, as clinic director, plagued the other staff members with his incessant demands for requisitions, reports, and obeisance. In addition to less effective supporting characters who never developed the depth or range allowed the previous cast, the plots for *Doc's* second season seemed more mechanical, trite, and provoked less empathy. In the first season nearly half of the shows concerned the Bogert family, although scenes from Doc's medical practice were always included. The topics, always humorous, often touched upon such serious topics as death and aging. Some of the stories about patients were wildly creative given the general run of television health care. For example, Doc, against his better judgement, agreed to sew up the wound in a dog's paw and later faced malpractice charges from the dog's owner; a criminal burglarizing Doc's office had a gall bladder attack and required immediate care; Annie tried to convince Doc to return to church, but he was more interested in finding a new poker partner; Doc had misgivings about renting his upstairs apartment to his daughter and her family; Fred Fenner had another woman; a shy widower had a crush on nurse Tully. The four second season entries centered upon the Westside Clinic: Tully disliked working for Stanley Moss and quit her job; Joe worried about retirement and considered another job, in Toledo; Stanley forgot to renew the Clinic's lease, and it appeared that Westside Clinic would be replaced by a delicatessen.

Although the series focused upon the old-fashioned medical services of Doc Bogert, a nurse character appeared in every episode and occasionally assumed center stage. Brief summaries of two episodes offer a better idea of plot development as well as demonstrate the role of nursing in the series.

"Nurse Annie" (January 24, 1976) found Annie Bogert back in uniform after a twenty year hiatus during which time she raised her family. When Tully unexpectedly had to leave for a few days to help a sick aunt, Annie volunteered to help out in the office. Joe immediately refused, but Annie's enthusiasm and the thought of a few dollars saved overrode his better judgment. Annie returned to the office stunningly attired in her uniform and took great pleasure in Joe's compliments, but the day proceeded badly for Annie; short-tempered patients, confusing phone messages, and Doc's imperious demands totally disoriented her. Tully stopped by to tell Doc that she would be off another day; after he assured her that it was all right, he called the nursing registry for a replacement. However, Annie assumed that Doc had decided to let her work another day and gradually she picked up a little confidence. That evening when she discovered that she had been fired, fireworks exploded in the Bogert apartment—until Joe recognized his mistake and begged Annie to return to work in the morning. Presumably Annie's second day was better than the first, but Doc was delighted at Tully's eventual return.

"Benson Hedges" (November 11, 1975) brought romance into Tully's life in the form of a shy widower patient of Dr. Bogert's. Mr. Benson confided his interest to Doc but confessed that the closest he had been to Tully was the time she gave him a B-12 shot. Amused and amazed, Doc advised the straightforward approach. Tully failed to pick up Mr. Benson's overly subtle lunch invitation, so he settled for making an appointment for a B-12 shot. Upstairs over lunch, Doc reported this development to Annie who schemed a way to promote the romance—dinner with the Bogerts the following evening, and Tully eventually became totally involved with Mr. Benson. After a week long romance, Benson proposed, leaving Tully with the difficult decision of whether or not to give up nursing for marriage. Tully felt that the decision was tough, but before she answered, Benson backed out of the proposal. Tully assured him that her answer would have been no, but no one really knew if this were true or not. The next day, hypochondriac Ben Goldman remarked that Tully was on time for work, and Tully proved her resilience by reverting to form: with a pointed look at Goldman she said, "I love nursing. This is where I belong. Among the suffering and infirm."

Not counting Annie Bogert or Ruth Sanstorm of "Hospital Diary," *Doc* protrayed two nurse characters: Beatrice Tully, Doc's faithful nurse of fifteen years for twenty-four episodes and Scotty, Doc's faithful nurse for the limited duration of three episodes. Thus, little can be said about Scotty's character, except that the show's producers probably intended that she be Tully-like in her devotion to Doc Bogert and in her personal friendship with him. Both nurses were middle-aged, unmarried (Tully never married; Scotty widowed), not particularly attractive, put in long hours, seemed competent and quick thinking, liked their work and were loyal. Tully appeared more acerbic and sharp tongued than did Scotty, but both nurses knew how to defend themselves verbally. In terms of nursing activities, there was a distinction between the types of things Tully did and those Scotty did in the second season. While in private practice, Doc performed almost all the patient care activities from injections to surgery, and nurse Tully ran the office, occasionally administering a drug or shot, but more often found in secretarial tasks. "Nurse Annie" emphasized the type of jobs that Tully did—telephone answering, patient placating, and chart location. Generally the nurse remained in the reception area, but Doc might summon her to perform such activities as prepare a syringe for his use. In Tully's only appearance at the Westside Clinic she did less paperwork and public relations, but she was still limited to putting patients into treatment rooms to await the doctor. In one scene Tully helped save a man's life, under Doc's supervision.

Scotty contributed more uniformly to patient welfare and performed skilled tasks requiring some judgment. In "Come Scrub with Me" Scotty not only did a routine prenatal exam by herself, but she also initiated plans for the patient's delivery when labor began unexpectedly. She prepared medications for Doc to administer and gave evidence of good nursing judgment. In "Westside Clinic and Deli" (the final episode), she examined a patient's throat, diagnosed it, prescribed a treatment, and sent the patient on her way. In addition, Scotty went to the scene of an accident and brought back those victims not in need of hospital, acute care (triage-type judgment). The abrupt cancellation of the series makes it difficult to determine if these last examples were indicative of a new trend for the nurse character or were simply isolated cases.

Both Tully and Scotty proved their loyalty to Doc and suggested that their professional goals always came second to Doc's aspirations and intentions; that is, they considered his work to be very important and worthwhile and felt that their most important contribution to helping others was to help Doc fulfill his altruistic ambitions. Much more can be said of Tully's relationship to Doc because of her longer participation in the series. She emerged as a member of the Bogert clan, privy to family secrets, and as a staunch friend in crisis. In the office Tully played a role similar to Annie's role upstairs, doing all the housekeeping-type tasks associated with running a physician's office. Although she performed few skilled jobs and did no patient care of her own, Tully retained an equality with Doc on a personal level, and she was free to disagree with or criticize his decisions, generally unrelated to patient care.

When in one episode, "EKG and Vote for Me," (November 9, 1976) a television show came to the clinic to publicize a politician's visit, the staff was interviewed. Scotty told about her job: "And I've fallen in love with the place. Of course, I've known Dr. Bogert for years—and I've always been in love with him." "Professionally and/or otherwise?" a reporter prompted. "And/or whatever way you want to take it," answered Scotty. In another episode Scotty revealed that her late husband had been a dermatologist, so perhaps she did know Doc from earlier days. However, there was no suggestion of romantic involvement between Doc and Scotty. Their greatest intimacy came when he confided to her his indecision about a Toledo job offer, which she proceeded to relay all over the clinic.

The non-nurse characters all responded positively to the nurses, even if on the surface much friction occurred. In the Tully/Doc format, Tully feuded constantly with two of Doc's regular hypochondriacs, but the viewer knew that she actually felt great affection for them. Doc's family included Tully in its plans and considered her an aunt. Judging by other episodes, had the series lasted, Scotty might have assumed a mother role among the young staff members.

In conclusion, the overall image of nursing emerging from this series must be considered positive, although many individual episodes and instances portrayed the nurse as merely a secretary or yes-person to the physician. However, the positive attitudes of most characters toward the nurses and their demonstrated competence and skills in limited instances, created a good impression of the nursing profession for the average viewer. The trend of the second season, limited to three episodes, suggested that the nurse would play an expanded role in servicing the nursing needs of the patient population of the Westside Clinic. The original format focused so much attention on Doc's old-fashioned practice of medicine, that the nurse character was left with little to do with regard to patient care. The Tully–Doc team also reinforced certain ideas about the often familial and intimate physician–nurse relationship if it developed out of a long association between one nurse and one physician. Although personal equality might exist in such a relationship, it still reinforced stereotypic ideas about the feminine role of nursing and the fatherly, masculine role of physicians.

The NBC series *The Practice* which began in January 1976 and ran 27 episodes until cancellation in January 1977, revealed an uncanny resemblance to *Doc* in both its theme and format. *The Practice* centered on the activities of a gruff but loveable general practitioner, Jules Bedford (Danny Thomas), who worked on Manhattan's west side and waged a continuing campaign to shame his doctor-son David who practiced on Park Avenue and invested in real estate. The Thomas' blend of pater familias and emotional wisdom permeated the personality of Jules Bedford.

Although the series became a vehicle for Danny Thomas to present his well-known bag of tricks, the writing of the scripts and the development of characters demonstrated above average quality for the half-hour sit-com format. Certainly the concept of a gruff but loveable physician was anything but innovative, and plot development followed standard formulae, but many of Thomas' one line, barbed retorts deserved audience chuckles. The supporting characters, with the possible exception of the too-dumb-to-be-true receptionist, achieved a certain credibility rare in such shows because of the ongoing development of their personalities. For example, the show's creators did not stereotype David Bedford (David Spielberg), but fleshed out his character by showing him in situations calling for a range of emotional responses. David's family—wife Jenny (Shelley Fabares), and children—provided Jules with the needed outlet for his patriarchal energies. Back at his own office, Jules received the well intentioned but often unreliable help of his receptionist Helen (Didi Conn) and the protective and affectionate support of his long-time nurse and girl Friday, Molly Gibbons (Dena Dietrich). Supporting characters, while often sympathetic in their own right, served primarily to draw out one or more of Jules' well-known quirks or biases. Born in a lower class neighborhood of New York City, Jules worked his way through school from a tender age, graduated from medical school, opened practice on the west side, lost his wife early, raised his only son David, and sent David to medical school. At the time of the show Bedford lived alone and devoted himself morning and night (including housecalls) to the needs of his patients and to meddling in his son's life with intuition, empathy, wit, and vast experience. Despite his insults and ridicule his patients remained steadfast in their loyalty to him, preferring him to the more sophisticated and mysterious ways of young doctors. For example, in one episode David and Jules vied for the right to treat a mutual friend for a wrist ganglion. David awed and confused the man with complicated explanations and prescribed surgery, so Dad simply took the man's wrist and smashed it against a hard surface, bursting the cyst. As a father Jules Bedford also believed in the old-fashioned verities and took seriously his role as head of the family, despite David's pleas to stop meddling and despite Jenny's revolts.

Molly Gibbons (Dena Dietrich), an attractive woman in her early 40s, had worked for and was devoted to Jules Bedford for fifteen years, ever since the death of her husband. Although a nurse and probably proud of it, most of her activities on the show concerned Jules' personal problems. She ran the office; supervised Helen; took blood and X-rays; administered medications; and, more important, she coddled Jules and worried about him. Her moods alternated between warm affection toward the grouchy doctor and stern rebukes about his temper. In one episode in which she considered marrying another man, she recounted her life with Jules and emphasized that her love for him stemmed from his dependence upon her. But her attitude toward the doctor was not always maternal; almost every episode showed her flirting with Dr. Bedford and his enjoyment but resistance.

Helen the receptionist talked to the plants and radiated optimism and good cheer; she was Bedford's nemesis because her lack of normal comprehension made her impervious to the doctor's sarcasm and mordant wit. Although unable to chew gum and walk at the same time, Helen managed to hang on to her job as receptionist, and Molly defended her to Jules.

Almost every episode of *The Practice* featured a father–son feud as either the focus of the show or as a skirmish fought to the side of the main battle. About half the shows concerned the treatment of a patient with an unusual problem, and the other half usually dealt with Bedford family complications. Brief summaries of two episodes illustrate plot development and the role of nursing in the series.

In "Molly and Jim" nurse Gibbons met an attractive new patient and began to date him. Jules hid his feelings about her romance and refused to advise or dissuade her from marrying the man despite Molly's desire for his response. However, when Jim proposed, Molly realized that she could not accept because of her responsibilities to Jules Bedford and because she loved Jules, "in a way." Jules took the news of her intention to stay calmly, but as soon as he was alone, he danced and sang with joy, indicating his true feelings. This episode showed how much both Jules and Molly cared for each other, but that they would be content with a rather unofficial romance because of the demands of Jules' practice.

In "The Choice" (February 27, 1976) a notorious drug pusher came to Bedford's office and demanded that he be treated for recurrent headaches. Molly repeatedly warned Jules to refuse because she was concerned for his welfare. Jules, however, could not turn down anyone in need of health care, and he discovered the man's diagnosis; he made a deal with the crook: in exchange for Jules' telling the surgeon how to treat him, the dope peddler would have to donate $150,000 to a drug rehabilitation program. The patient was cured only to be gunned down some weeks later. The show explored the ethical considerations faced in treating criminals. Molly and Jenny argued against helping the man while Jules and, reluctantly, David chose to give the man needed health care. The show presented physicians in a humanitarian light, while implying that nurses act out of more practical and less altruistic motives.

As seen in the above plot descriptions, nursing per se played a very small role in *The Practice*. Jules Bedford's old-fashioned medical office retained the services of a full-time registered nurse who spent more of her time worrying about Jules Bedford than worrying about the patients. In most episodes, she announced the arrival of a patient, reported lab results, gave injections, or took blood and X-rays; apparently she managed the business aspects of his practice because once she urged Jules to remind his patients to pay their bills. Although Helen the receptionist was constantly being chased back to the waiting room, Molly remained at Jules' side during many of his interviews with patients or with friends. In the first season, three of the episodes featured Molly as the central character: Once, she entered the hospital with a possible diagnosis of cancer; the following week she worried Jules with the possibility of her leaving her job for marriage; and once she accidentally overdosed a hypochondriac patient with some allergy serum. Although Jules considered her the best nurse in New York, Molly actually performed few nursing tasks in any one show. She followed Jules' orders on all matters of patient care and only occasionally suggested that Jules' method of treatment might get him into trouble; for example, she warned him against treating the drug pusher, and she thought his close relationship with a young, abandoned child patient might be dangerous for the child's emotional welfare. In "Molly and Jim" none of the reasons Molly stated for not marrying Jim included her helping Jules in a professional way. She believed that she was the only nurse who would put up with Jules' temperament, thereby uniquely qualifying her for the job. Her nursing identity was completely submerged in the larger, more demanding personality of Jules Bedford, and Molly and Jules shared a pseudo-marital relationship reminiscent of the Nurse Tully and Joe Bogert relationship in *Doc*. She flirted with him on several occasions; he enjoyed that. She chided him about his treatment of Helen as if she were their child; once Bedford acknowledged their domestic arrangement by mentioning that if Molly ever decided to marry again, they would have to discuss who got custody of Helen ("Molly and Jim"). On a few occasions Molly pressed Jules to declare his feelings for her, but most of the time she accepted their *understanding*—no official recognition of any special relationship between them.

In all, the only nurse character in *The Practice* was positively presented because she was universally popular among the other characters and because her patience, good humor, compassion, and toughness endeared her to the viewers. But the doctor–nurse relationship exhibited all the typical traits of an old-fashioned practice in which the unmarried nurse devoted her entire life to the service of the doctor and to the fulfillment of his dreams and aspirations.

Both *Doc* and *The Practice* featured despotic but beloved old physicians as protagonists and paired each of them with devoted and middle-aged nurses who also served as surrogate wives. In some ways *Doc* and *The Practice* were comedic take-offs on the values expressed in *Marcus Welby, M.D.* Old fashioned and mature G.P.s who still made house calls assumed the center stage while their devoted assistants were mature but younger nurses, reputedly skilled and intelligent but shown as maternal, domestic, and occasionally romantic. Consuelo Lopez is not far removed from Tully or Molly in terms of her value judged in terms of the aid she gave the physician's professional and personal life.

Doc and *The Practice* both gave attention to human values and to ethical conflicts, albeit in a humorous vein. When these shows failed, comedy producers, still convinced that doctors and nurses were funny people, returned to farce and slapstick. In 1977 ABC brought out a sit-com based on the 1959 movie *Operation Petticoat*. The zany show concerned another chapter in the hilarious, fun-loving adventures of U.S. boys and girls during World War II. Representative of the war-can-be-fun school so clearly delineated in *McHale's Navy, Hogan's Heroes*, and *Mr. Roberts, Operation Petticoat* depicted the nearly calamitous but always successful fortunes of the crew of the submarine, *U.S.S. Sea Tiger* and its unwanted guests, five Army nurses. The Pacific Theatre of war never saw such eager sailors and pretty nurses as inhabited the leaky pink submarine. The comedic premise of the series was that a barely seaworthy submarine (painted pink), assigned an optimistic commander eager to prove himself a contributing member of the war effort and given a supply officer who considers the ownership of property a minor nuisance, provide the ingredients for a funny show. But by adding one more element, five of the Army's prettiest nurses confined to the sub for various reasons, the results will be explosive and contagious humor. Even a brilliant recipe for fun such as this could sour if the producer were too heavy-handed, the plots improbable, the characters stock.

According to the series' pilot film, Captain Matt Sherman (John Astin), a desk bound naval department officer, had at long last been assigned to active duty as skipper of the submarine *Sea Tiger,* but when he arrived in Manila on December 8, 1941 he discovered that his ship had been badly damaged by the Japanese and that the Navy was preparing to scrap it. Sherman, loathe to give up his command, assembled a skeleton crew, and with the help and connivance of his supply officer

Lieutenant Nick Holden (Richard Gilliland) scrounged up enough spare parts to make the vessel seaworthy if not exactly fit for a recruitment poster. To Captain Sherman's delight his ship received its sailing orders, but to his dismay she was limited to transport and communications functions. Sherman, a decent officer, determined to carry out his orders (always hoping for the opportunity to prove the *Sea Tiger*'s martial prowess), even if he had to turn his head to avoid seeing his nemesis and savior, wacky Holden arrange some nefarious scheme to procure both needed parts and supplies as well as frivolous extras for his personal use. Usually Holden-inspired situations created the comedic complications for each episode. Other crew members included: Lieutenant Watson (Raymond Singer), the spit and polish executive officer who often nearly ruined the plans of his less orthodox mates; Chief Sam Tostin, who, as the head machinist responsible for keeping the creaky craft afloat, found the presence of the nurses most disconcerting; Hunkle, the owlish but inarticulate yeoman; and Chief Molumphrey.

The *Sea Tiger*'s first mission had her island hopping in pursuit of an admiral who needed transport to Manila. At one of the islands, Holden discovered five stranded Army nurses and brought them aboard; the nurses caused a queue at the shower and improvised laundry lines which exasperated and embarrassed the crew. The arrival of the nurses marked another source of conflict for the Captain and for Holden; Sherman, while sympathetic to the nurses' plight, wanted to contain the effects of their presence, but Holden seemed bent on taking advantage of the situation and turning the *Sea Tiger* into a cruise ship. Events played into Holden's hands, and, because of enemy interference, the nurses had to remain with the *Sea Tiger* for an unspecified amount of time. The five Army nurses adjusted to submarine life fairly well, but never gave up hope for a return to a real nursing assignment. Their senior officer, Major Edna Hayward, begged, pleaded, and encouraged Captain Sherman to find them a way off the ship; despite his interest in complying, he could not disobey orders to suit the nurses. Major Hayward was a short, redhaired woman in her late thirties who, though attractive, seemed rather matronly compared to the younger nurses who wore their makeshift clothing with as much sexual emphasis as possible. Major Hayward appeared in baggy or at least unsuggestive apparel. Hayward emerged as the real leader of the nurses, marked by having the largest speaking part, and she often expressed concern and worry for her girls' welfare. Though Edna was a rather excitable woman, she had uncanny mechanical ability to improvise parts and repairs from available materials. For example, she first appalled the machinist Tostin when she rigged up one of her girdles as an engine belt. She maintained an ongoing battle with Tostin over her role in the engine room. Major Hayward appeared to be a more seasoned veteran of war and wartime situations; she was more suspicious of the crewmen's attentions to her nurses than were the younger women, but she displayed warmth and good humored flexibility in light of the many odd events aboard the *Sea Tiger*.

Lieutenant Dolores Crandall (Melinda Naud), an attractive, tall, buxom blonde, had the most pronounced personality trait of the four nurse-lieutenants— she was a clutz who menaced the safety of all aboard by her propensity to trip, fall, and drop things. She accidentally set off torpedoes, ran an ambulance into a truck, dropped mailbags into the ocean, and inflated a lifeboat inside the conning tower. In addition, she was apologetic, friendly, and good humored, and gradually she became endeared to all who knew her, even Captain Sherman. The other nurses, Lieutenants Barbara Duran, Ruth Colfax, and Clair Reid, remained less differentiated, sharing positive traits of camaraderie, sociability, resourcefulness, friendliness, and good humor. All attractive, young women in their early twenties, they gladly suffered the inconveniences of life aboard a submarine.

Brief summaries of two episodes will indicate the type of plots presented as well as the role of nursing in the series. "Gray is Beautiful" (November 19, 1977) centered on the embarrassment of the captain and crew over their submarine's unfortunate pink color since the crew had gotten into a fist fight with other sailors who insinuated that the sailors of the pink ship must be less than virile. The nurses bandaged their wounded mates and overheard Captain Sherman and Lieutenant Holden discussing the problem of getting gray paint. The base commander had confined the crew to the sub and ordered that no gray paint be issued to Navy personnel from the *Sea Tiger*. The nurses managed to purloin the paint and disguised their cargo as contagious patients on stretchers. Holden was a little upset that the nurses succeeded where he had failed, chicanery being his forte, but they all rejoiced in painting the *Sea Tiger* a normal shade. They put out to sea and began painting the sub when orders arrived to return to the base at once—the theft had been discovered and they were all headed for court martial. However, all ended well when it was discovered that the nurses stole water soluble paint; when the *Sea Tiger* sufaced at the base, it was bright pink again.

In "On a Clear Day You Can See a Bulkhead" mechanical breakdowns and growing claustrophobia of the Army nurses created problems for Captain Sherman and the crew. In their tiny quarters, the nurses tried to dress in the limited space. Just as the nurses convinced Holden to "do something," Tostin was burned in an engine room explosion. The nurses quickly examined the injured man and concluded that he would be fine in a few days. While Tostin was led to the sick bay, Hayward examined the engine and informed the captain that the sub would not move until the shattered fuel pump could be replaced. As luck would have it, an abandoned island was nearby, and Major Hayward went ashore with her nurses to scavenge the needed part. While she worked, the nurses gamboled over the island enjoying the trees and air. A U.S. plane landed on the island and everyone ran to greet the pilot who agreed to take the nurses along with him to Port Moresby and accompanied them to the sub to retrieve their belongings and to install the fuel pump. The news of the nurses' impending departure raised mixed feelings among the crew; sorriest to see them go was Lieutenant Holden who unsuccessfully schemed to keep them aboard by pretending to the pilot that the nurses were deranged. As the nurses said goodbye, another engine room explosion occurred; the piston trouble seemed unlikely to be repaired with Tostin sidelined and Hayward leaving but at the last minute the nurses changed their minds. Major Hayward went to take a look at the piston, and the pilot, unable to wait, departed without his passengers. As a gesture of gratitude, Holden and Sherman had a scenic view, window and curtains, painted on the wall of the nurses' quarters.

As seen from these plot descriptions, nursing per se played a limited part in the series. Most episodes featured the stranded women in non-professional roles. With limited supplies and equipment, and without formal orders to be aboard the sub, the nurses mainly waited for rescue. They appeared to be competent and able professionals when the need arose, for example, during Tostin's engine room accident; however, for the most part nursing never entered the plot development, and the nurses never discussed their motivations for choosing their careers nor their attitudes towards their profession. The significance of the nurse characters lay in the fact that they were five women confined to close quarters of an all male submarine. Nylons and bras identified these characters more than did thermometers and stethoscopes. In fact, the sexual attractions and tensions between the crew and the nurses represented an ongoing theme of the series. At one point both men and women were portrayed as having to take lots of cold showers because of the effects of close quarters upon their libidos.

Given the limited identification as nurses, these characters did emerge as positive characters. They were friendly, resourceful, flexible, good humored, energetic, and attractive. They displayed a sense of loyalty to each other as well as to their adopted home, and they risked military punishment to help in the completion of any scheme deemed important to the ship's success. In addition, the nurses showed compassion and solicitude for the problems faced by the crew members.

The nurses' less attractive traits provided some of the comedic situations but did not prejudice the viewer's attitude toward the nurses in general. For example, in a fit of boredom, Lieutenant Claire Reid read the palms of the nurses and crew; when a few of her predictions came true, the nurses inspired a wave of hysteria that nearly sank the sub for good. Occasionally the nurses petulantly complained about their confinement, but more often they were cheerful. At their worst they were clumsy, hairbrained females intent upon fulfilling the stereotypes about dizzy blondes. But in all they remained loveable and sympathetic characters within the context of the series.

In the spring of 1977 CBS introduced yet another military situation comedy entitled *The Nurses*. The network clearly intended to ape their own success, *M*A*S*H*. The show was set in a M.A.S.H unit and featured the predictable array of nurse and physician characters: two young and attractive nurses, Jacqueline "Jackie" Morse and Elizabeth "Liz" Baker, who acted much like Hawkeye and B.J. in drag—lots of practical jokes masking sincere, committed concern for the welfare of their patients; Major Charlotte Hinkley, a formidable career Army nurse, who her subordinates referred to as "Big Momma" or, "B.M;" a sensual Turkish nurse named Sophia ("The Turkish Delight"); a clumsy, plump and over-compensative nurse, Shirley "Scoop" Nichols; Drs. Harris, O'Brien and Rogers, who put considerable effort into pursuing the nurses.

The storyline of the series' pilot (the show never made it to a permanent slot) concerned Jackie and Liz's attempts to stage a surprise birthday party for an about-to-be-21 Army corporal facing serious surgery. They had been carefully warned by Big Momma that any activities that were against regulations would result in the loss of their much awaited ten-day leave in Tokyo. Jackie and Liz argued a bit over the party, as Liz insisted that Jackie could not give so much of herself to every patient without slowly eroding her own sanity; in the end, Liz saw that Jackie was right and helped to keep the affair from Big Momma's attention. Everything turned out well when the Colonel saved the day by commending Big Momma for thinking up such a marvelous idea.

The description of the characters and much of the dialogue conflicted with the writers' attempts to make the leading characters sympathetic and positive human beings. Clearly the writers intended the young nurses to be Hawkeye-like in their compassion, pacifism, and disregard for military protocal and they were skilled surgical nurses who still found the time and energy to make their patients feel like real human beings. Unfortunately, the writers resorted to the unbearable clichés about certain feminine types and allowed the physician characters to sprinkle all conversations with the nurses with sexually suggestive remarks. Although this pilot never made it into a series, the development of a program concept featuring nurses as comic protagonists was quite interesting. It would appear that in the 1970s screenwriters could not abandon their insistence upon the sexual traits of military nurses, so blatantly exploited in the early years of *M*A*S*H, Operation Petticoat,* and *Black Sheep Squadron.*

CBS tried out another sit-com about a medical student who returned to school after experience in an unsatisfying career. *Annie Flynn,* a pilot that aired in January 1978, told the story of a nurse who wanted to be a doctor. Of course she was pretty and surrounded with loveable companions. The first and last episode of the series recounted her difficulty in handling the delicate situation of dating her anatomy professor. Other than her identification as a registered nurse who had returned to school, the series' one episode made little use of the character's nursing identity. The unfortunate single impression made by this entry would be that nursing does not provide a challenging opportunity for career-minded women.

In the spring of 1978 CBS, still trying to create a female version of *M*A*S*H,* broadcast a situation comedy pilot featuring nurse characters in leading roles, *The Fighting Nightingales* again centered around the worries and actions of nurses in a field hospital during the Korean War. However, the series was not a slapstick comedy, and it presented the nurses as responsible professionals who worked under extremely dangerous conditions. The pilot episode focused on the arrival of a new nurse who was going to replace a nurse who was killed trying to rescue a prisoner of war. Lieutenant Hope Phillips (Stephanie Faracy) stepped out of the jeep dressed in dress uniform, gloves, and high heels. The three other nurses, dressed for action in fatigue pants, t-shirts, and boots, immediately sensed the new recruit's naiveté. In fact, Hope became extremely nervous at the sounds of war nearby and practically useless after learning the fate of her predecessor. The recruiting officer had given her a totally false picture of the role she would play in the war effort. Major Kate Steele (Adrienne Barbeau) gave the new nurse sympathy and encouragement, and gradually Hope began to pull her weight as part of the team. Kate led her nurses with tolerance and a sense of humor. She was brave, calm, efficient, and respected by her colleagues and the patients. The entire image of nursing rested upon the nurses' abilities to face their own problems and to find their own solutions. No physician characters took the lead or tried to protect the nurses. These nurses were on friendly terms with the doctors but were not treated like mascots or objects for off duty diversion. Unfortunately but rather predictably this female dominated show did not sufficiently capture the public fancy to warrant its development into a full series.

That same spring of 1978 ABC introduced yet another health care comedy, *A.E.S. Hudson Street* which ran for only five weeks before cancellation. This situation comedy focused on the staff and patients of the Adult Emergency Service of a beleaguered New York City hospital. The initial episode introduced the show's regular characters: Dr. Tony Menzies, sympathetic Chief Resident; Dr. Mackler, a woman chaser; Dr. Glick, a stereotyped psychiatrist; Rosa Santiago, a sarcastic and very pregnant nurse; Newton, a gay male nurse; Rhonda, a sexy and rather dim staff nurse; a sophisticated black nurse (supposedly a triage nurse) who sat at the desk (and who seemed to have a different name and be played by a different actress each week); and ambulance drivers/paramedics Foshko (female) and Stankey (male). The first episode dealt with a number of patients: an escaped mental patient who dressed up as a doctor and actually performed two operations; a crook who had hidden a stolen pearl in his nose and could not get it out; a hang-glider who was injured when he was mugged upon landing; and a cardiac patient who had received emergency cardiac massage from the phony doctor. In the midst of all this chaos, Mr. Karbo, a hospital administrator, tried to persuade Dr. Menzies to give a friend a secret (and unreported) vasectomy in his office. Menzies refused, but the operation was done anyway by the fake doctor before he was unmasked as a mental patient.

The four remaining episodes followed the same format as the first: unrelated incidents concerning two or more patients and predictable gags played off the stereotyped characteristics of the regulars. Foremost were the sexual jokes, and the possibilities seemed limitless since one nurse was pregnant, one coolly experienced, one male and homosexual, and one a blonde sexpot (in appearance anyway). Dr. Mackler, as obsessed with sex as any adolescent, added his tasteless banter with the nurses to the general sexual humor. Examples of this humor were numerous: "Dexter, are you troubled by sexual fantasies?" "No, doctor, I enjoy them" [(Title unknown), March 30, 1978]; "No, Dr. Mackler, I'm *not* sick, and I don't need bedrest—especially not in your apartment" [(Title unknown), April 20, 1978].

The psychiatrist, Dr. Glick, and Dr. Menzies were both relatively exempt from the sex jokes, but they represented the show's two other categories of humor—stereotypes and ethnic humor, respectively. When a would-be suicide refused to believe that he was still alive, Glick offered a series of absurd arguments to convince him, and failing, he finally said (with deadly predictability). "Let's talk about your relationship with your mother." [(Title unknown), April 13, 1978] Dr. Menzies, a man of hispanic descent, in moments of stress or excitement, dropped into high speed Spanish or heavily accented English, with his voice rising and his eyes rolling. Many of Menzies' exchanges were with Rosa, who was also hispanic and who was victim of some of the ethnic humor. Rosa displayed another brand of humor herself (aside from sexual and ethnic); she used a kind of bored, mock cynical sarcasm apparently bred from having seen too much too often in the emergency room. When a malingerer resisted Rosa's attempts to throw him out and demanded the treatment he deserved, Rosa said tartly, "If I gave you what you deserved, *then* you would need treatment." [(Title unknown), Feb. 23, 1978]

The plots rarely called for the nurses to exhibit any real nursing skills. Usually they stood around chatting with the physicians, wisecracking with the patients, or watching while a physician worked with a patient. What work they did seemed menial, for the most part, or at least unskilled; they made phone calls, ran errands, washed equipment, carried trays, manned the reception desk. Only Newton was shown doing anything much more serious: He drew blood; he helped in a cardiac resusitation; and he informed doctors about patients' conditions.

Of the physician characters, Glick virtually never interacted with the nurses, and Mackler only made sexual jokes or propositions and looked to the nurses for approval. However, Menzies (Gregory Sierra) was able, despite his awful jokes, to convey the idea that he knew, liked and respected the nurses. He gave orders but in a tone that emphasized his reliance on their help and his trust in their abilities. With Rosa especially he seemed to have a collegial relationship. He implicitly trusted her diagnosis of a patient's possible thrombophlebitis, sending the surgeon in to see the patient; and together, with unspoken agreement, they fell into a routine designed to scare a malingerer out of the emergency room (ordering stomach pumping, high colonics, exploratory surgery, and a cystoscopic exam). Even in the midst of the silliness, something suggested that these characters really were friends who respected one another's talents, and that quality gave the nurses' image a dimension beyond the skimpy scenes actually shown. It was not enough to redeem the show, but it helped.

The nurse characters also suggested by their attitudes more than by their actions that they might be taken seriously as real nurses. They were, at least, on the giving end of the sarcasm rather than on the receiving end. They were almost never the butt of the jokes, except for mild jokes that Rosa made about her own eighth pregnancy and sex life. All the nurses put Mackler firmly in his place when he made sexual advances, and all made sarcastic remarks to obstreperous patients. For all their sarcasm and apparent cynicism, however, the nurses maintained an air of calm competence, even in the midst of rather chaotic conditions, giving the impression that they were well trained, experienced, and professional (even when their actions failed to corroborate that impression). They exuded an air of having done their jobs for a long time. They showed no starry-eyed idealism; they seemed to have no illusions about their work. For all the unlikely Hollywood wit, the actress still managed to convey the attitude of caring that one hopes for in a nurse, but the good was never sufficient to outweigh the bad.

With the exception of *M*A*S*H*, producers in the 1970s were unable to find a winning formula for a situation comedy about nursing and physicians and health care, although as seen in the previous pages they certainly tried. Perhaps this failure was to the advantage of the nursing profession because few positive and strong images of nurses appeared amidst all the slapstick and failed wit. The two best series, in terms of writing and character development, were *Doc* and *The Practice*. These two shows also consistently attempted to project an ethical point of view and a hierarchy of human values. For example in *The Practice*, Jules and his son often feuded over proper medical treatment or how rich doctors should be, but routinely the series promoted the notion that humanitarian goals should take precedence over monetary ones. In both of these series the nurse characters emerged as sympathetic women and admirable nurses, but they each defined their importance and professional worth in terms of the physician they served. Both Tully and Molly dedicated themselves first to the personal service of their physician employers; their professional goals rested in their commitment to their employers' altruistic goals.

6

Suspended Moments: Nurses in 1970s Action–Adventure Series

Action–adventure programs, most often featuring crime or law enforcement themes, have been a staple of network schedules for many years; a seemingly insatiable appetite for daring rescues, car chases, and climactic shootouts has prompted producers to package their action programs in a variety of formats. Women usually play very limited roles in these series, leaving the pursuit of danger to the men. *Charlie's Angels* has been an exception proving the rule; in it beautiful young women demonstrate physical bravery and heroism in the normal course of their work. In three action–adventure series of the 1970s, nurse characters played regular albeit secondary roles: *The Rookies; Emergency!;* and *Black Sheep Squadron*. Each of these shows had a different format. *The Rookies* dealt with the adventures of young policemen; *Emergency!* followed the bold rescues of young paramedics; and *Black Sheep Squadron* recounted the exploits of marine air aces in World War II.

The nurse characters in these shows fulfilled similar purposes; they provided the calm emotional center for the wide ranging heroes. Nurse characters seemed especially suited to their roles to provide female companionship and feminine reactions because the dangerous nature of the adventure hero's occupation often found him physically injured or at least involved with the physical injuries of others. The nurse of *Emergency!* was slightly more integral to the show's identity than were the nurses in the other two series because the emergency room of a large hospital was a primary setting. Nevertheless, Dixie McCall of *Emergency!* served as the same emotional sounding board for physicians and paramedics as did Jill of *The Rookies* for her policemen, and the nurses of *Black Sheep Squadron* for their pilots.

The use of nurses as feminine counterweights to the masculine world of daring adventure leads the viewer to certain assumptions about the role of nursing.

In many ways these action shows presented the world of nursing as static and reactive in nature; any excitement found in nursing would come through association with men in more demanding and challenging work. The nurses may have contributed to the resolution of certain problems, but they did so because the problem was thrust upon them. They never went in pursuit of danger or sought out problems to solve. When a nurse character became involved in a dangerous situation, she generally required the help of the action heroes to extricate her from her predicament. More often than not the nurse characters did not become involved in the main action at all; rather they served as nurturing women who waited to patch up their male colleagues' wounds or to ease their emotional stress or confusion. In all there was little new or surprising about their roles. They portrayed the motherly and romantic roles assigned to them in so many other television dramas and comedies.

In 1972 ABC aired *The Rookies,* something of a hybrid descendant of *Adam 12, Mod Squad* and *The Interns* all rolled into one and parcelled out into tidy thirty- or sixty-minute episodes. *The Rookies* detailed the professional activities and off duty lifestyles of three patrolmen assigned to Station Number Seven of the Southern California Police Department. Representing a new breed of young recruits who were sensitive to human life, the rookies were reluctant to use firearms, and they attempted non-violent approaches to crime control. One of the regulars on the series, Patrolman Michael Danko (Sam Melville) was married to nurse Jill (Kate Jackson). The two other rookies, William "Willie" Gillies (Michael Ontkean) and Terry Webster (Georg Stanford Brown) who was black, were bachelors. Lieutenant Edward Ryker (Gerald S. O'Loughlin), to whom the patrolmen were responsible, offered a contrast to his young charges: He was a middle-aged, experienced veteran who gave cynical and hard to digest, but, in the end, valuable advice.

Whatever the writers' intentions might have been, *The Rookies* did not turn out to be a very realistic show. The format of the tyical episode did not show an average day in the life of a policeman; rather it showed the rookies concentrating all their time on a single crime, with other affairs rarely interrupting or interfering with their speedy success in bringing the criminal to justice. The rookies' intention to work without violence often failed since the show featured a good many high speed chases and shootouts and numerous injuries which required the services of Nurse Jill Danko at the hospital. With some frequency they were shot, bombed, taken hostage, blinded, paralyzed, or killed. Hence, despite its vaunted idealism, the show maintained a macho image designed to appeal primarily to men.

Another aspect seemingly designed to appeal to the male viewer was the vulnerability of those close to the cops, especially Jill, who was frequently portrayed as a victim or potential victim in need of protection or rescue by the men. Jill was attacked, kidnapped, held hostage, or threatened with rape and/or death with a regularity that would drive any normal woman to divorce her policeman husband at the very least. But she, like her husband and the other rookies, persevered in her chosen life; indeed, she helped to keep their ambitions bright.

Sometimes the rookies got discouraged by the hardship of their lot, and their struggle, always resolved in favor of idealism, was often the central conflict of an episode for one or another of the rookies. In fact, most of the plots focused more on the actions and interactions of the main characters than on any outside antagonists, giving the show a somewhat claustrophobic and unrealistic quality. Within this general framework, Jill played a variety of roles, wife, friend of the rookies and keeper of their ideals, nurse, and victim. Her image was basically positive, and although her priority seemed to be her marriage, much give and take occurred between the couple in terms of respect for each of their work roles. However, more often than not, Jill was shown off duty. She served many of the same functions in her role as friend of the rookies. Of course she maintained complete marital loyalty to Mike, but in a sisterly fashion she acted as a stabilizing force for the two bachelors too.

Jill helped with more than just personal problems. She also entered into the rookies' discussions about cases they were working on, offering her own intelligent suggestions, sometimes suggestions that got the rookies turned toward the solution of the crime. She soothed minor disagreements among the rookies, particularly when a new rookie, Chris Owen, replaced Willie in the series. Terry especially was reluctant to welcome the newcomer; but Jill soon made Chris feel accepted when she persuaded the other rookies to help him move in and to listen to his ideas in discussions. Furthermore, she helped the rookies keep their ideals shining, reassuring them that their new breed of cops were noble and worthy, even though the public seemed ungrateful, uncooperative, and unaware that the policemen were on their side. Several times she dissuaded one of the rookies from quitting. She would not let them get cynical or slipshod about their idealistic methods.

Jill was friend not only to the policemen but to their wives and girlfriends as well. She went to baby showers for wives; she nursed them when they were ill; she comforted them when their men had been wounded or killed; and she discussed health problems with them. In fact, Jill was the model policeman's wife, and a tough model to live up to.

Many times Jill's professional education as a nurse enabled her to help the rookies in their work even more than usual. She often explained health problems that had some bearing on one of their cases. When a teenaged, diabetic girl ran away, for instance, Jill warned the rookies of the danger of her going into a diabetic coma, and they speeded up their rescue efforts, saving the girl from almost sure death just in the nick of time. Always, Jill was available to tell the rookies about the condition of injured criminals or victims. Even better, she sometimes supplied the evidence to convict them. And she was always available to nurse the police through their own injuries. When Lieutenant Ryker was particularly worried about another policeman, an old friend, in surgery, Jill volunteered to be his link by serving as a circulating nurse in surgery, apparently a decision she could make without having to consult anyone else. In fact, Jill handily happened to be working wherever and whenever the rookies or the rookies' suspects or victims were brought into the hospital. Be it in the emergency room, surgery, maternity, isolation, or jail ward, there was Jill.

Although Jill was made, by inference, to seem very important as a nurse, she actually very seldom provided nursing care, and when she did, her nursing actions were quite simple ones—wiping foreheads, preparing medications, reporting patients' conditions, helping physicians with their surgical gloves, and the like. She was never seen nursing except when it involved one of the rookies' police cases.

If the writers really did envision *The Rookies* as a macho show with special appeal for male viewers, Jill's role of victim in need of male rescue as the seasons progressed would be explained. She was frequently kidnapped, threatened with rape, and wounded. In all Jill got involved in an unbelievable number of traumatic situations where either her life or her sexual integrity seemed doomed except for the speedy, brilliant actions of the rookies. To do Jill justice, however, one must point out that she usually assisted in her own rescue too. She might have been a victim, but she was not helpless; she would not passively accept the outrages offered her by the criminal and/or mentally ill. She was quite brave, sometimes to the point of foolhardiness. A number of times she saved her own or another person's life by knocking a gun from the criminal's hand at the crucial moment, sometimes just deflecting a shot, sometimes smashing the gunman with a chair. Other times, she facilitated her own rescue by cleverness and trickery. But even when Jill was at her most resourceful, she still needed help from the rookies for her ultimate rescue. A good example was an episode called "Journey to Oblivion" (March 16, 1976) in which Jill witnessed the murder of one of her patients by Blair, a rich and jaded young man. Blair hired a gunman to kill her, and together they kidnapped Jill, taking her off to a deserted quarry where they figured her body wouldn't be found. The hired killer, seeing how pretty Jill was, proposed to rape her before killing her, whereupon Jill made a sudden grab for the wheel, causing a wreck. Blair was critically injured by a piece of metal in his chest, a wound Jill, who was only scraped, promptly began to tend. The hitman was only worried because Blair had not yet paid him, so Jill played on his greed, ordering him to help her with Blair. Reluctantly he obeyed; meanwhile, Jill found the hitman's gun in the grass near the wreck, pocketed it for later use, and performed her first operation. Blair was so impressed at Jill's having saved his life and her arguments to him about ways that he could change and make something out of his spoiled, useless life that he tried to help her escape. When that failed he offered the hitman an extra thousand dollars not to rape Jill. Shortly thereafter the rookies arrived, shot the hitman, and completed Jill's rescue. It is ironic that Jill, who kept her head throughout the whole crisis and exhibited considerable courage and cleverness, in the end had to be protected by the men, one of them a helpless patient at that. Jill wouldn't use the gun she had found, handing it to Blair for self-defense after Blair had told her to make her escape. The hitman returned too soon, however, and got the gun back with pathetic ease, making the rookies' final rescue of Jill necessary. For all her clear thinking, Jill thought her only alternative with the gun was to shoot the killer, a violation of her respect for life. One wonders why she didn't just hold him captive at gunpoint or tie him up until help arrived. Still, the episode showed Jill's intelligence, courage, kindness, and honesty and her nonjudgmental understanding toward people.

Jill was honest, too, sometimes courageously so. As a nurse she had to sometimes bring unwelcome news about patients' conditions. She broke the news about death, paralysis, and amputation quickly, kindly, and truthfully. When Willie was shot, Jill talked frankly to his fiancee, letting her know exactly what kind of marital future she could expect if Willie's paralysis remained permanent, and admitting to the general hardships and worries of being a policeman's wife. When the girl expressed doubts about her abilities to handle such tensions, Jill did not soothe her with false assurances; instead she encouraged the girl to examine those doubts thoughtfully.

To be sure, Jill occasionally displayed some negative traits as well, just enough to make her seem human. She showed some jealousy when she feared her husband might be too attracted to a young widow he had helped; and when she suffered a miscarriage, she retreated for awhile into feelings of self-pity, anger, unfriendliness, and irritability. However, these were all just temporary aberrations from her usual good humor and were soon conquered. In all, she was an attractive personality. Such an array of good traits could not help but reflect favorably on Jill's image as a nurse, even though actual nursing scenes tended to appear only sketchily. Because Jill was clearly and frequently identified with nursing, the viewer tended to assume that all her excellent qualities got carried over into her professional as well as her personal life. As the rookies were part of a new breed of cop, Jill was a member of what could easily be called a new breed of nurses—tough but flexible, willing to bend the rules a bit to accommodate the needs of a friend or patient and, though proud of her independence, never actually rebellious against any bureaucracy; rather she was pleased to be part of a health care team and was dedicated to her work. Hence, she actually eluded stereotypes. She was neither matronly, brash, mealy-mouthed, mousy, nor manipulative; she was a gutsy woman who had more in common with the hip heroine of *Mod Squad* than with any previously analyzed nurse characters.

January 1972 ushered in a mid-season television entry which concentrated on young, uniformed rookies who served as both firemen and paramedics. This show, *Emergency!*, proved quite popular and ran for six seasons before going into syndication. In the course of those six seasons, the nurse character Dixie McCall developed significantly, gaining a better image. *Emergency!* purported to show the workings of the paramedics of Engine Company 51 of the Los Angeles County Fire Department and their liaison with the emergency department of Rampart General Hospital. There were ten permanent characters in *Emergency!*, five of whom appeared in virtually every episode, while the others appeared only slightly less frequently. Most important were the two paramedics of the Company 51 firemen. John Gage (Randolph Mantooth), an intense, handsome bachelor with an active mind, was always concocting schemes to improve his personal or professional life; these schemes often backfired. Roy DeSoto (Kevin Tighe) was the straight man in this team, a stolid, all American family man. Both men were rather ordinary, young men (25–30) with one area of rather extraordinary skill, paramedicine. The other three important characters were the two physicians and a nurse who cared for the patients brought or sent in by the paramedics, and who treated walk-in emergency patients as well. Dr. Kelly Brackett (Robert Fuller) and Dr. Joe Early (Bobby Troup) were the healer–heroes of the show, giving the paramedics radioed instructions about further treatment for the patient after the immediate first-aid had been administered. Nurse Dixie McCall (Julie London) was clearly a secondary member of the hospital team, although she appeared frequently. She sometimes took the paramedics' calls on the biophone and wrote down the information they relayed, but she rarely gave them instructions herself. Dixie's main role was to meet the paramedics at the door, point out the appropriate treatment room for the patient, and then assist the doctors in their treatment. She always seemed competent but rarely vital. Her unique contribution was sex appeal.

The five lesser characters in *Emergency!* were a black doctor and four firemen. The firemen frequently appeared in scenes designed to show the personal relationships with Gage and DeSoto, most often in homey situations in the living quarters of the firehouse. They also engaged in some of the spectacular rescues, but Gage and DeSoto claimed the most daring maneuvers. Dr. Morton (he alone was never called by his first name) was not a thoroughly developed character. He was presented as a fine, dedicated doctor in most episodes, but he was never seen in any personal situation or relationship.

The plot format for the episodes was unvarying. There were four or five emergency situations—usually one hospital walk-in case and four cases calling for the paramedics—all designed to show the varying skills of the emergency care team, and nearly all unrelated to one another. The episodes were given at least a hint of continuity by some idea which usually opened the show, recurred periodically, and then resolved itself in the final frame. Both the rescues and thread ideas fell into predictable categories. The paramedics rescued people from fires, high places, water, or wrecks of some sort, or, they treated such emergency conditions as heart attacks, food poisoning, hyperventilation, fainting, broken limbs, and choking. The viewer frequently saw them administering I.V.s, applying emergency splints or burn packs, requiring the patient to breathe into a paper bag (for hyperventilation), or using the defibrillator (for cardiac arrest).

The ideas tying these emergency scenes together also tended to fall into categories. Most frequent were those indicating the personal lives and relationships of the firemen. Less frequently the overreaching idea would be a professional one, as the episode in which the paramedics got into a running argument with Dr. Morton about the proper amount of caution to exercise in emergency situations. In this case (an exception rather than the rule), the various emergency incidents tended to illustrate both sides of the professional argument. Occasionally the patients would provide the touch of continuity for the show. In one episode, for example, a squabbling couple who believed in "therapeutic fighting" kept requiring the assistance of the paramedics as they inflicted increasingly serious damage on one another. Once in a great while an episode would show both the firemen and the hospital staff struggling with their respective versions of the same problem. Most often, however, the non-emergency scenes were personal, human interest ones.

The firemen, especially the paramedic firemen Gage and DeSoto, were the heroes in all episodes, while the hospital team played a secondary role. The intellectual level of the show seemed deliberately undercut in many ways for although the paramedics did an excellent job professionally, they were distinctly ordinary young men. The show conveyed rather a mixed message about nurse Dixie McCall, even though the writers obviously intended a favorable portrayal, and even though she did develop somewhat over the seasons. She was admittedly put into the show at first as nice scenery for viewers. In early episodes she was a rather laconic, pessimistic, hardbitten character who rarely smiled and who was rather contemptuous of the stupidity which brought many of the patients into the emergency room for treatment. Her professional role was skimpy indeed, lacking in authority, decision-making, and realism; she merely assisted the physicians with unskilled tasks. She had a pleasant personal relationship with the doctors, and there were occasional hints of a romance between her and Dr. Kelly Brackett. More often, however, she discussed problems with the doctors, encouraging and sympathizing with them. Within a few seasons her role developed a little more importance, and she gained status in both professionalism and in sympathy; however, the sexy image remained. Dixie was nice looking and neatly clothed in a white uniform. Her voice was low and attractive, and although her dress and speech were always appropriate to the situation, she never looked quite as professional as she sounded and acted. Perhaps her false eyelashes were responsible. On the other hand, she sometimes wore a stethoscope, which added to her professional image.

The actual nursing seen was rather simple, even in the later seasons. She took vital signs, helped patients onto stretchers or into treatment rooms, put dressings on wounds or burns, phoned for equipment (at the doctor's request), told orderlies to help transport patients, wrote down symptoms phoned in by the paramedics, sometimes gave the paramedics instructions for patient care, hung I.V.'s, used a ventilating bag on a patient, and did paper work at the desk. Over time these cumulative actions and the quiet confidence with which Dixie performed each of them suggested much more experience than was actually shown; therefore, the viewer tended to credit her with more professionalism than was warranted by the scenes themselves.

Some shows, however, definitely undercut Dixie's professionalism. The episode "Gasoline Crunch" was one example. Crowell, the new executive administrator, called Dixie to tell her that the hospital's stringent budget was forcing him to reduce the number of emergency room nurses allotted to the Saturday night shift—Dixie's busiest time. She wrote the administrator an angry memo and then worried about her audacity; the administrator, however, offered her a promotion to nursing supervisor. She considered, then finally rejected it, with a supposed self-sacrificing gesture, when the parents of a boy she cared for brought her cookies and told her what a great help she had been. Dixie appeared short-sighted and naive in her notion that she could be of more use in an emergency room than she could be as a nursing supervisor with greater and more far-reaching authority. Crowell attempted to convince Dixie to take the job by showing her the large office and executive washroom that would go with it, rather than discussing the job's heightened responsibility; at no time did she consider the political, power, or professional implications of the offer.

Only rarely was Dixie featured so prominently in an episode, and her usual appearances, though brief, portrayed her sympathetically, especially in her relationships with others. In later seasons she was seen only as a nurse, never off duty, but she was characterized by both professional and personal relationships with the doctors, the paramedics, and (to some extent) other nurses. The physicians discussed cases with her, counted on her help, and gave orders, confident in her ability to carry them out. However, it would be wrong to say that they were treated as equals. The doctors and the paramedics were the heroes; Dixie was their helper, but when she did occasionally appear alone, she used her own judgment. More than once her judgment was better than that of the physicians'.

Her relationship with other nurses was treated somewhat differently. In the first place, usually no other nurses appeared in an episode, other than those walking around in the background in an effort to establish a realistic hospital scene. When another nurse was featured in an episode, she usually served as a bad example of some issue. For instance in "The Bottom Line" another nurse showed insufficient concern about a boy's head injury, simply because he looked all right. Dixie, on the other hand, immediately recognized the possibility of concussion and had a doctor examine the boy without further delay. The two nurses had no direct dealings in this episode, but the intended comparison was unmistakable. In another episode entitled "Paperwork" a young nurse had just been established at Rampart as the new supply nurse, in hopes of increasing hospital efficiency. Fresh out of school, young nurse Patterson insisted on mountains of paperwork for every minor supply transaction; the paramedics bemoaned the loss of Dixie's easy, informal efficiency as supply nurse, and Dixie herself heartily disliked the new nurse's system. By the end of the episode, Dixie had actually sabotaged the new nurse by sneaking in and replacing supplies that had been out, thus completely confusing Miss Patterson's inventory figures. The resulting muddle caused the new job to be eliminated, and things went back to normal.

Given Dixie's remarkable wisdom, her image ought to have been even better than it was, particularly since that wisdom was supplemented by her attractiveness, good humor, intelligence, competence, and efficiency; but the viewers' idea of Dixie was much more indirectly controlled. Most important, other characters (doctors, paramedics, and patients) universally liked, admired, and respected her, and she exuded a genuine respect for other people, implicitly granting them their respective competencies. Somewhat neutralizing these favorable aspects were some unspoken negative ones. Foremost were Dixie's rather minor role and the relative unimportance of her actions compared to those of the other regular characters. Dixie, of all the team, had the least part in the lifesaving system. The paramedics had the most dramatic role, involving the most physical action, often requiring spectacular, danger defying rescues. The physicians moved in to administer the necessary treatment that would assure the patient's return to health. Dixie's role seemed to be rather tangential in comparison.

Baa Baa Black Sheep, an action–adventure series that featured a group of comely nurses, premiered on NBC in September 1976 and nurses routinely appeared only after a format revision of the series; it returned to the air in December 1977 after a half a season's absence, renamed *The Black Sheep Squadron*. This show was based on the real life exploits of Major Greg "Pappy" Boyington and his squadron of Marine air aces known as the "Black Sheep," who served in the South Pacific during World War II. Of a total of thirty-five episodes produced, less than a dozen featured nurses as regular characters.

Black Sheep attempted a slick hour of action based upon the squadron's successful forays against the Japanese (a.k.a. "riceballs," "zeroes, "zekes") and equally successful efforts to undermine military discipline. The two hour premiere described the formation of the unconventional unit: Greg "Pappy" Boyington conned his way into a Marine commission and promised to create the best squadron in the South Pacific. Having culled his crew from court martial records of the South Pacific theatre on the basis of their lack of brains and talent for trouble, Major Boyington disciplined the ragged misfits for the greater glory of the U.S.A. His squad was stationed on the front-line island of Vella la Cava from which the Black Sheep patrolled the enemy infested waters and air of the Solomon slot. Each episode began with a few seconds of wartime newsreel describing action in the Pacific before moving onto the week's offering of heroism and hijinks.

Robert Conrad who played Pappy Boyington easily established a devil-may-care attitude which switched to tough-talking Marine when the chips were down. The rest of the Black Sheep remained at the level of stock characters—eccentric kooks who could be counted on to screw up the most reasonable order but who came through in the clutch. General Moore (Simon Oakland) and Colonel Lard (Dana Elcar), the rear area brass, alternated their despair and pride in the antics of the 214th Marine Fighter Squad. No regular nurse characters appeared in the series until the second season at which time several nurses seemed to be stationed on the island of Vella la Cava. The very attractive young women who played the nurses were introduced each week as Pappy's Lambs: Ellie (Kathy McCullen), Dottie (Kathryn Cannon), Nancy (Nancy Conrad), and Samantha "Sam" Green (Denise Dubarry).

The first twenty-two episodes of *Baa Baa Black Sheep* recounted various missions assigned to the squadron or events which challenged the group to prove its reputation for incorrigibility. A few episodes featured one or more of the Black Sheep involved romantically with a nurse. The second half of the season featured plots similar to those of the first year, although nurse characters assumed a greater role in the action. A summary of two episodes from the second year of the series reveals the typical role of the nurses. In "Fighting Angels" the island of Vella la Cava came under attack by the Japanese, and nurses assigned to the hospital on the island had to help to defend it. The American Navy planned an all-out attack on Admiral Yamamoto's fleet and expected the Black Sheep to hold their own position as well as to participate in the offensive. Although the strategists did not think that the Japanese would attack Vella la Cava, they ordered the evacuation of all nursing and non-essential personnel. The nurses hastily packed their bags and exchanged warm farewells with the pilots. Head nurse Dottie went to Pappy's tent and, although embarrassed, suggested that they use their remaining time to become closer, but Greg, though he appeared very fond of the nurse, postponed their relationship until the crisis has passed. He gave her his good luck charm before she left. Colonel Lard arrived to supervise the evacuation of the nurses and discovered that the Japanese had already landed on the island, making the transport of the nurses impossible. Thus the nurses and other non-combatants prepared for the defense of the camp. Sergeant Micklin instructed the nurses on the way to shoot a gun and enjoyed every minute of the contact. The Black Sheep took to the air and kept the enemy at bay, but the next day when the squadron had to join the larger attack on the Japanese fleet, the nurses and Colonel Lard defended the island. The nurses put up a good fight but were outnumbered by the invading commandoes; however, just in the nick of time the Black Sheep returned and drove the enemy into the sea. The island personnel assessed their damages and discovered that head nurse Dottie was the only casualty. Greg's voice-over narration at the end of the episode noted that she had been a source of strength to everyone.

In "A Little Bit of England" the Black Sheep relied on a British coastwatcher to rescue a downed pilot and returned the favor by delivering medication for a sick native girl. When "England"—codeword for the island of Konga—was overrun by the Japanese as a result of a nurse's lengthy radio contact, the Black Sheep went to the rescue. The episode opened with a typical scene of life on Vella la Cava: Pretty nurse Ellie took a shower while two prankster pilots managed to hit a golf ball into the water tank above her head and, of course, had to look for it. Although Ellie remained unaware of their true intentions, two other nurses, Samantha and Nancy, arrived, sized up the situation, and ordered the pilots out of the area. Noting that her boyfriend was one of the golfers, nurse Nancy angrily called off their date for that evening. Later that day while on a combat mission, the golfing boyfriend, Lieutenant Boyle, failed to return with the rest of the squadron; the nurses tried to comfort a very upset and worried Nancy. Soon the Black Sheep determined that Boyle had been picked up by English coastwatcher Peter Buckley who had a secret camp in the hills of Konga, was not seriously hurt, and would remain hidden until a submarine rescue could be arranged. However, Buckley did need some medical advice about a native girl and described her symptoms over the radio; instructions for treatment were abruptly cut off by Pappy who explained that any radio transmission longer than two minutes could be traced by the Japanese and might endanger Buckley's hideaway. When Samantha stressed the seriousness of the girl's sickness, Greg arranged to fly in medication and fly out with Lieutenant Boyle; in so doing he had to leave behind another pilot. Before arrangements could be made to retrieve the other pilot, Samantha jeopardized Buckley's position when she radioed him with long, explicit instructions for administering the medication. Angered that Sam had ignored his warning, Greg again took to the air in order to rescue the little group of allies on Konga. Of course all went well; Pappy returned to the island with the pilot and sick girl, and Buckley moved his camp to another location.

Apparently the nurses were stationed on Vella la Cava for the purpose of providing fun for the hard working pilots of the Black Sheep Squadron. Very little attention was given to their duties as nurses; they seemed more like mascots than like professional nurses. The four or five young women who portrayed the Lambs were all in their early twenties, had spectacular figures, sported tight jumpsuits, and wore their hair in long, sexy waves. A striking contrast emerged between these nurses and the real nurses seen briefly in the show's use of newsreel clips from the war; the women in the newsreels wore starched, unrevealing, white uniform dresses and caps and appeared to be an average looking group of women of mixed ages. Since no medical officers were attached to the island's hospital, the nurses had complete charge of health care on the island; however, on only a few occasions did they display professional activity. A couple of times a nurse made a cursory exam of a wounded pilot and ordered blood, but there was no real sense of a nursing organization. For example, the nurses never seemed to be on duty, to change shifts, or to have routine tasks.

The women had no negative qualities, which perhaps accounted for their lack of believability as characters. They were beautiful, kind, courageous, sociable, young women who proudly served their country. The fact that they were present in a frontline unit suggested their bravery. When their evacuation was called off because of Japanese commandoes, they were frightened but quickly regained their composure. The nurses proved themselves to be good sports and concerned for the welfare of the Black Sheep when they reluctantly agreed to put on a USO show for the Seabees who refused to repair the badly damaged Black Sheep runway without a show. At first the nurses refused to parade around in front of a bunch of leering, drooling construction workers, but Greg promised to keep them from harm. Samantha finally relented, and the nurses donned shorts and halters and began to coo and flirt with the Seabees. To sweeten the pot, the Black Sheep auctioned off after-the-show dates with the performers.

Since there were plenty of men to go around, the nurses never showed signs of jealousy or competition among themselves. In fact, when two nurses, Sam and Dottie, both had a romantic interest in Major Boyington, they adopted a may-the-best-woman-win attitude, and they remained good friends until Dottie's untimely demise. If one of the nurse's boyfriends was shot down, the others comforted her and encouraged optimism until he was found. Most of the nurses seemed rather sophisticated and shrewd with regard to the intentions of the Black Sheep. When a new nurse arrived, Samantha Green, the other nurses warned her about the initiation rites in the Sheep's Pen. When one of the Black Sheep impersonated a doctor who had come to examine the new nurse, she quickly turned the tables on him by pretending to go along with his scheme, enticing him to undress, and stranding him in the nurses' quarters in his shorts.

Plot development made it clear that all the nurses, more than other women, were available for sexual relationships with the pilots, if they happened to fall in love. For example, when the Black Sheep discovered that the passengers of a C-47 were female pilots, they were visibly disturbed. One pilot noted that he knew how to talk to nurses but not to pilots.

Although none of the nurses received much individual attention, Samantha Green, daughter of Boyington's friend and C.O., received more than the others. She joined Pappy's Lambs late in the second season and seemed to have requested assignment to the island because of her romantic interest in Major Boyington. Dad became upset when he learned that Sam was on Vella la Cava because he was well aware of the Black Sheep's reputation with women. He implored Greg as a friend to watch out for his little girl; this posed a moral dilemma for the major who did have some romantic/sexual interest in the beautiful nurse. Although their mutual attraction was always clear, their relationship remained undeveloped because of her status as the General's daughter. Sam emerged as the leader and spokeswoman for the other nurses, although she had the same rank as they, and occasionally she gave even the pilots sound advice. (Only in "Fighting Angels" was a nurse identified as the head nurse, and she died.)

These young women contributed to the image of nursing as a decorative, sideline occupation. Although they had no negative qualities, the short shrift given their professional duties and talents suggested to the audience that nurses really did not do very much of value. Their addition to the all male cast served to make the series more sexy and to provide an ongoing supply of sexual jokes and risque situations. On the very few occasions in which health care intervention was required, the nurses appeared competent and well trained, but the general impression remained that these women had no real function beyond serving as cheerleaders for the Black Sheep.

The image of the nursing in *The Rookies* and *Emergency!* showed Jill Danko and Dixie McCall exhibiting many positive characteristics that endeared them to everyone. In both these shows, however, nursing appeared to be less exciting, perhaps a less demanding profession than being either a fireman or a rookie policeman. Despite the contributions made by Jill or Dixie, all the glory went to the young men in uniforms who had to be physically brave in pursuit of their duty. The nurse characters, essentially hospital-bound, lacked the freedom and responsibility enjoyed by their often younger and less educated collegues. Because these shows appealed to children and adolescents as well as to adults, the effect of the role of nursing versus policemen/firemen could have been rather detrimental to young people still forming their attitudes about the value and importance of various occupations and professions. The introduction of nurse characters into *Black Sheep Squadron* was simply a ruse to inject sexy women into an all male compound. The fact that the nurses were brave, intelligent, and fun did not erase the predominant image of their being sexual mascots for the boys' team.

7
Mixed Bag: Two Classics, One Early Demise, and Two Lightweights

The same year that saw such lusterless entries as *Temperatures Rising* and *Little People* also heralded two of television's most popular series—*The Waltons* and *M*A*S*H*—series that were still running and holding audiences in 1980–1981, their ninth seasons. These shows were different, both from the series previously discussed and from each other. *The Waltons* showed a poor Appalachian Mountain family in the 1930s and 1940s, while *M*A*S*H* portrayed a glib Army medical team in the Korean war during the 1950s. Despite the vast differences in format, however, the two series shared some characteristics that probably accounted for their popularity. Both shows successfully combined realism and idealism, and both emphasized positive, lasting values—love, hard work, and helping others. A sense of family also pervaded both series: a real family in one case, a drafted family in the other; and within their limited realms both families exerted a healing influence on the outsiders who passed through. Critics at first doubted these series' ability to survive network competition, forgetting perhaps that works appealing to hope and affirmation of human goodness have always been more enduring than those based on self-castigation, nihilism, despair, or scorn.

The Waltons, unlike most other series depicting nurses, always focused on an extended family, one of whose members happened to become a nurse. Although Mary Ellen's nursing was occasionally mentioned and even featured a few times, nursing was never a regular part of the format. Also different was the fact that the viewer was not presented with a fait accompli, an already fullblown portrait of a nurse. When *The Waltons* premiered in 1972, Mary Ellen was only fourteen-years-old and not yet decided on a career. Over the seasons viewers saw her develop both as a person and as a nurse. Because of *The Waltons'* powerful appeal, because the show was on for so long, and because viewers had a chance to watch Mary Ellen develop from a child to a woman, this series offered a very strong, thorough image of the nurse character even though audiences rarely saw her actually perform nursing duties until the 1979–1980 season. However, her desire to be a nurse related to her general longing to manage her own life, and nursing was seen as partly responsible for and partly symbolic of Mary Ellen's maturing.

Mary Ellen, even as a child, was the most restless and rebellious of the Walton children. Although she was sometimes headstrong, pessimistic, outspoken, pushy, or bad tempered, she was also a serious, practical girl, eager to help other people. After a few seasons she began to mellow to such a degree that her grandmother wondered, what had happened to the old Mary Ellen? Early on she showed an interest in nursing, reading aloud from *A Girl's History of Nursing*, and making it clear that she was concerned with the happiness and welfare of those around her. Her desire to become a nurse was probably enhanced by her general rebelliousness against the roles expected of her as a female and as a member of the large, closeknit, mountain family. For a while she refused to learn the womanly arts of cooking and needle work, and she impatiently bristled when her grandmother suggested that only the boys need have careers or such creative learnings as music or writing. Mary Ellen wanted to be a whole person in her own right, and in part, nursing represented to her the opportunity to become just that.

Mary Ellen's somewhat inchoate ideals about becoming a nurse met head on with reality in the 1975–1976 season when she went confidently to take the entrance examinations at the University of Virginia School of Nursing and miserably flunked the math and chemistry sections of the test, having never studied these subjects. She questioned her chances, and her desire, to become a nurse. Back home she went to talk to Nora Taylor, a ruggedly independent public health nurse who served the mountain families; Nora agreed to tutor Mary Ellen in return for the girl's help in caring for a destitute family with a dying mother and a depressed grandfather. This first contact with real nursing strengthened Mary Ellen's conviction that nursing was her true career, and she later went on to pass the examination.

Nora Taylor's portrayal offered some strong though unspoken suggestions about the requisites for mountain nursing. Nora worked alone, apparently without directions from physicians or anyone else, and she was obviously a needed and important person in the community. However, the price for this seemed to be total and utter dedication to her nursing, to the exclusion of all personal life. Although Mary Ellen introduced Nora to the town's handsome new doctor, Curtis Willard, Nora quickly denied any romantic interest in Curt and declined to go out with him again. Mary Ellen, unlike Nora, could not resist the charms of the outspoken Dr. Willard, and she left her fiance just days before her scheduled wedding in order to marry Curt instead. Having freed herself from the power structure of her large family, Mary Ellen then entered a three-level power structure with Curtis in his roles as a male, husband, and physician. Even the independent Mary Ellen did not seem to question his dominance; and she settled into more or less traditional roles as wife and nurse. She learned the womanly arts after all and was proud of her accomplishments. She briefly helped Curt with his practice and functioned in a completely old-fashioned style—nurse as handmaiden to the physician. She fetched his medical bag, chaufferred a patient, and helped decorate his office. The only thing that suggested a more important function for Mary Ellen was Curt's asking her to help him learn to interact better with folks in the community since he had already alienated a number of people with his blunt remarks. Mary Ellen retorted sharply that she was a nurse, not a miracle worker.

In the 1977 season Mary Ellen got pregnant, and that condition took precedence over her nursing. One episode, however, did show Mary Ellen acting as a nurse, and independently at that. Curtis had gone out of town, having denied Mary Ellen's request to accompany him. She was too close to delivery time, he said, so she obediently stayed behind. While he was gone, a call came from a woman who was about to deliver a baby. Mary Ellen went to aid the woman, slogging through storm and mud to get there, and delivered the baby herself. In the 1978 season Curt went off to the Army and Mary Ellen took an accelerated nursing course so that she could finish quickly and go work with Curtis at Pearl Harbor. Curt kept urging her to hurry, and Mary Ellen was eager to rejoin him; but the pressures of the extra work added to the duties of home and motherhood proved too much for her. She resorted to pills—uppers and downers—to get herself going and then to get herself to sleep. This state did not last long, however, as she kicked the habit by the end of the episode, and Curt apologized for pressuring her so much. Shortly thereafter Curt was killed at Pearl Harbor, before Mary Ellen could join him. In almost morbid fear of losing the only thing left of Curtis, Mary Ellen gave up nursing to take care of her baby, John Curtis.

The 1979-1980 season revealed significant changes developing in Mary Ellen's image for at least three reasons. First, the power structure in the family was altered with both Grandpa Walton and Curt dead; second, women's social position generally seemed somewhat changed by wartime conditions; and third, Mary Ellen returned to nursing. All three of these conditions brought increased independence for Mary Ellen. An early episode in the season showed Mary Ellen taking a leave of absence from her job at the plant to return to nursing when Nurse Nora Taylor suddenly joined the Army Nurse Corps and went off to nurse victims of an epidemic at an army camp. Nora left Mary Ellen a list of the people to be visited, describing their needs, ailments, and personalities, and she offered Mary Ellen an irresistible challenge when she suggested that Roni Cotter would try to scare her, but Nora felt assured that Mary Ellen would not let her. This episode offered interesting images, both of nursing and, specifically, of Mary Ellen as a nurse. A nurse to the back hollows folks seemed to combine the skills of nurse, physician, social worker, educator, and good friend. The nurse made regular rounds to all the mountain families to check on them, to be available if needed, to establish herself as a trusted friend. She had to win her way among the stubborn mountain people solely with her own strength, understanding, flexibility, and persistence. She exuded sturdy pioneer resourcefulness as she rode horseback up the mountain, clad in breeches and knee-high laced boots.

Mary Ellen presented a very favorable image as a nurse. She was conscientious and persistent about the duties she was asked to perform, and she displayed considerable cleverness, tact, and flexibility in overcoming the back hollows folks' reluctance to accept her. Mary Ellen finally seemed to have gained the kind of independence that she sought when she first decided on nursing as her career. She was running her own life like an adult, making her own decisions, and confidently following them out with success.

Another important long-running series whose nurse character developed tremendously over the seasons is *M*A*S*H*, a series that defies easy categorization. Like some of the other popular dramatic series, it portrayed older and younger doctor–heroes working together to save lives; but the younger physicians were the more skilled, and the older ones often deferred to their judgment. Like the health oriented comedies, *M*A*S*H* used funny dialogue and comic situations much of the time, but the lines were genuinely witty and intelligent, and the underlying philosophy was deeply serious and humane. Like the action–adventure shows, *M*A*S*H* depicted the practice of medicine in close relationship to some other uniformed profession and usually in emergency conditions; but the heroes hated the uniform, hated the profession it represented, and hated the insanity that made such a profession necessary.

M*A*S*H, which was in its ninth successful season in 1980–1981, offered a strangely limited premise to hold the public interest for so long a time, both in prime-time shows and in multiple reruns each week. The series quite simply dealt with the actions of a small group of Army personnel in a mobile surgical hospital (M.A.S.H. 4077) located somewhere near the front in the Korean war. Episodes generally concentrated on the mess tent, the operating room tent, and "The Swamp"—the surgeons' chaotic living quarters. The plots revolved around the horrifying variety and equally horrifying sameness of the endless stream of mangled bodies which flowed through the M.A.S.H. operating room; the problems of trying to work in wartime conditions; the conflicts between vastly different personalities under stress in confined areas; the various diversions by which the characters took their minds off the war; their different ways of coping with the situation; and the periodic intrusions of higher authorities who threatened to destroy the delicate albeit somewhat insane compromises which enabled this mismatched group to provide lifesaving emergency care for countless soldiers who would have otherwise not lived to reach the regular military hospitals.

To sum up the premise of *M*A*S*H* in a single phrase one could say that it was a show about different kinds of insanity. Overriding all was the gigantic insanity of war itself, of settling arguments by killing or mangling the fittest of the human species, none of whom were involved in the original argument. Closely related were all the individual insanities of the people who had to cope with the war, either voluntarily or against their wills. The characters tended to separate into clusters of varying aberrations, and those capable of the greatest abstractions tended also to exhibit the most extreme actions.

The focus of *M*A*S*H* was most frequently on the two maverick surgeons, Benjamin Franklin "Hawkeye" Pierce (Alan Alda) and John "Trapper" McIntyre (Wayne Rogers). They (Hawkeye especially) had a highly developed sense of humaneness and pacificism and were the main spokesmen for the show's underlying message. Having become a part of the war against their wills and against their principles, they coped by working past all normal endurance to counteract the ravages of battle and by ceaselessly wisecracking to camouflage the heartbreaking absurdity of patching soldiers up so that they could go out to be shot again. Beneath their teasing, their sometimes excessive drinking, their lighthearted pursuit of the nurses, and their practical jokes lay the only real sanity that the show espoused—the serious reality of people caring about other people, trying to make life better for them, treating them as human individuals instead of as objects, symbols, or numbers.

Hawkeye, a thoracic surgeon from Maine, was the heartbeat of the camp, and his glib flippancy covered a complex character and a sometimes painful sensitivity and anger. Trapper, rakish, handsome, and married, was replaced in the fourth season by Captain B. J. Hunnicutt (Mike Farrell), who made an even better foil for Hawkeye than did Trapper. While he shared Hawkeye's intelligence, medical skill, dedication, and sense of humor, B. J. had, in addition, a solidity, a sense of serenity and responsibility, a certain sweetness of character that Hawkeye lacked. B. J. was a happily married, loyal, family man who was buoyed, even in the midst of his sometimes piercing homesickness, by his assurance of love and communication with his beloved Peg and his little girl. Although he, like Hawkeye, almost constantly joked to help get through the war's death and pain, B. J. never tried to disguise his feelings of tenderness, which, in the absence of his wife, spilled out to those around him. Hawkeye, for all his casual sexual jokes, nudist magazines, and avoidance of commitment, evinced an enormous amount of respect for B. J.'s marital loyalty.

In contrast to these pacifist physicians was the incompetent surgeon Major Frank Burns (Larry Linville). He too governed his actions by principles, but his principles appeared to be a rather jingoistic patriotism and a rigid sense of discipline through regulations. Hence, his actions, too, seemed a bit insane, but less pleasantly so. The show's most frequent conflicts occurred when the various characters applied their particular principles to the same situation.

The series was improved when Frank, who was too silly to be believable, was replaced by a more worthy adversary for Hawkeye and B. J., Major Charles Winchester (David Ogden Stiers) in the sixth season. The stately Winchester was a cultured, intelligent, lordly, overbearing, arrogant Bostonian of the bluest blood and a talented surgeon besides. Despite his faults he was a likeable person, genuinely witty, sometimes touching, sometimes almost noble (briefly anyway) in his willingness to admit his errors. Pitting such a character against Hawkeye and B. J. produced much more interesting battles.

Major Margaret Houlihan, the series' major nurse character, had principles which were somewhere between the abstract extremes represented by Frank and Hawkeye. Whenever she was functioning as a nurse, she displayed her more humane characteristics, working earnestly and efficiently to the patients' best advantage. Insofar as she aligned herself with Frank, however (as she frequently did because of their longtime sexual affair), she displayed the insanity of blind, inappropriate adherence to Army regulations and ideals. As the seasons progressed, Margaret was gradually made a more sympathetic character than her initial role as regular Army clown. As she gained in depth, understanding, and complexity, she rid herself of Frank and increasingly became allied with the other surgeons.

Other characters in the series were also somewhere in the middle of the continuum, tending to work out purely personal means of coping with the war rather than acting in accordance with some overriding principle: Lieutenant Colonel Henry Blake (MacLean Stevenson), the unit's commanding officer and general surgeon for the first four seasons most typically drank, watched dirty movies, joked around with Hawkeye and Trapper, and let them make major decisions for him. Frank and Margaret were actually correct in their accusations that he was an ineffectual commanding officer, but because Blake was philosophically on the side of the show's underlying principles, he, not Frank and Margaret, gained the viewers' approval. In the fourth season he was killed, and Colonel Sherman Potter (Harry Morgan), a much more believable commanding officer, took command of the M.A.S.H. unit. Like Blake, Potter had warm feelings toward his maverick surgeons and was willing to bend military regulations to accommodate them; but unlike Blake, he had genuine authority in the camp and was not afraid to use it. Potter commanded both affection and respect from his subordinates.

In *M*A*S*H,* the physician-heroes shared many of the classic attributes of the good doctor; they were aggressive in their stand against war and mutilation; they were attractive; and they were single-minded in their pursuit of the patient's welfare. However, each of the doctor-heroes was demonstrated to possess serious weaknesses, weaknesses that led him to depend upon others for help. Hawkeye turned to alcohol, the friendship of B. J., and the authority of Colonel Potter to help keep him sane. Colonel Blake was an indecisive man who escaped the burdens of authority whenever he could. B. J. was homesick for his wife and child and that often undermined his equanimity. Even the Boston-bred and Harvard educated Charles Winchester occasionally fell into despair because of loneliness, or else he allowed his conceit to lead him astray. Colonel Potter, a career Army doctor, recognized that he was coming to the end of his career, and occasionally that awareness affected his stability. The major nurse in this series, Margaret Houlihan, possessed more weakness and character flaws than did all these doctors put together, at least at the series' beginning, yet the writers of the show were able to develop her and to repress some of her negative characteristics while emphasizing her more positive features.

The other main characters—all showing varying degrees of peculiar action—might be classified as the innocents and, above all, humane: Father Mulcahy (William Christopher), whose basic goodness seemed to insulate him from many of the unpleasant realities of the war; Corporal Walter "Radar" O'Reilly (Gary Burghoff) who coped by remaining a child, clinging to his teddy bear at night, making father figures of Henry, Hawkeye, and Trapper and drawing comfort from them; and Corporal Maxwell Klinger (Jamie Farr) who waged a constant battle against the army, not out of higher principles, but because he wanted out. Aside from the regulars, a fairly consistent parade of outsiders also appeared in the *M*A*S*H* episodes, and all of them contributed in some fashion to the idea of various kinds of wartime insanity: the patients, the unending influx of mutilated bodies that testified most forcefully to the idea that war was crazy; enemy soldiers and local citizens; and high Army officials, the most consistently satirized.

The weekly episodes which focused on the relationships among these characters scarcely had classic, deathless plots, but they served as vehicles for some consistent messages, characterizations, and situations that appealed to the viewing public. Since *M*A*S*H* premiered on the heels of America's distasteful involvement in the Viet Nam war, its anti-war sentiments were widely popular. In addition, the consistent humor of the show attracted people, as it was generally a kindly, clever, affirmative sort of comedy that was distinctly anti-war. This fundamental battle against death, and even more the concomitant affirmation of life made *M*A*S*H* appealing. Despite the military setting, the show consistently dealt with underlying issues with which audiences could identify. Here, as in civilian life, people confronted their priorities and acted according to their deepest beliefs; they learned how to work with conflicting personalities; they faced, with varying abilities, dreadful conditions, and they learned to cope. The heroes who faced these problems in *M*A*S*H* were flawed human beings, but they made a stand for decency and did something constructive. In their strange way, they were creating order and goodness in a situation that made no sense and that defied personal control. However insane the sanctioned slaughter around them, Hawkeye showed a consistent respect for life, for people. Overwhelmingly the philosophy of *M*A*S*H* concentrated on healing, not just in the sense of treating injured and diseased bodies, but also in its emphasis on life, sanity, the creative forces of love, cooperation, and caring for others. In this affirmation of life lay the only inoculation against, or cure for, the large insanity surrounding the show's heroes. Hawkeye, Trapper, and B. J. consistently refused to conform to the trappings of the military machinery. They were virtually never in uniform; they flouted the military hierarchy of command; they ridiculed propagandistic views of the situation. Instead they emphasized the non-military. They talked of home; they brewed liquor in their still; they arranged affairs with the nurses; above all, they made jokes even in the grimmest of times.

Since the show's inception, the nurses in the M.A.S.H. compound have, with few exceptions, been associated with this affirmation of life, and their image has been primarily positive. To get an accurate perception of the image of nurses in *M*A*S*H*, one must consider Margaret Houlihan separately from the other nurses as well as considering both the nurses' professional work and their off duty appearances. Until the seasons of the late 1970s, the show presented a somewhat dichotomous image of the nurse, however favorable. They were excellent professional women in the operating room, but off duty the emphasis was on their potential as sexual diversions. Professionally the nurses were accorded respect on *M*A*S*H* from the beginning. The opening shots of each episode, as the credits rolled, showed nurses and doctors alike running to the landing area to get the wounded soldiers off the helicopter and into the operating room as quickly as possible. The nurses were all business in their fatigues, and they ran as quickly as the men to get where they were needed. Also most episodes included operating room sequences in which the nurses appeared to good advantage. The nurses played a distinctly secondary role to the doctors, but they were always shown as the doctors' allies, encouraging, inspiring, and exemplifying the emphasis on life rather than death.

The majority of nurses in *M*A*S*H* appeared anonymously: Viewers saw them only when they were in the operating room, their faces covered with scrub masks, their conversations limited to "Yes, Doctor," "Clamp," "Sponge," etc. They obeyed the doctors' every request, and the efficiency of their work was unquestioned. They were virtually never criticized; they put in long hours without complaint; they kept working even when bombs fell nearby, when supplies dwindled, when lights malfunctioned, and when sleep was a distant memory. Their professional value was never in doubt. It was, however, sometimes taken for granted. While the doctors showed signs of strain and exhaustion, the nurses stayed trim and composed under the same circumstances, and thus seemed more like machines than like vulnerable human beings who were sacrificing their all for the good of the patients.

Another dehumanizing factor in the portrayal of nurses was that they were rarely seen interacting with the patients. They aided invaluably in the medical mechanics of the operating room, as assistants to the doctors; but until later seasons the viewer almost never saw a nurse with a conscious patient. Hence, a nurse rarely appeared in those professional situations where her competence exceeded that of a doctor. Nevertheless, as the seasons progressed, *M*A*S*H* gave increasing recognition to the distinctive role that nurses play until, by the 1979–1980 season, it offered the most genuinely professional view of nurses to be seen on television, despite the comedy format of the show.

The nurses assisted competently in the operating room in all seasons, occasionally doing minor surgery themselves to free the physicians for more urgent patients when the influx of wounded created emergency situations. Only rarely did the nurses need correction or instruction in the operating room, and they accepted added responsibilities confidently. But, despite their obvious professional competence, the early years of *M*A*S*H* emphasized their off duty activities. They participated in most of the games and diversions that occurred in the M.A.S.H. compound. They played baseball, danced, drank, went to movies, helped stuff a jeep, had parties, and arranged affairs. Naturally enough, they were the object of considerable sexual attention in this camp full of men. There were countless sexual jokes and propositions, albeit good-natured and admiring in tone; most of them were not meant to be taken seriously. In the first two seasons, however, a few episodes made rather insulting assumptions about the women. In the first episode of the first season, Hawkeye and Trapper raised tuition money for their Korean houseboy by raffling off tickets for a weekend pass to Tokyo with a friendly nurse companion. Hawkeye convinced one of the nurses, Lieutenant Dish, to be the prize in this raffle, even though she was engaged. Although the men arranged for Father Mulcahey to win the raffle, thus sparing the nurse any sexual performance, the demeaning assumption was still there: The nurses were objects that the men could use for barter. No one was supposed to notice that in the noble scheme to send the Korean boy to college, the nurse was being treated like a piece of merchandise.

This assumption that the nurses were the doctors' property to dispose of as they deemed fit, occurred at least two other times. Once Hawkeye promised a visiting plastic surgeon a "barracuda" nurse if he would perform prohibited plastic surgery on a private who was depressed because of his large nose; and once the doctors promised the nurses' attendance at the Engineers' Ball if the engineers would quickly design and produce a certain kind of clamp needed in surgery. Another time, the nurses threatened to go on strike romantically unless one of the men befriended a cute but dangerously clumsy nurse who was upset by her lack of success in love.

These demeaning episodes were rare, however, and disappeared altogether after the first few seasons, though the jokes and propositions continued for some years. With those exceptions, the women's role as objects of sexual interest has had more positive aspects than such a role has had traditionally. Although there was much talk about affairs, there was much more arranging of them than there was consummation. Either the propositions were not meant seriously, or else everyone was too busy or too tired when the opportunity actually presented itself. Also, women and sex were very much associated with the affirmation of life that the show so celebrated; sex was not viewed as wicked or secretive. Furthermore, the women were as active and independent in making arrangements for affairs as were the men; sex seemed to be as much a positive choice for them as for the men. Hence, the viewer did not see them as being used by men. Finally, their sexual activity in no way diminished the doctors' respect for them as women or as nurses. On the contrary, the men often seemed to feel that the nurses represented the only remaining bastion of sanity and mental strength in an otherwise absurd environment. Thus, a position of apparent weakness was, in fact, considerably stronger than it first appeared.

As feminism became increasingly influential in the United States in the mid 1970s, and as people's awareness of the insulting implications of traditional views of women was heightened, *M*A*S*H* began to tone down the sexual repartee on the show, to focus less on the nurses' off duty potential as playmates, and to give increasing attention to the nurses' professional capabilities. Each season included several episodes which concentrated on the nurses' importance, and later seasons tended to show the nurses' functions not only as important but also as distinct from physicians' roles, as something more than the physicians' handmaidens. Everyone lent a hand, for instance, in lavishing love, food, and health care on a group of refugee children that needed shelter for a few days. Physicians and nurses alike were somewhat maternal as they told stories, hugged the children, carried them to bed, and comforted their fears. Another time the nurses proved themselves to be the physicians' equals (and then some) as they all worked a dreadful 48-hour stint in the operating room while the casualties from an assault relentlessly poured into the compound. Still another episode emphasized the nurses' importance when they were evacuated, leaving the men to cope for themselves, and it was clear that the physicians were the worse for their absence, both personally and professionally. Everyone pitched in to help with the nursing chores in the operating room, but it was soon evident that nursing was a special skill, not just something anyone could do well. To Father Mulcahey, who was assisting with more good will than effectiveness, Hawkeye said, "Keep those sponges coming, Father. Remember, 'nurse' is also a verb." Not only was nurse a verb, it was a different verb than doctor; and audiences noted that the doctors obviously lost some of their own powers to perform well when the nurses were absent.

Nurses took on even more professional responsibilities in later episodes. In the 1978–1979 season, Margaret started a triage training program for her nurses, and within days the nurses learned to assess the nature and seriousness of the patients' injuries and to speed them in order of their need to the operating room. In an episode in the 1979–1980 season, nearly the whole camp came down with salmonella, leaving only Margaret, Charles, and Father Mulcahey to care for the patients. Margaret enlisted the two men to help her with the nursing care. Charles at first imperiously refused to help with the nursing because he was not a woman, but Margaret soon shamed him into it, and it developed that Charles did not wash the sheets clean enough to suit Margaret; and he fell into exhausted sleep before he could finish his duties, only to be roused by a wrathful Margaret. Father Mulcahey, on the other hand, was in his glory. As a nurse he worked tirelessly and happily, finding it good to feel so useful. The two men together emphasized to the public both the difficulty and the nobility of the nursing profession.

The increased focus on the nurses' professionalism had several results. There was a concommitant decrease in emphasis on their off duty life, thus lessening the nurses' roles in the weekly plots; their image lost in quantity as it gained in quality. There were, however, more scenes with patients in the post-operative ward where nurses were seen working independently of the doctors. Primarily, though, the result was that Margaret became responsible for about ninety percent of the nursing image, and she developed into a genuinely complex, believable, and sympathetic character.

Although each season of M*A*S*H had episodes which emphasized nurses, either individually or collectively, only Margaret was developed as a continuing character. She always had a central role in the plot. An attractive, blue-eyed, blonde in her late thirties, she was one of the few characters who was in the Army by choice. Her father had been a spit and polish Army colonel andd her mother an Army nurse, and Margaret was both proud of following the family tradition and ambitious to further her career. When the series began she was a rigid, bullying, hypocritical character who represented the military mind that the series so satirized, and Hawkeye rarely passed up an opportunity to tease or antagonize her. Margaret's development over the years might best be seen in terms of her search for independence, power, and self-respect. It might seem that she had all these things at first, both professionally and personally. She was, after all, an officer and a head nurse; she was single, with no husband to hamper her movements, and she felt free to have sex rather promiscuously with no restraints and certainly no sense of guilt. However, in both her professional and her personal lives, she had little actual power, particularly as long as she was allied to Frank Burns, who had most of her faults and none of her redeeming features. Margaret (or "Hot Lips," as she was mockingly called in early seasons) and Frank Burns early in the series' life provided the main opposition for Hawkeye and Trapper because of their rigid, unthinking insistence on the very letter of every Army regulation, however little sense it might make. Many early episodes showed Margaret trying to curtail the influence of Hawkeye and Trapper in the camp and doing her best to short-circuit their offbeat schemes. She had legitimate problems to complain about. The physicians often treated her with disrespect and blatantly disobeyed her even in situations where she had the right to command; the other nurses often went along with the physicians. In these early years, the only people who usually obeyed Margaret were the other nurses along with Radar and Frank Burns, and they obeyed primarily because they were afraid of her irrational temper. The more Margaret tried to insist on her power and authority on the basis of Army regulations, the less power she actually had. Although Margaret got little respect on the basis of her military title, she did wield considerable authority as head nurse, unless she was using that authority to meddle in her nurses' private affairs. Even in her most unflattering portrayals, Margaret was always acknowledged to be an excellent head nurse, and she kept the operating room running smoothly, often under adverse circumstances. Her strictness appeared in a more favorable light in the operating room than it did outside where she was associated with military power and the military mentality.

Margaret was often unreasonably strict with the nurses in early seasons; in one of her testy moods she even snapped at a nurse in the operating room to sneeze on her own time. She was scornful of the nurses' affairs, even though she hypocritically carried on with Frank, and she showed little understanding and made little allowance for any personal problems her nurses might have. Even so, she exhibited a desire to get closer to her staff. The simmering feud came to a boil in the fifth season, when Margaret finally confronted her wary nurses and plaintively asked them if they had ever shown her friendship. Margaret had finally come to grips with their (usually justified) reservations about her. The last scene of this episode showed Houlihan, Baker, and the other nurses sharing a helmet full of illicit homemade fudge. In the rest of the year's showings, Margaret was depicted as a firm, sometimes pigheaded, but ultimately fair administrator who demanded only respect.

The simple respect Margaret sought came only gradually over the next two seasons. The area in which Margaret manifested the most change was in her relationships with the physicians and with men in general. At first, Margaret seems to have had the upper hand in male–female relationships, as she often had affairs with high military brass, and clearly she had almost complete control over the hapless Frank Burns. In fact, Frank was the main source of Margaret's bad image. He was such a pompous, incompetent idiot, that Margaret's affair with him made her look bad. Unlike Frank, however, Margaret was never an unrelievedly unsympathetic character, even at her worse. Each season, even when she was clearly the adversary, Margaret showed signs of being a basically very good human being who cared about other people. For instance, when the camp thief turned out to be a Korean boy who was stealing to help his family, Margaret was the first to volunteer to let him keep her things. And however unreasonable Margaret might have been in some respects, however angry she might be at the doctors, her patients never suffered from any slip in her nursing efficiency. In fact, Margaret's professional excellence proved to be one main bridge for the steadily improving relationships between her and the physicians. Hawkeye, Trapper, B. J., and the commanding officers always acknowledged that Margaret was a fine nurse and did not hesitate to thank her for her help or compliment her on a good job. She, in turn, unequivocally admired their surgical skill and dedication, however often she might rail at them personally.

When she and Hawkeye went to the front ["Comrades in Arms" (Part I), Dec. 6, 1977], they found a tremendous number of casualties waiting for treatment. Hawkeye was thankful for her help as she set to work without instructions, and he entrusted her with jobs usually performed only by physicians—closing up after surgery, initiating surgery—knowing that she was competent. Much later, they sank to the ground into exhausted sleep, Margaret murmuring proudly, "We did it!" When she nervously asked about snipers, Hawkeye moved closer to her and gently covered her with half of his own blanket, and all hints of their usual verbal squabbling were set aside. On the way back to the 4077, Hawkeye kissed her on the cheek and told her seriously that she was his favorite officer in the Army, and then resumed his usual kidding. The experience visibly touched Margaret. When Frank eagerly came to her tent that night, she snubbed him, commenting dreamily, "Dr. Pierce and I performed together like a well-oiled machine, under very difficult circumstances, and it was an exhilirating experience." Later, when the others were all complaining bitterly about such minor trials as camp food, Margaret and Hawkeye exchanged smiles that acknowledged the genuine difficulty they had overcome together, and they raised their coffee cups in silent tribute to each other.

The change in Margaret also had its roots in the show's fifth season, when Margaret became engaged to Lieutenant Donald Penobscott and gave up Frank Burns; but it did not really bloom until the seventh season, when the short, troubled marriage dissolved in divorce. In a Jan. 29, 1979 episode entitled "Hot Lips is Back in Town," Margaret received notice of her final divorce decree, which so distracted and depressed her that she was brusque and absentminded in the operating room. Charles, whom she was supposed to be assisting, sarcastically remarked, "You will phone me when you get back in town, Margaret?" After O.R., Hawkeye and B. J. sympathetically took Margaret to the bar to cheer her up, and she began to rethink her relationships with men in the past. With growing joy she realized that a divorce was not the end of her life, but a beginning, an opportunity for a new independence. For the first time she sensed that she was a whole human being, in charge of her own life. The realization exhilarated her. She woke Colonel Potter to tell him her discovery: "Colonel, I'm going to make the Army my career." This seemed less than earth shaking to Potter, who dove disgustedly back under the covers. But Margaret realized that she had turned an important new corner: "I always saw my future in terms of men. I got lost in all those men. . . . I finally realized that I don't need anyone to help me live my life. I'm in control. And I'm going as far in this man's Army as a woman can go. Maybe even general." It was at this point that she set up a rigorous program to train her nurses in triage and confidently invited her old friend, Major General Lyle Weiskopf, to inspect in three days' time. She persuaded Charles to lecture the nurses, and she drilled them constantly, with such effectiveness that the inspection was spectacularly successful. Later, as she and Weiskopf relaxed with a drink, they had a conversation which emphasized the old and new images of Margaret. Margaret was proudly recalling her nurses' fine work, while Weiskopf was thinking of the old times when he and Margaret had spent nights together drinking. He offered her a promotion to Lieutenant Colonel on his nursing staff in Tokyo; only gradually she realized that Weiskopf was talking about "romantic suppers, . . . late night strolls. . . ." When she did realize what the General had in mind, she exploded in anger: "Colonel in charge of what? Your boudoir? I'm a head nurse, and a damn good one. What did you think this whole demonstration was for anyway? . . . . General, get the hell out of my tent. And that's an order."

This episode marked Margaret's baptism as a liberated woman. She did not automatically become a perfect character, but both her professional and her sexual images were permanently changed. Like most newly liberated women, she had to struggle to redefine herself, to recognize the proper boundaries of liberty, to balance self-interest against consideration for others. She did base her ambition increasingly on her own talents as a nurse and an officer. She began to display an awareness of the appropriate use of authority, of when to bend regulations for the sake of a higher order.

One episode, "Preventive Medicine" (Feb. 19, 1979), emphasized both her new professionalism and her new attitude toward sex. Handsome Colonel Lacy came to visit his injured men at M.A.S.H. 4077, and Margaret was tremendously attracted to him. She ignored Hawkeye's and B. J.'s hatred for this man who was responsible for the greatest percent of casualties, until she herself heard him cavalierly dismiss the prospect of thirty percent casualties in his plan to take a useless hill for his own glory. Her attraction to him suddenly vanished, and she walked away from him in disgust. Later, when the doctors were about ready to give Lacy an unnecessary appendectomy to keep him from taking all his men off to get killed, Margaret showed up in the operating room, sent Nurse Able out, and demanded to know what was going on. The doctors tried to divert her attention, but Margaret bluntly observed, "It's my nurse and my O.R." Unfooled by Hawkeye's evasive chatter, she quickly sized up the situation and snapped, "Forget it. It's unethical, it's illegal, and I won't let you." Recognizing her authority, Hawkeye finally said, "You can stop us if you want, Margaret, but who's going to stop him?" Margaret considered that a moment, then asked if Nurse Able knew what was going on. Assured not, she warned, "Keep it that way," and turned to leave. "Thank you, Margaret," B. J. responded with feeling. "Don't thank me," she retorted; "I was never here."

This presented an interesting view of Margaret in several ways. First of all, her power was finally recognized by the men who have always played the strongest roles in the series, and they stood ready to obey her decision. Second, she had several options, and she made her decision after weighing both sides. Finally, her decision was strictly non-regulation, a bending of the rules which would have been unthinkable in Margaret's earlier years when she was characterized as a mindless adherent to military regulations, however insane or inappropriate.

There are many indications that Margaret's sexual image also changed in the late 1970s. Although she still had a sexy figure, she was rarely seen in clothes that emphasized her sensuality. Usually she appeared in ordinary fatigues or scrub uniforms. The old nickname, "Hot Lips," vanished totally. The sexual jokes about her almost disappeared, except for Hawkeye's occasional, mild sallies (for example, working with a badly frostbitten patient, Hawkeye flippantly suggested that Margaret kiss him and bring his temperature back up to normal). She herself had a much greater sense of self-respect as far as sex was concerned. She was a sensuous woman, but gave sex more sensible proportions in her life. Her self-respect came before her sexual desires; viewing audiences could see this in her rejection of the handsome Colonel Lacy because of his inhumane ambition, or her rejection of Weiskopf's offer of a promotion in return for her sexual favors. Also, she showed a new sexual independence which indicated that she no longer felt that she must define herself in terms of men's desire for her. After a one-night fling with a handsome reporter who came to the 4077th, she dismissed his profession of love in favor of her own freedom.

As if to underscore the turnabout in Margaret's sexual image, the writers gave her an episode ("An Eye For a Tooth") in which she played a practical joke on Hawkeye and B. J. that was very much like a joke that was played on her in the original *M*A*S*H* film. In a campaign of practical jokes between her and Hawkeye and B. J. (both sides secretly spurred on by the scheming Winchester), Margaret sneaked into the shower when the two men were there and removed their clothes and towels. The two men made an embarrassed dash to their tent only to find it filled with laughing nurses who were awaiting the show, eating popcorn, and calling out remarks to the nude doctors. Margaret was no longer the victim in sexual matters, be they jokes or affairs. She had become a controller, an independent agent, sharing with the other nurses an image of more sexual equality than was usual for television shows.

The 1979–1980 season of *M*A*S*H* was a fascinating study of the new Margaret—fascinating precisely because so much of the old Margaret was still recognizable. While the script writers had transformed Margaret from one of the bad guys to one of the inner circle of heroes she was not suddenly glossed over as a perfect character; she was still a flawed human being (as, indeed, Hawkeye and B. J. were). Her old faults were forgivable, however, because her main priorities were right. For her, as for the doctors, people now took precedence over institutions or regulations; and her decisions were born of humane understanding rather than of inflexible militarism. As a nurse, as an officer, and as a woman, Margaret was a changed woman, and yet somehow she remained forever, essentially Margaret.

Actually, nursing was the aspect that changed least in Margaret's transformation; in 1979–1980 as always, she was an excellent nurse, maintaining high standards. She could be flexible when the situation demanded it, however. For instance, when Hawkeye and B. J. had to do an unsterile, emergency operation on a dying patient, Margaret would not give them a requested clamp until it was sterilized. But when minutes and seconds determined whether the patient would suffer irreparable brain damage, Margaret instantly abandoned proper procedure to obey the doctors' call for help, even though she complained that she hated it. With her nurses, too, Margaret seemed to have an extra measure of understanding. She was still quite strict and authoritative with her staff, and she still did not seem to form any close relationships with the other nurses. But there was a noticeably more friendly atmosphere among them, and their obedience seemed much more the result of genuine respect rather than fear of Margaret's famous temper.

The mixture of old and new in Margaret was also evident in her attitude about being an officer. Unlike the men, Margaret was in the Army because she wanted to be. She had not done an about face by 1979–1980. She still gave orders with a sharper air of command than did anyone else; she still used titles more often than did the others; and she sometimes became tense and Army-like when the military brass arrived, but the new version of her military side was sometimes humorous and sometimes touching. In one episode she raged at Klinger (now the company clerk) to order her a new footlocker. The lock was broken on hers, and—like the Margaret of old—she accused the others of stealing or peeping at her underwear. Klinger insisted that the Army regulations prohibited replacing a footlocker unless it was damaged in combat. Margaret then calmly took a gun and blasted her footlocker full of holes; she then ran out of her tent with the ruined trunk and told a wild story about finding an enemy soldier behind the trunk ready to attack. She got her new footlocker. Thus did the new Margaret abide by Army regulations.

A far more serious view of Margaret's professional side appeared when a senator's aide came to investigate a report that a Communist agent lurked in the 4077 camp. Margaret was, at first, a little flirtatious with the aide, thrilled as always to be associated with someone important from Washington. But then she discovered that she was the one the aide suspected of being a Communist simply because she previously went with a man (Wally) who later became friends with someone suspected of being a Communist. At first Margaret and the doctors laughed at a charge built on such a ridiculously fragile tissue of paranoia, but the aide grimly insisted that unless Margaret told all she knew about Wally and gave the names of all his friends, she would be charged with un-American activities. Given the choice of betraying old friends or of facing public humiliation herself (and thereby humiliating her military father as well), Margaret sadly decided that she could only resign her beloved career altogether to avoid hurting others. She was now a far cry from the old martinet that had used every ounce of her military authority to make life miserable for Hawkeye, Trapper, or anyone else who displeased her. Now, the men gathered around her protectively and devised a scheme to blackmail the aide into dropping the whole ridiculous charge. Rank meant little to Hawkeye and B. J., but because it meant much to Margaret, they helped her to protect it.

It is a happy irony that the *M*A*S*H* series, which sprang from an offensively sexist movie, changed to offer the most genuinely respectful and professional image of nurses to be found on television. Furthermore, because of the show's longevity, both in new, prime-time shows and in reruns, that image has been repeatedly reinforced. With its witty entertainment and its consistent espousal of positive values, *M*A*S*H* gives a strong presentation of nurses as independent, highly professional human beings, who are distinct from and in some ways superior to doctors. As the seasons developed, the nurses were shown in expanded roles, confidently taking on more and more responsible duties.

In September 1979 CBS introduced *Trapper John, M.D.*, and ABC offered *The Lazarus Syndrome;* only *Trapper John* flourished, while *The Lazarus Syndrome* quickly faded from the network schedule. In December 1979 CBS premiered *House Calls,* a half-hour comedy situated in a hospital setting. In general, the image of nursing in these series conformed to the limited range of stereotypes previously offered on television.

The most popular of these new series, *Trapper John,* derived from the storyline of CBS' *M*A*S*H*. The protagonists of this show were two irreverent but extremely skilled surgeons who worked at the fictional San Francisco Memorial Hospital. The older doctor of the duo was none other than *M*A*S*H* veteran Dr. "Trapper" John McIntyre (Pernell Roberts) some twenty-five years after Korea and considerably mellowed. He had become the chief of surgery in a large metropolitan hospital and rarely participated in practical jokes. Divorced from his wife Melanie because of his dedication to this work, he still hoped to win her back. The younger doctor was Dr. Alonzo "Gonzo" Gates (Gregory Harrison), former *M*A*S*H* surgeon from the Viet Nam era. Gonzo scorned all rules and regulations; he lived in a scroungy motorhome called The Titanic which he had moored in the doctors' parking lot, and he wore blue jeans, plain t-shirts or loud printed Aloha shirts, and running shoes. Trapper saw some of his own youthful high spirits and anti-establishment vigor in the young surgeon and quickly adopted Gonzo as his best friend. The two were frequently seen sipping vintage wine atop The Titanic after the successful conclusion of one of their many problems. The traditional relationship between older and younger doctors had been reduced to almost nothing; Trapper rarely availed himself of the opportunity to pass along wise sayings to his younger colleagues. More frequently, Gonzo was called upon to awaken Trapper's dormant sense of nonconformity.

Two other physician characters, Dr. Stanley Riverside and Dr. "Jackpot" Jackson, contributed to establishing a *M*A*S*H*-like atmosphere. Stanley, the son of the hospital's chairman of the board, was a prissy, wishy washy man who ran the emergency room with skill but who caviled at any breach of regulations. He toadied up to the wealthy and powerful and disdained Dr. Gates who did not look like a doctor. Jackpot, an intern who seemed to work only in the emergency room, made book for anyone in any situation but also happened to be a promising young doctor. However, these colorful attempts fell very short of recreating *M*A*S*H*'s well written, bitingly humorous, and frequently touching episodes. *Trapper John* had much more in common with *Medical Center*, its thematic predecessor. This was not surprising since the producers of *Trapper John*, Don Brinkley and Frank Glicksman, also wrote and produced the saga of Joe Gannon for CBS.

As with *Medical Center*, *Trapper John* settled for technical accuracy rather than striving for broadly based realism. Lots of technical jargon and sweaty browed surgical sequences were included to convince the viewer of the doctors' great skill. Yet the phoniness of *Trapper John* rivaled that of its predecessor. For example, in one episode, the writers would have had the audience believe that a wealthy Arab sheik presented his daughter, decked out as a streetwalker's version of an Arab princess, to Dr. Gates as a "thank you" for successful bile duct surgery. One wonders who does not know that Moslems are notoriously puritanical about their female children in the era of petrodollar diplomacy.

More serious than the ridiculous flights of fancy were the liberties taken with hospital routine and nursing practice in the episodes. The presentation of nursing as a separate profession, composed of intelligent and skilled practitioners, was nowhere found in *Trapper John*. The nicknames and characteristic features of the two regular nursing characters were "Starch" (Mary McCarty), the epitome of the no-nonsense, tough talking nurse who threw her considerable weight around in her dealings with all and sundry, and "Ripples" (Christopher Norris), a sexy blonde in a tight uniform who brought out the most absolutely predictable dialogue from every male character over ten. Despite these offensive labels, both nurses were obviously valued members of the nursing staff and nearly indispensable to the physicians. Starch's relationship to Trapper followed the standard pseudo-wifely tone so often observed when middle-aged, fictional nurses have worked with the same doctor for many years. In this case Starch had met Trapper when they were both stationed in a M.A.S.H. unit in Korea. Starch's job in the hospital seemed to be Trapper's factotum. In one episode, "Have You Hugged Your Nurse Today?" Starch accepted a social invitation for Trapper, planned what gift he would give, and suggested what he should wear. When Trapper protested and told Starch to keep out of his personal affairs, they each got angry and Starch quit. She then went to the nursing personnel office, which seemed to function like a computer dating service, and demanded a transfer. The chief of nursing first talked to Starch like a marriage counselor hoping to save a shaky marriage between nurse and doctor. When Starch insisted that she and Trapper could no longer work together, the chief nurse looked through her records, noting that all the good doctors were taken, and finally assigned her to Dr. Stanley Riverside. In the meantime Trapper had been assigned nurse Dottie Pitt, a fatuous middle-aged woman with an adolescent crush on Trapper John. Of course, Trapper and Starch eventually reconciled. The entire story presented the nurse as part professional, part secretary, and part mother. Dottie's first service for Trapper, during her brief tenure, was to redecorate his office with homely touches of chintz and bric-a-brac.

Although Starch often performed menial tasks for Trapper, she did not see herself as his inferior. She felt free to tell him what was on her mind. She would often tell him to hurry up in surgery, or to use a certain suture, or she would hand him equipment before he asked. These actions did not make Trapper seem incompetent, but they did make Starch appear knowledgeable. Despite their close professional association, Trapper did not really discuss patient care with Starch, unless the patient happened to be a personal friend of hers. Their relationship was even closer on a personal basis. Starch was the only person from whom Trapper asked advice about his putative natural son. Likewise, when Starch's boyfriend was in the hospital for a coronary bypass, Starch turned to Trapper in her fear and confusion about what would be the best thing for the patient.

In many ways Starch was a sympathetic representative of the nursing profession, yet the producers insisted upon undermining her strength with certain demeaning traits. First, there was the nickname, and second, there was the wide range of responsibilities she had assumed by working with Trapper. Obviously in real life hospitals do not routinely assign individual nurses to specific doctors. A scrub nurse with Starch's expertise would normally work only in the operating room. She would not, as Starch did, pull shifts in the emergency room, keep the surgeon's appointment book and social calendar, and order his lunch. Finally, there was the nurse's physical appearance: Mary McCarty was an attractive, middle-aged woman, but she was extremely large. Her size, combined with her nickname, give her a comic dimension not shared by any of the physician characters. Her appearance underscored the stereotype of the authoritarian, not physically beautiful, unmarried nurse who had devoted her whole life to nursing.

The second regular nurse character, Miss Gloria "Ripples" Brancusi, did not play as large a role as did Starch. For the most part, she pushed carts through the hallways as evidence of her abilities, or she stood behind the desk in the emergency room, or she served as the focus of sexual attraction. She wore her blonde hair pinned up while on duty, but her uniform was rather tight and short. She wore nylons and white high heels rather than the more practical uniform shoes. In her defense, it must be noted that she did not act the role of sex goddess that had been assigned to her by nickname. She did not try to manipulate orders by using her physical charms, nor did she encourage the sexually provocative remarks often made to her. She and Gates developed a brotherly/sisterly affection.

Thus, in their relationships to the two protagonists, the nurse characters appeared in a positive light. However, whenever the nurses were shown with other nurses, or in capacities separate from their relationships to the two heroes, they appeared less capable or at least less respected. Perhaps the best illustration of the show's first season treatment of the nursing profession appeared in an episode entitled "Strike!" (February 24, 1980), which opened with Ripples Brancusi handing out information leaflets to nurses entering the hospital. One young woman refused the proffered pamphlet with the excuse, "I don't wanna get involved." Meanwhile Gonzo Gates began the seduction of beautiful nurse Denise, whom he readied with a glass of rare and expensive wine; she gulped it down as if it were Pepsi Cola. Just as they began a passionate embrace, Denise heard the efforts of her colleagues and guiltily invited them all into the Titanic to get out of the hot sun. The action then shifted to the hospital where Gonzo unloaded his burden on Trapper; the talk of a strike was affecting his love life.

Perhaps the worst feature of the entire story was that absolutely no attention was given to the nature of the nurses' demands. The only reason mentioned was money, but there was no attempt to determine whether the nurses' demands were legitimate or not. When Starch told the younger nurses that sanitation workers earned more than they did, the younger nurses expressed surprise. None of them seemed to understand the strike at all. Nurses usually do not call strikes unless the conditions of employment and financial recompense have been deteriorating for a long time. No one in the show expressed any sympathy for the nurses; indeed, the nurses themselves barely mentioned their grievances except in the most general and unconvincing terms. Certainly the doctors did not take their position seriously. Trapper found the interruptions more irritating than anything else, although he did worry about the patients and blamed the strike for causing a labor negotiator to change his mind about surgery, and Gonzo's attitude toward the strike was succinct: It was ruining his sex life.

Of almost equal insensitivity was the presentation of the nurses as incapable of leadership and intelligent discourse. Not a single nurse participated in the negotiations with hospital administrators. Their union had hired a male non-nurse, a professional negotiator, for them; his presence would not have been so bad were he not assigned the role of playing truant offier to the unsophisticated and undisciplined nurses. The meeting between him and the nurses revealed the distance between them: He could not discuss the issues but had to spend his time trying to calm the hysterical ladies. Nurses did not participate in the resolution of the strike. It was brought about only when the professional negotiator and the hospital administrator finally talked.

The short-lived *Lazarus Syndrome* promised to be a much more realistic effort than *Trapper John*. The show broke several traditions in health care drama, which may have spelled its doom. The hero of the show was a thirty-seven-year-old black, married cardiologist, Dr. MacArthur "Mac" St. Clair (Lou Gossett) who worked in a large southern California hospital. He had come a long way in a short time, but the effects of his dedication to his career had taken their toll on his fifteen-year marriage to Gloria (Sheila Frazier). He had taken to working every day and all hours in order to avoid confronting his domestic problems. On one such working afternoon [(Unknown title), Sept. 4, 1979], he received a phone call from a vague acquaintance, Joe Hamill (Ronald Hunter), who described to him the symptoms of a heart attack. After Mac met his new patient in the emergency room of Webster Hospital, Hamill went into cardiac arrest. After successful resuscitation, Joe was sent to the C.C.U. where he began an uncomplicated recovery after what turned out to be a relatively minor heart attack and the two men began locking horns. At one point, Mac firmly refused to become involved in Joe's personal problems, and accused Hamill of falling into the "Lazarus Syndrome: the feeling that doctors are gods who cannot only cure physical ills but also cope with any other problem." Mac was eventually asked to take over the hospital administration and accepted with the proviso that he could hire an administrator to handle all the non-medical problems. He then offered the job to none other than his feisty patient, Hamill. Thus began the partnership and friendship of Hamill and St. Clair, the series' protagonists. The subplot of the pilot concerned Mac's attempts to salvage his marriage and Joe's attempts to end his own.

No regular nurse characters appeared in the series, although nurses always appeared in background scenes performing such typical nursing tasks as monitoring equipment, making notes in charts, and carrying trays. In brief appearances nurses were presented in a favorable light. For example, in the pilot, the nurses were shown to have the major responsibility for the care of patients in the C.C.U. When Joe Hamill awoke in the middle of the night after his heart attack, it was a nurse who appeared at his side and reassured him about his condition. She explained that his physician would not be around until the following morning. This nurse was not the overly solicitous, maternal figure common to health care drama; she simply told him the brief facts of his situation and reassured him by her own calm attitude. In this same episode the physician asked for and accepted a nurse's assessment of a patient's condition and generally allowed the nurses to work at their own level of competence without burdening them with superfluous orders.

In one episode a nurse character played a major role. The September 11, 1980 entry featured Olivia Cole as surgical nurse Pamela Quinn, an attractive black woman in her mid-thirties. The opening scenes of the story established that she worked in tandem with a surgeon, Dr. Kobuk, and enjoyed a collegial, friendly relationship with both her employer and Mac St. Clair, who appeared in the scrub room after an operation. Soon thereafter Pamela was raped at knifepoint by a stranger. Her attempts to deal with the incident by returning immediately to work and by depending upon Mac as an emotional anchor constituted the remainder of the story. The whole incident became complicated by the fact that she and Mac had had a love affair many years earlier and her dependence upon him, which he encouraged because of his sympathy for her situation, then threatened the delicate reconciliation between Mac and his wife. Pamela handled the rape incident by trying to forget it. She received a lot of support from her employer, Dr. Kobuk, who willingly rearranged his surgery schedule to accommodate her recovery. Other staff and nurses defended her from the prying eyes of the press and offered good wishes and sympathy. She explained to Mac that her work was her life, and that she could find no comfort in her lonely apartment. Although Mac worried that she was covering up her emotions rather than dealing with them, he allowed her to proceed with her own method for recovery. Finally Hamill pointed out to Mac that he was putting his own marriage in jeopardy and not helping Pamela, because he would soon end the relationship with Pamela, leaving her with nothing. Mac confronted Pamela and insisted that she recall the rape incident and express her anger, which she finally did. The episode ended with Mac preparing for a long weekend away from the hospital with his wife.

This particular story unfortunately presented the nurse as a victim as well as allowing the physician to be the catalyst to her recovery. Nevertheless, the handling of the story and the presentation of Pamela's character were quite positive. She was reputed to be a strong, independent woman; her temporary refuge into emotional dependence was predicated by unusual and terrifying circumstances. The viewer could assume that she would be able to return to her productive and satisfying life. Furthermore, this nurse was appreciated by the staff and recognized as an important member of the team.

As in many health care dramas, this series sinned by omission; that is, it neglected nursing care in favor of the physician's role. The series at least did not present physicians performing nursing tasks. Physicians did not administer medications or sit by patients' beds for hours at a time. It was unfortunate that the series was cancelled so soon because the producers hinted that they were able to conceive of realistic stories that did not distort normal hospital routine in an effort to be dramatic.

The newest health care series, *House Calls,* a thirty-minute situation comedy, premiered in December 1979. The show, based on a 1978 feature film of the same name starring Walter Matthau and Glenda Jackson, was set in a fictional California hospital, Kensington General, which suffered from erratic administration and leadership. The Chief of Staff, Dr. Amos Weatherby (David Wayne) was beyond the legal age of retirement, short-sighted, and forgetful, but he was determined to hold onto his office. He no longer operated as a surgeon, but he did see patients. The hero of the story was Dr. Charlie Nichols (Wayne Rogers), a handsome, unmarried, very skilled surgeon who, because of his affection for Dr. Weatherby, made sure that the older physician did not harm anyone. Charlie was something of a swinger as the series began, but he was on the lookout for an attractive, intelligent, mature woman with whom he could develop a permanent relationship. She arrived, as if by divine intervention, in the form of the new assistant administrator, Mrs. Anne Anderson (Lynn Redgrave), an attractive, red-haired divorcee. Anne was also British and, with her clipped accent and brisk manners, she made a nice complement to Charlie's more informal personality.

The attraction was mutual, and the relationship was quickly a regular and serious one. However, they managed to frequently disagree and squabble about trivial matters, which kept their love affair interesting in a comic way.

The other regularly featured characters included Dr. Norman Solomon (Ray Buktneica), an unmarried Jewish physician with a roving eye for women but who was dominated by his mother; Mrs. Phipps (Deedy Peters), the omnipresent Gray Lady who roamed the hallways of the hospital radiating saccharine optimism and cheer; and a nurse called Bradley (Aneta Corsaut) who appeared at the nursing desk across from Anne's office.

No single first season episode featured a nurse in a major role, but several images of the profession could be found. In the first show, a sexy, blonde nurse was lounging by a doorway and making provocative remarks to handsome Dr. Charlie. In one story (January 21, 1980) Norman had his eye on a particularly attractive nurse, Linda. Charles suggested that Norman introduce himself and make a date, but Norman felt inadequate. Norman's introduction to the nurse was forced when he found himself quarantined with her and several others. When Norman and his dream girl finally met, it was clear that the makings of true love were missing. She seemed to have the mental development of a fifteen-year-old. Her typical answer to most remarks was "Wow, that's heavy." When Norman mentioned his interest in the ballet and music, she told him her musical preferences were disco and, for serious music, she liked the older folk singers like Burl Ives, Harry Belafonte, and Orson Welles.

Such brief displays of nurses at work in the hospital painted an unattractive view of the profession. The nurses were never seen performing skilled tasks. Bradley, the nurse seen most often, appeared to run a clearinghouse for hospital messages. She did seem to have some supervisory position over younger nurses, but not consistently so. The work depicted was menial: they answered the phone, babysat for children, occasionally administered medication, and ignored frantically signaled call buttons. *House Calls,* to date, has not taken great pains to present the nurses sympathetically or as skilled professionals.

The image of nurses on 1970s prime time comedy and drama continued to be deficient in quality although two important series, *The Waltons* and *M*A*S*H,* which developed significant nurse characters began in 1972 and as of 1980 were in their eighth season. This modest progress was soon diluted by the negative representations of nursing offered by *Trapper John, M.D.* and *House Calls.* The best hope in terms of portraying a realistic view of the hospital world via entertainment, *The Lazarus Syndrome,* met an early cancellation. As television usage increased to more than 6.6 hours per day per household and public debate over the restructuring of health care roles emerged as an issue in television news, the stereotypes of the "God-like" doctor and "handmaiden" nurse persisted in television entertainment. A point of view aimed at highlighting the emergence of nurses as unique and important health care providers was almost totally absent, yielding perpetuation of anachronistic images and ideas about nursing.

8
Montage: Fragmentary Images of Television Nursing

Not all television treatment of nurses and nursing occurs in network series, and thus this chapter will discuss a miscellaneous grouping for non-network programs; these include syndicated series, made-for-television movies, and assorted public television programs. Syndicated series are sold individually to local stations for broadcasting during those hours when the national networks do not provide programming, as well as to local, independent stations that do not broadcast network programming at all. Syndicated series are primarily seen during the late afternoon and early evening hours, in the gap between daytime network shows and prime time programs, and in the late nighttime slots following local news shows. Syndicated series have been in existence since the early days of television broadcasting; however, there has been a declining interest in producing shows solely for syndication because most successful prime-time series are eventually repackaged as syndicated offerings. Feature length films made especially for television have been a phenomenon of the last decade. In the early 1970s, networks began showing feature length films, drawing from a large number of recently made films and film classics that had never been shown on television. However, the rate at which television consumed these films soon exhausted existing supplies and major film studios began making movies designed for television only. Generally low budget creations, and similar to the B-films made up until the 1950s, these films are rarely shown in theatres. Often the profits from the relatively inexpensive telefeatures keep film studios in the black and allow them the luxury of making more elaborate films for theatrical release. Both syndicated series and telefeatures have a very mixed quality.

Generally, Public Broadcasting System affiliates have shown programs about nursing or nurses that reflect a more intelligent and realistic treatment of the profession than those shows usually seen on commercial television. In the early days of public television programming was almost always referred to as educational television in the sense that the entertainment value was always secondary to the didactic purpose of the show, with the exception of presentations of classical music. However, in the last decade or so, with many successful BBC productions, public television has begun to attract an impressive number of viewers. Unfortunately, no nurse characters have regularly appeared in any of the popular PBS series. Discussions of nursing have usually been relegated to the less popular discussion formats and documentaries.

Syndicated series date from the early 1950s; the latest health care theme series was produced in 1972. The syndicated series involving nursing or medical themes appeared in two distinct periods: in the mid-1950s and in the early 1970s. The syndicated shows produced in the early period shared the same views of nursing and medicine as seen in the prime-time shows of that decade. Medicine appeared to be a near priestly vocation, while nursing appeared to be primarily maternal and romantic. The syndicated series of the 1970s reflected the typical attitude toward nurses in current health care drama: a mixture of benign neglect, derogatory images, and random compliments.

Several production companies prepared series with health care themes for syndication in the 1950s: *Dr. Christian,* made in 1956, *Janet Dean, R.N.,* 1954, and *Dr. Hudson's Secret Journal,* 1955. These series appeared at varying times all over the country and lasted until the early 1960s. Obviously, *Janet Dean, R.N.* is a good indicator of prevailing attitudes toward nursing because the central character of the series was a registered nurse. Thirty black and white, thirty-minute films were produced for the show by Cornwall productions, purportedly to sell the nursing profession, and to point out that many illnesses are actually psychosomatic. Janet Dean was an unmarried, attractive woman in her early thirties. She had been a military nurse during the war, but on the show practiced as a private duty nurse out of a New York agency. Unlike other nurses on television in the 1950s, Janet was not portrayed as a romantic figure in any of the episodes. Often she appeared as the savior and protector of the weak. Janet's greatest nursing skill was her ability to identify emotional problems and handicaps which contributed to a patient's health status. In this respect she followed in the *Dr. Christian* and *City Hospital* tradition. Her efforts to rehabilitate her patients often found her becoming involved in family conflicts. For example, when she nursed a small boy she discovered that part of his difficulties stemmed from over-protective parents. The most frequent theme, found in one-third of the episodes, portrayed Miss Dean in a criminal or disastrous situation calling for extraordinary bravery or solutions, rather than for nursing knowledge and skills. For example, she agreed to enter an elevator caught between floors and hanging by a thread in order to treat the injured within; she faced a bank robber determined to kill the only eyewitness to his crime (he happened to be Miss Dean's patient). The critics found the series heavy handed and noted that Janet Dean applied her psychological interventions with or without the doctors' approval or help. The critics felt that Ella Raines as Miss Dean was attractive and competent but particularly appealing in those episodes in which she was still a nurse and not yet immersed in the more Freudian aspects of the case. Although nursing responsibilities and knowledge infrequently received attention, the nurse character emerged as a dynamic woman, a problem-solver, and an individual who used initiative. In many ways Janet Dean was to nursing what Dr. Christian was to medicine.

Dr. Christian starred MacDonald Carey in the title role of Dr. Mark Christian, nephew of the fictional giant Dr. Paul Christian (Jean Hersholt appeared in two early episodes of the series to establish continuity). Although *Dr. Christian* sought to cash in on the tradition of Jean Hersholt's famed country doctor of radio and movie fame, the small town setting of the series was in sharp contrast to the types of problems faced by Mark Christian in his practice. More often than not the doctor-hero was involved in foiling criminals, sleuthing, or treating such rare diseases as bubonic plague and radiation poisoning. At least half of the approximately thirty-six episodes dealt with crime/detective themes. Three actresses appeared as nurse characters: Cynthia Baer, Jan Shephard, and Kay Fayllen. The only focus on nursing occurred in the final episode of the series in which three patients accused Dr. Christian's nurse of blackmailing them with information taken from their medical files. The show so focused on the exploits of the physician character that nurses remained firmly in the background.

Perhaps the best known and most popular of the syndicated series of the 1950s was *Dr. Hudson's Secret Journal* based on Lloyd C. Douglas' best-selling novel of the same title. In keeping with the didactic themes common in 1950s television, the syndicated *Dr. Hudson's Secret Journal* sought to establish a dramatic vehicle for delivering moralistic statements about the human condition. The series had a melodramatic tone, and the plot usually involved a character who benefited from Dr. Hudson's wise influence. Again in the early 1950s tradition, psychological problems and moral dilemmas preoccupied physicians more than did physical ailments. The pilot film depicted the moral transformation of Dr. Wayne Hudson (John Howard), a brilliant surgeon, who, after the death of his wife, had become cynical, withdrawn, and bitter. Hudson's involvement with a famous artist brought him to a new understanding of himself and his powers. The artist, who died at the end of the series, passed the secret of personal power and success to the physician: to aid others secretly, as suggested by Jesus in the Sermon on the Mount. After Hudson accepted this revelation, his success as a physician increased, and he kept a written account of his deeds in a handwritten ledger which he placed in his safe at the end of every episode. The show intended to inspire, teach, and reinforce the values of democracy, positive thinking, and Judeo–Christian morality.

The regular cast, in addition to Dr. Hudson, included his nurse Ann Talbot (Frances Mercer); Dr. Means (Phillip Tonge), the hospital administrator; Tacky Schultz (Blossom Rock), nurse and switchboard operator; Kathy (Cheryl Calloway), Hudson's daughter; and Mrs. Grady (Olive Blakeny), Hudson's garrulous housekeeper. But Hudson dominated and became a living legend because of his brilliance, his hard work, and his dedication. Ann Talbot, Hudson's nurse and confidante, was the second most important character of the series and appeared in at least half of the stories. The nature of her hospital position remained rather vague, but she was considered a nurse of importance and stature in the hospital. At times she appeared to be a staff nurse, a supervising nurse, and a superintendent of nursing, but her most important duty was as Dr. Hudson's personal assistant. A tall, attractive woman in her forties, Ann had worked years for Hudson and handled many of his domestic and family problems as well as helping in his professional work. One episode told the story of their relationship; in "The Ann Talbot Story" Hudson recalled the way in which his daughter Kathy, after the death of her mother, had tried to get him to marry Ann. Although Ann loved Hudson, the doctor explained to his daughter the reasons that he could not marry the faithful nurse, and she seemed, thereafter, to be content to work with him and to be a big sister to Kathy.

Tacky Schultz, a homely woman in her fifties, also appeared in nearly half the episodes but played a very minor role. Although she always wore a nurse's uniform, she never did any actual nursing care. Her duties were confined to the switchboard where she answered the phone, made calls for Hudson, and relayed information among the various folks that came to her desk. Nurse Hakopian (Natalie Norwich) appeared in a few episodes as a flighty, romantic, attractive young woman who provided a much needed comic relief in the series. The image of nursing in *Dr. Hudson* rested upon the contributions of these and a few other one-time-only nurse characters. The nursing profession was portrayed, in general, as a noble calling; nurses often provided help and care that doctors could not. Despite the positive associations surrounding the nurse characters, the actual scenes projected an image of nurses as wife and mother substitutes and as loyal handmaidens to the physician.

Ann Talbot's character provided most of the series' attention to nursing. Despite her great loyalty to Hudson and her respect for him, Ann managed to retain a sense of independence, and she occasionally criticized Hudson for harsh attitudes. However, the overall impression of Ann's professional role was that she was first, Hudson's executive secretary—privvy to his thoughts but still responsible for typing them up—and second, his medical assistant, occasionally discussing patient care and helping in surgery. In no case did Ann deliver nursing care to a patient on her own. On a few occasions Ann gave moral support or criticism to a fellow nurse, but usually she left nurse related conflicts to Hudson for solution. Other nurse characters did not correct the impression of the nurse as a peculiarly feminine vocation calling for domestic skills and female intuition. "Love in White Shoes," a rare comic episode, told the story of young Nurse Hakopian, at her wit's end because she was twenty-three years old and had no prospects for finding a husband. In walked two new residents and Hakopian set her cap for first one and then the other. Throughout her scenes in the hospital, the nurse appeared absent-minded, clumsy, and negligent of her routine duties. She set out to entrap a luckless British doctor who insulted and rejected her; at this, Hakopian quit her job at the hospital and appealed to kindly Mrs. Grady to teach her to cook so that she could really snare the doctor. When Hudson discovered Hakopian's resignation, he insisted that the offending doctor apologize. Hudson explained that Hakopian was affectionately esteemed by the entire staff; she may have been unorthodox, but she was an extremely effective nurse whose real talent lay in her ability to empathize with critically ill patients. Hudson credited Hakopian's nursing with saving patients he had given up for lost. Of course, this episode ended with Hakopian marrying her doctor and promising never to enter a hospital again, except for the purpose of enlarging her family.

In "Betty's Story" a young nursing student breached medical ethics by revealing a secret surgical procedure performed by Dr. Hudson. It was later discovered that she had become a nurse only at the insistence of her mother and was, in fact, a talented artist. Hudson rescued the girl by helping her realize her true vocation; he got her a job in an art supply store. "The Livingston Story" recounted the case of the middle-aged, spinster head nurse Beatrice Livingston who terrorized her nursing students with her perfectionistic demands. Of course Hudson saw through Livingston's facade and recognized her nursing talent. He elicited the story of her life, and found out that while nursing her fiancé, she had made a mistake which led to his death, thus leading to her current perfectionism as compensation.

Scenes of nursing care, sporadic and in the background, rarely featured nurses performing skilled tasks. Although Ann Talbot represented a positive image of nursing, the overall impression gleaned from the series was that nurses were women who played an important role of comforting patients and doctors, but they were, after all, only women and could be forgiven transgressions because of their romantic or scatterbrained natures.

In both *Janet Dean* and *Dr. Hudson,* nurses were predominantly seen in a positive light, but Janet Dean was most often seen as more a detective than a nurse, and Ann Talbot generally basked in the glory of Dr. Hudson.

In the early 1970s, three syndicated doctor series aired on U.S. television stations: *Dr. Simon Locke; Police Surgeon;* and *Young Doctor Kildare.* The first two of these series were Canadian productions; in fact, *Police Surgeon* turned out to be a drastic revision of the *Simon Locke* format which first appeared in 1971 and starred actor Sam Groom as young Dr. Locke, a combination of medical genius, pioneer, and detective all bundled into one handsome package. *Simon Locke* took place in a small Canadian town, Dixon Mills, where old Dr. Andrew Sellers (Jack Albertson) had advertised in a medical journal for an assistant in his practice and subsequently hired Simon Locke, a brilliant physician, chief of internal medicine at a large, metropolitan hospital; he had tired of the city's impersonality. Dixon Mills was needy enough, for there were no other physicians around for hundreds of miles, and the only approximation of a hospital was Dr. Sellers' office/home, with its examining and hospital room. The two physicians worked with the help of two other regular characters—Nurse Louise Wynn (Nuala Fitzgerald) and Police Chief Dan Palmer (Len Birman).

Life in Dixon Mills was a perpetual series of dire emergencies, often with illegal or criminal overtones. In a typical episode ("The Man Who Hunted Hunters") an unknown assailant kept shooting hunters with tranquilizer darts, tying branches to their heads to look like antlers, and trussing them up on their own car fenders. The victims were all brought to Dr. Locke, and finally, as Locke had feared, a small hunter was hit with a tranquilizer dose that was too large; the man could scarcely breathe and was in danger of dying. Locke cleverly rigged an endotracheal catheter from beach balls, tubing, and an oxygen tank. Meanwhile, Police Chief Palmer (who often helped Locke) went into the woods dressed like a hunter to lure the dartman, bearing with him an antidote shot to the tranquilizer, in case the dartman found him first. Unfortunately, he did not expect the dartman to shoot him twice, so Dr. Locke, having saved the hunter's life, had to then go find Palmer and revive him as well. The misguided dartmen died in Locke's arms, ironically the victim of a hunter who mistook him for a deer; a brash reporter ended up in jail for helping the dartman escape after Palmer captured him.

Nothing fazed Locke. He could fashion lifesaving equipment from any spare parts and he could also out-talk nervous killers with guns and track down fugitive typhoid carriers in order to administer a cure. Dr. Sellers helped Dr. Locke in all of these shows, but the glory clearly belonged to the younger doctor. They had a congenial relationship, and they thoroughly respected one another. Sellers recognized that Locke was a better physician than he would ever be himself, but the townspeople tended to give their loyalties to the older man.

This paragon of medical ability would hardly seem to have required any assistance, but there was, in fact, a regular nurse character in the series. The credits listed her as Mrs. Louise Wynn, but she was consistently referred to as "Wynn." She appeared in a majority of the episodes, and although she never had a major role, she emerged as a pleasant, sensible, middle-aged woman. At first, it was tempting to dismiss her as the very image of the typical country doctor's loyal helpmate—more housekeeper than nurse—but some episodes soon dispelled this image and revealed a skilled and confident nurse whose actions bespoke years of experience. Over the season Wynn carried out a variety of nursing (and other) responsibilities, acting in numerous ways to help the physician practice medicine efficiently and to comfort the patients. She had an excellent relationship with both doctors, especially with Sellers, with whom she shared an easy understanding that bespoke years of cooperative association. She worked swiftly, either with wordless obedience or without any orders from the doctor, always understanding perfectly what was necessary in the situation at hand. Without instructions she removed a comatose patient's shirt so the doctor could treat him; she monitored vital signs; she told the doctor when a patient's heart had stopped; she asked if a patient was allergic to any drugs; she calmed nervous patients.

In one episode, "The Perfect Specimen," aired Sept. 23, 1971, another nurse appeared and gave quite a different image of nursing. This time it was a beautiful young woman of about twenty-five, Andrea Howard, obviously Simon Locke's former girlfriend from his big city days come to persuade him to return to the city. Ms. Howard accompanied Dr. Locke as he rushed to help Jeanne Jordan, a woman whose husband was so proud of her perfect health that she dared not admit that she had been in pain for some months. The nature of her serious condition was never explained, but Simon had to do an emergency surgery. Ms. Howard assisted the doctor with perfect efficiency, both during the initial examination and later during surgery. Afterwards, however, Mr. Jordan (to Andrea's astonishment) accused the doctor of being a "needle happy quack," and other patients soon were closing their doors to the young doctor. Ms. Howard was disgusted with these ungrateful people who didn't seem to appreciate Simon's talent, and she tried even harder to persuade him to return with her to the big city. Instead he asked her to stay, telling her that there was plenty of work there for a surgical nurse with her ability. She pointed out that the people didn't even want him, but he shrugged, knowing another emergency would come along to prove him necessary to them again. "That's the life you want?" she demanded, "Waiting for emergencies to prove yourself to THEM? I'd die watching you suffer so." Nonetheless, Dr. Locke insisted on stayng, and Ms. Howard left forever.

Ms. Howard's response to Locke's dedication in conjunction with her admitted talents for nursing projected a cool, impersonal image of the nurse. She had many virtues to recommend her. In nearly every way possible, Ms. Howard's few scenes established her as an excellent and efficient nurse. Still, her image contrasted sharply with that of Wynn, who was also an excellent nurse. Andrea maintained a cool detachment about her profession which would preclude self-sacrifice for patients over her own needs. Wynn was strongly in tune with the good country doctors, while Andrea Howard remained forever the modern city girl. Locke, Sellers, and Wynn did appear to be throwbacks to another age. Wynn was an excellent nurse in her own right, but she never received anything like the sometimes cloying adulation bestowed on the doctors.

Simon Locke's talents did not long remain hidden in the wilds of Dixon Mills. After a single season, Dr. Simon Locke was cancelled, and the brilliant young doctor was switched to a spinoff show entitled *Police Surgeon*. In this new series Simon worked in the Emergency Medical Unit of the Metropolitan Police Department in Toronto, Canada, and Dixon Mills' former police chief Dan Palmer worked as a lieutenant with him. Diseases and/or injuries occurred as regularly as did the crimes in every episode, so both men had plenty to keep them busy.

Certainly nothing seemed to escape Simon's keen eye, and he seemed to solve mysteries and crimes faster than did the regular policeman.

This combination of popular television heroes—physicians and policemen—apparently appealed to the public more than the earlier show since *Police Surgeon* ran for three full seasons. Typical format for the series focused on a crime in which either the criminal or victim was injured or sick. Locke typically traced the criminal by detecting slim clues about an ailment which would eventually give him away; or he unhesitatingly walked into dangerous situations in order to give medical aid; or he administered some spectacular emergency rescue treatment (or all of the above). Plots relied heavily on a limited selection of criminals including syndicate gangsters, young street gang hoods, and ex-cons. In the course of solving the crimes, Locke treated such medical problems as broken bones, injuries from beatings, gunshot wounds, electric shock, heart attacks, food poisoning, diabetes, and iritis. When Dr. Locke was not detecting, he was making brilliant emergency treatments or rescues. He set a broken leg with a broomstick, his necktie, and a belt. Most impressive of all, perhaps, was his rescue of an alcoholic who had fallen into the metal structure of a railroad trestle against which a live wire was hanging and throwing off sparks. Not even the threat of electrocution stayed this doctor from his noble work. He accosted some cannery workers, put on their rubber gloves, rubber boots, and rubber aprons, climbed down the trestle with a rope, lowered the man to the ground, and restarted his heart with an injection of adrenaline. Such examples typified the show. This medical superman needed a nurse even less than did the Dr. Locke of Dixon Mills; and, indeed, there was no regular nurse character. In fact, nurses made few appearances in this syndicated series.

Yet another bright young doctor—this time still a learner—arrived on the television scene with the introduction of the syndicated series *Young Doctor Kildare* in 1972. Produced by MGM, this half-hour series featured Mark Jenkins as an idealistic young intern and Gary Merrill as Kildare's wise and paternal mentor, Dr. Leonard Gillespie. Blair General Hospital remained the background for Jim Kildare's trials and triumphs, and each week he matched his skills and moral character against an assortment of hostile or mistrustful patients and/or staff. The supporting cast for the show consisted of three nurses: Marsha Lord (Marsha Mason), Edith Ferris (Dixie Marquis), and Nurse Newell (Olga James). In addition, other nurses or doctors supported the main characters when the plot demanded, and, of course, featured players (usually patients) changed from week to week providing Dr. Kildare with new health care challenges. Any slight nods to realism in this show were overbalanced by bows to the romanticized simplifications. Over the weeks Kildare treated patients whose health problems included cancer, pneumonia, encephalitis, venereal disease, mongoloidism, acute allergies, and psychosomatic deafness. Also routine were injuries resulting from falls, car accidents, riots, or radical bombers. Substance abuse problems were also seen in the series. Kildare came into contact with all these problems because each week he worked in a different section of Blair Memorial. Since he was only an intern, he was on rotation among these different departments in order to learn the various medical specialties. It was, however, hard to believe that Kildare was a green young intern since he appeared omniscient, almost in charge of the whole hospital. He was never baffled by a patient's symptoms; he instantly made correct diagnoses. The physicians themselves showed concern for their image. In "Housecall" both Gillespie and Kildare were somewhat nonplussed by a patient who seemed to know as much about her condition as they did. The lady diagnosed her problem, prescribed for herself, and contradicted Gillespie's suggestions for X-rays. Gillespie snowed her into silence with big words. Kildare said he thought the patient was right about having a kidney stone. Gillespie agreed, but he did not want a civilian to tell them their business. The scene was played for light humor, but the underlying assumptions were quite plain, and not too humorous: Complete, unquestioning faith in the superior knowledge of the physician is the only acceptable attitude in a patient. A patient's expression of interest, knowledge, or preferences concerning his own diagnoses and treatment clearly trespasses on the physician's privileged territory.

The idea of physicians as wise, kindly, altruistic, and skilled miracle workers is so ingrained in our heritage that it is difficult to judge objectively just how realistic the writers meant *Young Doctor Kildare* to appear. Sometimes the episodes addressed genuine and complex problems with a fair degree of honesty, only to undercut them with startlingly abrupt and unlikely endings. For example, in "Unfinished Child" Kildare had to tell a middle-aged father, Gregory Lanzo, that his newborn child—a long awaited girl after three boys—was a mongoloid, and that the baby had an intestinal blockage which would prove fatal unless surgery was done. Lanzo, a lawyer famous (and poor) for his defense of life's downtrodden, found this an unbearable blow and refused to authorize the operation. Kildare was horrified at the idea of watching the baby needlessly starve to death. A genuinely moving confrontation between Kildare and Lanzo was set up as each convincingly presented his side of the argument, Lanzo telling of the financial and emotional struggles he had had for years. Kildare skillfully argued him out of his decision, and the whole episode suddenly ended happily. Mr. and Mrs. Lanzo turned to each other with mutual satisfaction and gazed at their baby, and Mr. Lanzo burbled happily about how much his son had wanted a baby sister. Somehow, magically, all his former worries disappeared without a trace. A number of other episodes had these sudden and unconvincing sunset endings in which genuine problems evaporated after a few words from Dr. Kildare.

Nurses in *Young Doctor Kildare* had a minimal involvement in the action. They got equipment, relayed messages, reported test results, prepared syringes for the physicians, and watched them work. They took orders from the physicians, but the execution of these orders rarely figured in the narrative and almost always occurred offstage. Indeed, there was not much for the nurses to do with Jim Kildare around. He provided the nursing care himself, everything from giving injections to comforting and talking to patients and families. Only twice did nurses display even a hint of protest at the doctor's patronizing assumptions about their roles. Once Nurse Newell said she would do it herself when a doctor reached to take the hypodermic; but the doctor insisted on giving the injection herself. In another episode Kildare was teasing a maternity nurse about becoming a mother herself someday if she was lucky, and she promptly reminded him that she was a nurse because she wanted to be a nurse, not to find a husband. Such minimal protests were hardly sufficient to offset the overpowering evidence that Blair Hospital nurses served mostly as standard hospital scenery and flattering background for the doctors. Even Kildare sometimes treated them as extraneous matter. When Gillespie came into the emergency room with a minor cut, a nurse began to treat the wound, but Kildare waved her aside and did it himself.

This benign neglect of nurses was not the only factor that adversely affected their image. Several times the physicians sent the nurse out of the room when they wanted to discuss a patient or talk to a patient's family. Such exclusion implied that patient information was none of the nurse's business or that the nurse could not be trusted not to gossip. In "By This Sign" the doctors were trying to eliminate the public hullabaloo surrounding a very religious and very suggestible girl who got bleeding stigmata in her hands every Friday. A nurse, however, proceeded to tell another patient about the girl who then demanded that he see her before he died. Another reference to nurses' unreliability occurred in "Accident," when an emergency room nurse suggested morphine for the victim, only to be sharply reminded by the physician that morphine was not suitable for a patient with a head injury.

One might possibly dismiss the small blots on the nurses' image except that in the very few instances in which nurses played a more important role, they also appeared unfavorably. In only three episodes did the nurses have more important roles, and in only one episode did the nurse appear at the center of the main plot. The first story, "The Chemistry of Anger" opened with nurses and interns criticizing the unpopular female resident, Dr. Keefe. Five or six nurses under her authority had already requested transfers to another service, and when Kildare came on rotation, the remaining nurses sympathetically welcomed him to "Devil's Island." Since Keefe was truly an abrasive human being, the nurses' attitude was understandable; but again, they compared unfavorably to the heroic Kildare who persistently worked to win Keefe's friendship, learned important medical lessons even from her unpleasant way of teaching, and vigorously defended her when Dr. Gillespie refused her application for chief resident.

The second story began with a negative image of a nurse and subsequently softened somewhat. The "bad" nurse was an outsider, Emily Connors, the supervising nurse at a county sanitarium for retarded persons. She was shown bringing in one of the inmates of the sanitarium, a terrified and uncooperative young girl (Kelly) with abdominal pains. The Blair nurses tried to gently calm the patient, but Nurse Connors told them they were wasting their time since retarded people didn't understand anything. When Kildare arrived she informed him that Kelly's problem was probably appendicitis and suggested that he start surgery immediately. Kildare furiously reprimanded her for speaking in front of an already frightened patient and asked her what kind of nurse she was. Later he questioned her angrily about the sanitarium's practice of tranquilizing the patients daily and of feeding them all pureed food because some of them had trouble chewing or swallowing. With equal anger, Nurse Connors lashed out at Kildare, asking if he had ever so much as visited a mental hospital. For all the daring exposés of conditions there, she said nothing was ever done about the overcrowding, understaffing, overworking, and underfinancing and viewers were shown that her harshness was born of angry disillusionment at the constant compromise her job entailed, at the insidious destruction of sensitivities that such compromise caused. She did not appear in the central part of the episode which concentrated on Kildare's attempts to teach Kelly and his triumphant discovery that she was not, in fact, retarded; but in the end, Connors appeared genuinely touched at this discovery and by the fact that Kelly had spoken at last.

In the third story, the only episode in which a nurse was the main character, Nurse Amy Marvin had fallen in love with patient Jack Beale, a diabetic dying of cancer, being kept alive only by machines. His son refused to authorize Mr. Beale's release from the machines so that he might die with dignity, although Ms. Marvin pleaded with him to do so. The patient was soon found dead from an insulin overdose; Amy Marvin was accused of giving the medication, although she denied it. At the hearing the prosecution revealed that Mr. Beale had willed the nurse nearly all his money, some half a million dollars, and had left his son nothing at all; this information took Nurse Marvin completely by surprise. She subsequently admitted to her lawyer that she did in fact kill the patient because she couldn't bear to see him suffer. The lawyer proved that the son deliberately let his father suffer, egging the nurse to administer the merciful shot, because he knew that the legacy would revert to him if she were convicted of murder. The judge decided not to bring the case to trial; Amy went free but she lost her nursing license.

Such syndicated series of the 1970s as *Young Doctor Kildare* offered very little difference in terms of the image of nursing than those seen in the prime-time series (*Medical Center* or *Marcus Welby*, for example). At best nurses, while less dedicated than the physicians, shared in their reflected glory; at worst they were seen as short-sighted, problem-prone women who needed the firm guiding hand of a male doctor to set their troubles to right.

While special made-for-television movies have not often dealt directly with nurses or nursing, the handful of films that have emphasized nurses have usually done so in a negative or frightening way. For example, in "Nurse Killer," a 1978

ABC *Mystery of the Week* movie, a group of nurses living in a psychiatric hospital became the victims of an unknown assailant. The nurses themselves were less than admirable. One nurse was addicted to morphine, another was involved in an unhappy marriage, and still another was having an affair with the hospital administrator. The heroine nurse had taken the job in the psychiatric hospital to be near her father, the administrator, and to recover from the suicide of her husband. As it turned out, the killer was herself a nurse, the head nurse of the institution who had been keeping her retarded, illegitimate child in the institution for years and had finally decided to revenge herself on others.

In "Night Cries," a 1978 film made for ABC, a young mother, despondent after the death of her newborn daughter, experienced powerful and frightening dreams in which the delivery room nurse appeared as a villainous character. The dreams persisted, convincing the young mother that her daughter had not died. In fact, the dreams turned out to be psychic manifestations—proving the strength of mother love—which led the heroine to discover that the delivery room nurse had kidnapped her baby and planned to sell it on the black market. Not only was the nurse shown to be a criminal, but also a psychotic from having worked in a delivery room for years without having children of her own.

"Nurse Will Make It Better," a 1977 ABC *Mystery of the Week* movie, told the weird tale of a nurse who managed to cure an incurable paralytic. The patient's sister suspected the nurse of some strange activities but was unable to prove her suspicions until she herself posed as a paralytic. Eventually the truth emerged; "nurse" was in fact a minion of Satan, working on earth to collect souls for her beastly boss. Bullets passed harmlessly through her body, but finally the heroine emptied the guarded box which held all the "collected souls." As soon as the souls were dispersed, "nurse" vanished, and the once paralyzed sister returned to her paralytic state.

As can be seen, nurses in mystery movies have not been the source of much positive feeling. However, in April 1980 CBS presented two special feature length films devoted to nursing topics. The first to appear was *Nurse* and the second *Portrait of a Rebel: Margaret Sanger*. Given the disappointing treatment of nursing in regular network series during the most recent season, these two films did a little to balance the scales.

Nurse offered the viewer an unusual look at the world of nursing in a large, big city hospital—unusual because it presented the nursing profession with both sympathy and realism. Although this television version of a best-selling novel changed certain characters in the book, it did retain the book's sense of the inherent drama captured in the day-to-day experiences of a real staff nurse. The story followed six months in the life of a recently widowed woman, Mary Benjamin (Michael Learned), who had returned to nursing after an absence of eighteen years. Despite this long hiatus from the profession, Mary took a job at the hospital where she worked eighteen years previously, and because she once held the position of head nurse in the hospital and had also completed her B.S.N., she was immediately appointed as head nurse of a medical-surgical unit. She had been married, living in a large, suburban home with her physician husband and her son when her husband died of a heart attack. She explained to a friend that returning to nursing somehow had given her back an identity that she had lost during marriage. In order to live close to work, she moved into a rather small and dreary apartment which her husband had used when he had to stay in town to be near a patient.

Mary's son Chip (Jon Matthews) had gone away to college, and she began her new life alone. She plunged into her new job with energy and with a few misgivings. Before taking over her job as head nurse, she attended the hospital's refresher course and orientation for new employees. Within a seemingly short time, however, she took charge of a 36 bed ward. Mary's job was complicated by her staff, her patients, her own self-doubts, and one physician who was demanding and rude. Most of Mary's nursing staff appeared to be cooperative, conscientious, and friendly women of mixed age, ethnic background, and appearance though they did present her with problems. The patients on Mary's floor generally gave her satisfaction despite their often rude demands. Mary and the nurses cheerfully worked with feisty, uncooperative patients. Dr. Rose (Robert Reed) was the staff terror; he was a demanding and arrogant physician who clearly wanted as little to do with the nurses as possible. He distrusted Mary as head nurse because of her long absence from nursing. He was laconic in his dealings with her, merely giving her his orders, and seemed uninterested in anything she had to say about the patients. Mary tried to accommodate him but did not mutely defer to his pronouncements.

Mary's main problem stemmed from her own mixed feelings about returning to nursing. She told a friend on a visit to the suburbs that her memories of nursing were idealistic but her current job was drudgery and low paid drudgery at that. She was not at all comfortable with the presssures of the job either. Her first crisis undermined her shaky confidence. When a physician ordered penicillin to be given to a patient, she administered it without first asking the man if he had any allergies. Intravenously injecting the medication, within seconds the man was in an anaphylactic shock. She immediately initiated emergency procedures, and after defibrillation, the man was saved. Nevertheless, the experience deeply affected Mary who found herself confronted with her memories of trying unsuccessfully to revive her own husband after his heart attack. Mary completely broke down and admitted to one of the other nurses, Toni, that she had no business coming back to work, that she was too old to handle the pressures. Toni calmed her down but agreed that maybe she ought to escape back to the suburbs. Toni referred to herself as a lifer, hooked on her job, but she admitted that if she had the option of leaving the profession she certainly would. In a later interview with the personnel director who had hired her, Mary promised to try to stick out the job for at least a few more weeks. As if to complicate her life, her son Chip quit school and insisted that he was going to get a job. In the days between Christmas and New Year's Mary finally saw her life settling into some kind of order, with the nurses cooperating, Dr. Rose becoming more accepting of her, and one patient telling her to quit dealing with her life in half measures. After her conversation with Kelly (the patient), Mary drove out to Scarsdale and put her house on the market. She packed up her favorite possessions and turned her drab apartment into a real home. Her son came back from his ski trip, and they continued their argument about his living at home with her. She was afraid that she would grow dependent on him, but finally, with the surprised acquisition of a cat, Mary realized that she was at home in a new life. Her son would stay with her and might, as he announced, even become a nurse like his mother.

The plot of *Nurse* simply followed Mary's personal and professional development over the period of a few months; yet the dramatic content, composed of small setbacks and triumphs for the show's protagonist, managed to entertain and satisfy the viewer. The rhythm of the show rested on an episodic look at the nurse's life, a back and forth description of her new experiences in nursing with her handling of her personal life. There was an interesting contrast between her two lives; for most of the show nursing provided her with challenges and pressures, a reason for getting up in the morning. Her private life seemed almost stagnant, a few bittersweet visits to her suburban life and many solitary evenings in her new apartment. However, by the end of the show, when she finally realized her satisfaction with her new professional life, she turned her home, her private domain, into a warm and welcoming place. Without doubt Mary's return to nursing provided her with the self-confidence and purpose she needed in order to adjust herself to her changed personal circumstances.

The image of nursing in *Nurse* took its most definitive form in Mary Benjamin's reactions to her renewed commitment to her profession. The image of the profession was overwhelmingly positive without being romanticized or distorted. First, Mary returned to nursing because she sensed that she needed some new purpose in her life to help fill the gap created by her husband's unexpected death. That she returned after an eighteen year absence suggested that her identification with nursing had always formed a very important part of herself, even though she had not considered active participation in nursing throughout her marriage. She went back to school after her son entered the first grade in order to get her B.S.N., but again she did not put her nursing knowledge to use. Nevertheless, the viewer sensed that this attractive, intelligent, and wealthy woman had always thought of herself as a nurse and the enduring, albeit shelved, commitment suggested to the audience that nursing was much more than a job; nursing for Mary Benjamin had been an important part of her self-development and had provided her with a ready professional identity which sustained her at a critical juncture in her life. Although Mary returned to nursing with almost no reflection, her sudden immersion in the hospital forced her to examine her motives and commitment to the profession. Almost immediately she realized the distance between her idealistic memories of nursing and the physically demanding drudgery of her new job. She promised little to herself or her employer about staying on the job. As head nurse, she was shown carrying out direct nursing care responsibilities, from bed-making to medication administration, as well as administering the personnel and overall nursing care on her floor, but she was exhausted at the end of the day. Her first emergency, which she skillfully handled, totally unnerved her later.

It was very clear to the viewer, as well as to Mary's hospital colleagues, that as a well-to-do widow she had many options to consider; she was not economically bound to continue her work as a nurse. Yet the tide of Mary's doubt turned, and by the end of the show she managed to handle her job and her life with both humor and confidence.

Beyond the presentation of Mary Benjamin's reinvolvement with her profession, *Nurse* focused a good deal of attention on the true work of contemporary nurses. The world of nursing seen in this show lacked the presence of many well known nurse character types: the eternal mother–nurse; the authoritarian spinster nurse; and the nubile young nurses. Instead, in *Nurse* the hospital corridors were populated with a variety of nurses: women who were determined to protect their own interests yet who conveyed a firm sense of compassion and conscientiousness. To be certain, there were irritating discrepancies in the story, but more than any recent dramatic look at nurses, there was consistent reference to the real world of nursing.

The realism with which the profession was presented began with the story's depiction of the hospital environment. Shot on location in a New York hospital, the background activity was totally convincing. There was none of the mindless scurrying about noted in a lot of hospital drama. The organization of the hospital was seen in nursing terms—patients needing common types of care were grouped on the same floor. There was an obvious hierarchy in the nursing world. The personnel director was an attractive and chic woman who managed the hiring, firing, and scheduling of the nursing staff. She did not wear a uniform, but was seen in purely administrative terms. Mary Benjamin, the head nurse, seemed responsible for monitoring the work of her nurses and making sure that all the patients were being cared for. She became involved in trying to accommodate the work of the floor with the individual needs of her staff members; for Mary, each of her staff represented a different human approach to her work. Unlike nurses seen in most hospital drama, the nurses were not homogeneous and indistinguishable.

Although the story did not explicitly identify the nurses, the different levels of nursing functions were seen. Mrs. Donovan was probably an LPN. She had worked at the hospital for sixteen years, and acknowledgeable viewer could assume that her professional growth was limited by her educational qualifications. Furthermore, she did none of the more skilled tasks, but was limited to morning care routines and helping to move and lift patients. In a few scenes, women wearing blue uniforms and no caps appeared to be helping Mary change a bed, and they would appear to be nurses' aides. In many ways, the show's ambiguous presentation of nursing distinctions mirrors reality; many, many patients in hospitals have little idea of the educational differences and spheres of authority of the many women and men in white uniforms who minister to their needs.

According to most television health care fiction, nurses engage in limited activities, particularly in hospitals: For the most part they stand at the nursing station and answer the phone and deliver messages. In *Nurse* a ward clerk obviously had these secretarial responsibilities. The nurses worked according to the obvious fact, so often ignored in television, that their patients need care twenty-four hours a day. The presence or absence of physicians seemed little noticed by the nursing staff, unless an emergency situation required a physician. The nurses provided continuous care and supervision of their patients; the physicians occasionally gave new orders to be followed but did not set the pace for nursing care. Even in emergency situations, the nurses began emergency treatments, only relinquishing their role when the physician arrived. In one case, the nurse performed the lifesaving feat of removing an object from a patient's throat. The show captured the vast range of nursing responsibilities. It revealed that much of a nurse's job involves such physically demanding tasks as lifting and moving heavy patients; constantly running back and forth between patients; and such menial tasks as cleaning bedpans or changing beds and removing soiled laundry, and that nurses also concern themselves with the emotional well being of their patients. The show also made it clear to the viewer that nurses approach their job in a professional manner. One very important scene, for the image of the profession, was the depiction of the nursing staff's daily conference. The nurses were shown meeting together and discussing their problems and plans for care of a particularly difficult patient. Although it was clear that the nurses were simply fed up with catering to the somewhat crazed "King of Europe," as the patient called himself, it was also clear that they considered his situation according to objective standards.

Because of the enormous physical demands of nursing and the multitude of tasks, nurses were also shown making errors or becoming less than cooperative. In one scene, Toni forgot to administer an insulin dosage. The physician berated Mary and her staff for the intolerable mistake, and indeed, the nurses seemed to agree that the physician was correct in his demands, if a bit rude in his manners. Toni immediately took responsibility for the incident and became very upset, noting that she had never before made such an error. Only a conscientious nurse would have reacted with Toni's sincerity and guilt.

The nursing staff on 8 Cook was composed of several women in obviously different circumstances: a group of women with different reasons for working as nurses. Not all had the idealistic dedication of Mary Benjamin, but all seemed to perform to relatively high standards of nursing care. In addition, the presence of physicians did not dictate the schedule of nursing care. Aside from a brief and unnecessary scene in which young Dr. Benson asked Mary to have an affair, there were none of the romantic and sexual relationships between physicians and nurses that so exist in much television health care drama. The relations between medicine and nursing in this show were not shown to be very cooperative. What basically emerged was the sense of there being two separate sets of concerns in the hospital—nursing care and medical interventions.

Given the lack of physician domination in the show, it naturally emerged, much in the manner of *The Nurses* in the 1960s, that nurses handled their own personal and professional problems. In all, *Nurse* brought into the open many aspects of the nursing profession that are ignored in most television fiction. The story revealed that there is a shortage of nurses. Mary Benjamin had no trouble finding a job even after an eighteen year absence; placing her in a head nurse position was unrealistic, but the hospital's willingness to retrain older nurses is a practice utilized by hospitals to recruit nurses. At one point, Mary was asked to work a second shift after completing one eight hour day. In fact, many hospitals routinely expect their nurses to work overtime; if *Nurse* did not develop the nursing shortage in its most acute form, it nevertheless mentioned it. Furthermore, Mary demonstrated the classic symptoms of "reality shock" often faced by new nurses: the conflict between their ideals and the divergent demands of their jobs, which often preclude the delivery of quality patient care. Mary's son, Chip, also articulated a new attitude toward the profession in that he suggested that he might decide to become a nurse.

Nurse was the best fictional presentation of the profession since the demise of *The Nurses* in 1965, although dramatically the older series was much better constructed. CBS developed a continuing series with this story's concept and, if it turns out to be a successful series, TV may have an opportunity to rectify a good deal of its past treatment of the nursing profession. CBS's April 22, 1980 production entitled "Portrait of a Rebel: Margaret Sanger" focused exclusively on Sanger's early involvement with the birth control movement from about 1912 to 1920. It was difficult to identify the exact years encompassed because the movie frequently strayed from an accurate chronological narrative of Sanger's life. In fact, the television biography offered very little substantive information on the content of Sanger's theories or her development as a political activist. The movie was poorly written and constructed, and none of Margaret Sanger's visionary strength emerged in Bonnie Franklin's portrayal. But despite the rather shoddy production, it was heartening to see television show some interest in the lives and contributions of great American nurses, and in its way, "Portrait of a Rebel" did present Margaret Sanger as a courageous, outspoken, forward looking leader who placed the needs of individual women above the hypocritical standards of post-Victorian society. The movie began with scenes of Margaret Sanger working as a public health nurse in some unidentified, lower class neighborhood in New York, after the turn of the century. Wearing a long, light blue dress with a white nurse's cap, Mrs. Sanger hurried into the tenement home of a woman suffering the aftereffects of a self-induced abortion, and immediately she confronted an unsympathetic doctor who referred to his patient as a stupid woman; the physician instructed the nurse to make the patient comfortable and await the inevitable. Sanger asked him why he could not tell the woman how to prevent pregnancy, and the doctor responded that such information was against the law to dispense. The woman predictably died in great pain after sharing her anguish with Margaret Sanger. Later, at a party she attended with her artist husband Bill, Sanger met a feminist journalist named Anita who immediately signed Margaret up to write for her paper, *The Call,* because Sanger had been expounding on the need for birth control. Even though the newspaper could not print most of what Sanger wrote, she was asked to cover the Lawrence, Massachusetts textile strike for the paper. She was seen herding a group of children onto a train, singing "Solidarity Forever" with the tykes. Then the action cut to a Senate hearing on the strike, during which Sanger changed the subject of the children's poor living conditions to make a plea for revoking the Comstock Law so she could disseminate birth control information. Thereafter she immersed herself in research (the topic of which was left unknown), much to the dismay of her husband who espoused radical rhetoric, but seemed to really want a subservient bourgeois wife. Bill, dismayed by his wife's increasing activism, left for Paris, and during his absence, Margaret organized a small group of women to help her disseminate her work. She compiled a new journal, *The Woman Rebel,* which was confiscated by the postal authorities for being obscene. To thwart these authorities, Margaret and her group mailed them individually so they could slip through the censors. Eventually she was arrested by federal authorities; in her adversity, her father changed his mind about her work, and her sister Ethel also joined the cause. There was a lot of pretrial publicity which Sanger tried to exploit. She had a meeting with a Machiavellian-looking Catholic monsigneur who warned her to stay away from Catholic women; with great pluck, she paraphrased Pope John XXIII with anachronistic flair, promising to open the doors and the windows and let in the light.

An unsympathetic judge refused her request for a postponement, and with great anguish about leaving her children, she fled to England to prepare her defense and there met Havelock Ellis who not only introduced her to current literature and leaders in matters of human sexuality and contraceptive methods but also fell in love with her. After an idyllic affair with Havelock, she journeyed to Amsterdam where she discovered the diaphragm. Soon she was disturbed by nightmares that her daughter needed her; before she got home, the child was dead. In her torment, she maniacally repeated that she wanted her child back yet had the presence of mind to ask Bill Sanger for a divorce because she was in love with someone else.

Shortly thereafter she was arrested again, but the indictment against her was dropped because the authorities did not want her to test the Comstock Law in court. On her way out of the courthouse, cheated of her day in court, she announced to her supporters that it was the time to open the birth control clinic. Soon all the women working in the clinic were arrested and tried individually. Ethel, Margaret's sister, was the first tried, and she was convicted and sentenced to thirty days in the workhouse. She promised a hunger strike and carried out the threat, causing the prison officials a great deal of trouble. She was finally released, near death. Margaret's trial also found her convicted. To her lawyer's dismay, she refused to stop her work while her case was being appealed. She bravely and cheerily faced her thirty day incarceration, although she did not go on a hunger strike. While immured she befriended the other prisoners, mostly prostitutes, and tried to educate them about birth control. She wrote love letters to her dear Havelock and made her final stand by refusing to be fingerprinted before her release. The warden, so anxious to be rid of her, relented, and Margaret said a fond adieu to the wonderful inmates of the prison and to the sympathetic matron. The movie ended with a voice-over narration of H.G. Wells' dictum: "When the history of our civilization is written, it will be a biological history and Margaret Sanger will be its heroine."

It would be easy and probably fruitless to dissect this movie's errors with regard to the presentation of Sanger's life, but in that Sanger is identified as a nurse, it is necessary at least to discuss the way in which her nursing influenced her work as an advocate of birth control as well as the inaccuracies regarding her role as a nurse. The first scene of the movie not only established Sanger's nursing identification but also provided the most dramatic explanation of Sanger's commitment to finding a way to prevent pregnancy. The viewer was made aware that her work among poor women together with her belief that her own mother died indirectly as a result of too many pregnancies forged in Sanger a revolutionary passion for the cause of birth control. Unfortunately, there was no discussion of Sanger's early training as a nurse nor of her reasons for working as a nurse. As the wife of a supposedly well-to-do (another mispresentation) artist and architect, she did not need to work; and married women usually did not work outside the home unless economics made it necessary. Aside from elliptic references to her father's labor radicalism, there was little hint of the source of Sanger's leftist ideas. The only statement relative to her nursing was made when she told the dying woman who wanted information about birth control that she too was ignorant of proper techniques because nurses know only what doctors want them to know. When Sanger quit nursing because she could no longer stand to watch women suffer, there was a sense that she was escaping from her work; her commitment to a greater role as birth control advocte was slow in developing.

In the television film Sanger underwent an intermediate career as a journalist for a radical newspaper. While it may be true that she was asked to write feminist articles for the paper, she was not an investigative reporter, and, in fact, Sanger went to Lawrence because she was a nurse and a socialist and was asked to make sure the children of the striking workers did not starve, as happened earlier in a prolonged strike. She was asked to testify before a House of Representatives (the television version called it a Senate) committee investigating the strike and the conditions of the children of the strkers; according to the published transcript of this hearing, she testified only to the condition of the children and did not use her role as witness as a platform to lobby against the Comstock Law. In the film as well as in the transcript, she did refer to herself as a nurse, assuring the investigating congressmen that she was qualified to judge the conditions of the children. After this initial phase of the movie, no further reference was made to Sanger's nursing background. Although the opening scenes concerning her work as a public health nurse were important, they were not sufficient to impress the viewer with the importance of Sanger's nursing identification to her future role as a reformer. Thus, the role of nursing in Sanger's development and in her social conscience was considerably diminished by the writer's selection of what points of her life to emphasize and at times by his distortion of people and events. The producers and writer of the show seemed intent upon portraying Margaret Sanger as a feminist, which she was, who used the rhetoric of the 1970s, which she did not. Important facets of her political development and reference to her change of strategy in the 1920s were excluded. Nevertheless, since few enough people would be aware of the inaccuracies of this television version of Sanger's life, she was presented as strong and courageous, and association of her with nursing would have nothing but positive repercussions for public sentiment about nurses. As a point of comparison, a 1980 episode of *Nova,* a public television science series, devoted an hour to recapitulating the achievements of Margaret Sanger's life.

This PBS version offered a much more intelligent discussion of her life in a biographical sketch that revealed the development of her thought as well as the contradictions inherent in her personality. The format for the *Nova* production was a dramatization of a 1955 interview with Mrs. Sanger; the episode consisted of flashbacks to important scenes of her life and segments of the two day interview. Piper Laurie played Mrs. Sanger. The value of the PBS version lay in its presentation of Mrs. Sanger's whole life and not simply her rabble rousing days. According to the PBS story, Sanger's relationship with Havelock Ellis was exceedingly important not so much for its romanticism as because of his channeling of her energies into more productive efforts. Under Ellis' guidance, Sanger started to work for the establishment of contraception as a subject of scientific study, working to convince respected scientists to consider the topic and toward gaining support from philanthropists. According to the *Nova* version, her affiliation with radical labor agitators and her street corner organization did her cause more harm than good. *Nova* also recounted her role of the international organization of the birth control movement. Perhaps most interesting was the personality of Margaret Sanger, which very clearly emerged in the *Nova* production. Sanger

Fragmentary Images 157

ended her life as the widow of a wealthy industrialist. During her interview, she sipped champagne and laughed at the incongruity; she admitted that she had always been a radical although she drank champagne. Finally, the *Nova* production made clear that Sanger's political vision, profoundly influenced by Malthus, in which she saw the entire world reformed through population control, was in fact more of a motivating force in her life than her concern for the suffering of individual women, as suggested in the Bonnie Franklin impersonation.

The *Nova* treatment of Sanger's life included the segment on her experience as a public health nurse, and the death of Sadie Sachs because of a self-induced abortion. Mrs. Sanger told the interviewer that the case of Sadie Sachs was the third such death she had witnessed in one month's time and noted that abortion was the leading cause of female mortality in New York during those years. In this brief treatment, Mrs. Sanger appeared to be a much more objective nurse than in the CBS version in which she seemed to react with purely emotional horror rather than in an informed manner. According to the *Nova* version, which followed the facts more closely, Margaret Sanger did not turn immediately to the birth control movement nor to female suffrage; she dabbled in the labor movement and radical politics for at least four years before turning her attention to the advocation of birth control. Nursing per se did not receive a lot more attention in the *Nova* version than it did in the CBS movie; however, *Nova*'s greater credibility would undoubtedly enhance the image of nursing if it were to be compared to the Bonnie Franklin nurse character.

In general, public television offers the viewer more intelligent productions. Unfortunately for the nursing profession, public television has never broadcast a whole series featuring a nurse character. Occasionally, however, information or educational shows will feature either a fictional nurse or a real nurse discussing issues relevant to the profession. One such show, *Meeting of Minds,* created and hosted by Steve Allen is of the talk show variety, but the guests that appear on the show come not from the present but from the past. Two episodes featured Jayne Meadows impersonating a ninety-year-old Florence Nightingale who joined Martin Luther, Voltaire, and Plato in discussion. When Florence Nightingale was interviewed, what emerged was the standard story of her life: her early call to God's service; her work in the Crimea; her later retirement and reform accomplishments. During the interviews with the others, Miss Nightingale occasionally offered a comment or asked a question revealing the range of her reading or her particular interests. In all, the discussion revealed her to be a self-confident woman who took interest in a variety of topics ranging from religion to intellectual freedom.

Other public television shows have emphasized the new roles of nurses in the field of health care. For example, two PBS shows, *Woman* and *Handle with Care* introduced the public to the concept of nurses working as practitioners in expanded roles. PBS also broadcast "Inside the Cuckoo's Nest," a documentary on the psychiatric hospital used as a setting for the film *One Flew Over The Cuckoo's Nest*.

Obviously public televison, with its commitment to educational programs and quality entertainment, is the forum in which nursing has been treated with the greatest respect. Unfortunately, nursing is very rarely a topic for public television; in addition, the audience for public television programming, although growing, offers no competition to the commercial network's control of the airwaves.

9

Join Us Tomorrow: Nurse Characters in Daytime Drama

Serialized daytime television drama (soap opera) has long been scorned by critics of television as unworthy of serious attention. Within the last several years, however, recent observers have discovered what fans of the soap operas have known all along; that is, daytime drama is more reflective of real life than the much glossier prime-time dramas that get all the attention in the newspapers and *TV Guide*. Long before the nighttime shows could deal with controversial topics, the daytime serials were featuring stories about rape, abortion, drug addiction, alcoholism, illegitimacy, and promiscuity—all within the context of typical, middle-class, American family life. More than one trained social observer has found the soap opera to be a valuable telescope for the examination of social attitudes and contemporary life. Because of the high incidence of health care professionals in the populations of fictional soap opera towns, it is not surprising that nurse characters appear or have appeared in almost every daytime serial. Thus, an examination of the soap opera genre and the image of nursing in this type of drama seems warranted.

The first television soap appeared in 1950. *The First Hundred Years* lasted for only two years; however, producers continued to try to transfer the serialized drama, created for radio, to a video format and by 1960 soap opera had become strictly a television commodity.

In mid-1980 there were 12 serialized dramas on television, accounting for 52.5 hours of network time per week; the average age of these shows was 17 years. The extraordinarily long runs of these shows, compared to prime-time offerings, reflect the intense audience loyalty built up among viewers of the series. However, compared to prime-time audiences, soap operas draw many fewer viewers. An average daytime serial counts about 6.7 million viewers; overall, there are an estimated 20 million viewers of soap opera in the United States. An article on soap opera (*New York Times Magazine,* March 23, 1975), pointed out the somewhat surprising facts that at least 11 percent of the viewers were men and that the social, economic, and educational composition of the audience was a true cross-section of the country.

The daytime serial, because of its daily installments, must pace its stories to be glacially slow, and each episode needs to include a certain amount of recapitulation of events. The slow pace has the side effect of allowing credible character transformation and a real sense of personal development—a luxury unknown in most prime-time drama. In addition, the cost of producing these shows is much less than what is spent on prime-time offerings because of the limited amount of shooting on location and the hiring of relatively unknown actors. Plots mapped out months in advance, limited rehearsal time, a small number of sets, and the housebound nature of shooting imbues the shows with a certain humdrum appearance. Yet, despite the obvious drawbacks to producing daily episodes on a limited budget, the overall quality of acting and direction is surprisingly good.

The populations of the fictional communities of daytime drama include a high proportion of physicians, lawyers, and successful businessmen. All the important soap opera families count at least one respected physician in their midst and two soaps, *General Hospital* and *The Doctors,* are composed almost exclusively of physicians and their families. Where there are doctors, there are inevitably nurses, and several of the most popular soap opera heroines also wear or have worn the white uniform of the professional nurse. The large concentration of health care professionals in daytime drama can be explained in several ways, most of which depend upon the inherent plot opportunities in the health care world.

One journalist reported that Irna Phillips, the creator and long-time dominating figure in the soap opera genre, was something of a hypochondriac and simply wrote her own fascination with doctors and disease into her stories. Yet other more practical reasons help to explain the phenomenon. In the first place, the occupation provides several plot necessities: physicians' financial security allows for well-appointed homes and well-dressed characters. Also, physicians are not tied to an inflexible nine to five work schedule; they may be in any locale at any time of the day or night without seeming to neglect their work, and they act as natural magnets to troubled characters. Psychiatrists in particular become very easily involved in the emotional conflicts of other characters. Problems of pregnancy and childbirth, frequent health issues for characters, involve the physician in helping his client with her social adjustments to her condition. Finally, every hospital constantly acquires new nurses and physicians, so new characters can enter the story with little explanation. In addition, the hospital provides natural ways for characters to come together and meet both on purpose and by accident. In addition to the doctors, nurses, aides, and volunteers (a formidable percentage of the fictional town's citizenry), the staff members' families and friends can be brought onto the hospital floor in search of their relative, for lunch, for coffee, for serious confrontations. Of course the patients in the hospital and their visiting family and friends allow for changing population to be found in the hospital. In other words, the general hospital provides a good public crossroads for fictional townspeople. This natural crossroads is made an even better locale by its obvious association with the dangerously ill; not only does a brush with fate stimulate the victim to reassess his or her recent actions, but also it draws together or shakes apart weakened families or marriages. Alliances of love and friendship are often rearranged upon the aftermath of a serious illness. For example, Dr. Althea Davis of *The Doctors* decided against divorcing the husband she did not love in order to marry her true love because her current husband needed her after he was stricken with paralysis. Chuck Tyler of *All My Children*, who in 1979 had thought of divorcing his wife Donna, regained some of his former love for her when she nearly died as the result of a mugging.

Compared to the typical treatment of nurses in prime-time health care series, nurses in daytime drama emerge as much stronger and more influential members of society in general and the hospital in particular. One reason for this is that women are accorded much greater respect and equality in the fictional world of daytime television than normally seen in nighttime drama. Also, the health care world of daytime television offers a non-heroic view of the role of the physician in society. Although physician characters enjoy their share of dramatic surgical successes, they never appear in the same god-like position enjoyed by such prime-time physicians as Ben Casey, Dr. Kildare, Marcus Welby, or Joe Gannon. Doctors in daytime drama suffer the same types of personal and professional problems as all of the other characters. Thus, in the daytime health care environment nurse characters do not compete against the deified physician for audience sympathy. Perhaps these two points need further amplification in order to understand the values inherent in daytime television.

In the radio format and older television serials, stories were often based upon the presence of tent-pole characters, usually a middle-aged or older married couple with a large family. The mother and father of the family remained nearly immune from trouble, although they certainly suffered along with their children who generally faced a variety of disasters. In each case, the couples were older than most of the remaining cast of characters, their marriages secure, and the wife stayed at home while her husband worked in some established profession, such as law or medicine. Although this stay-at-home wife served chiefly as a comforter to her family in time of trouble, there was never a hint of condescension in the treatment of her by other characters; her opinions were valued and sought after by a host of relatives and friends.

The age of the female characters determined, to a great degree, their social and familial roles. The oldest characters continued traditional patterns: The father worked and the mother kept house, reflecting social reality in that many women who married before World War II have never left their homes to seek outside employment. In middle-aged families of daytime drama, often both husband and wife work outside the home; they are approaching marital security but occasionally they too experience some threat to their marriage. Usually, too, these middle-aged couples have grown children and become involved in the problems of their more trouble-prone offspring. Some of the best examples of these working couple marriages are found in the combination of health careers. Obviously, in this pattern of working husband and wife, the wife commands additional respect as a result of her professional position outside the home. These professional women often continue in their role as maternal comforter to their family and friends, but in addition they earn the respect and admiration of their patients or colleagues. The youngest members of the daytime serial communities are the most volatile and undependable. The young women in these series almost all seem to become pregnant, usually before marriage, and the experience of motherhood is one of the most important character forming events in their lives. Nevertheless, young women appear no more inconstant, selfish, promiscuous, or troubled than do the young male characters. Young men cope with premature parenthood as frequently as do young women. Very few of the younger characters enjoy any prominence based upon their dependability or role as problem solver and counselor, but there is an equality between males and females in this category, with both young men and women revealing the same types of emotional insecurities.

Outside the male–female relationships, soap opera society reveals numerous examples of strong women who are able to take care of themselves, both within and outside of marriage. These single women often do suffer and struggle for the sake of love or family, but they generally survive their problems with most of their sanity intact.

Despite all the social and familial equality seen between men and women in daytime drama, the virtues and values most frequently lauded remain rather stereotypically female in nature. A character's essential goodness is most often derivative of his or her relationships to family. Thus, a female character can rarely be judged good or bad until she is seen in conjunction with her first child. Her concern for her child's welfare and her capacity for self-sacrifice are the hallmarks of her goodness. A man's feelings for his children also characterize his essential goodness, but great sacrifices are rarely demanded of him. The establishment and preservation of strong families remain the greatest virtues in soap opera society. Although independent, working women in respected positions frequently appear, the underlying scheme of the soap opera world still emphasizes the satisfactions to be found in solid marriage and family relationships.

Because the position of women in soap opera society is quite positive and respectable, nurse characters (always women) automatically share in the general equality and strength found in female characters. In addition to the generally favorable position of women in soap opera, health care realism is not of major concern to daytime drama. (Even such health care oriented soap operas as *The*

Doctors and *General Hospital* do not pay much attention to the technological side of medicine and nursing.) In all soap operas, doctors spend as much or more of their time counseling friends and family as they do in surgery; because so much of the role of the physician is directed toward his or her personal relationships, the physician stands in a more nearly equal relationship to other health professionals and non-professionals on the hospital staff. So too, the nurse characters, depending upon their social and familial standing, are able to offer the kind of emotional support, counseling, and advice often reserved for physicians only in prime-time health care drama.

Also important to the role of the nurses is the fact that doctors are not omnipotent heroes in the world of daytime fictional health care. Nurses are frequently found trying to help distraught physicians cope with their emotional problems or professional concerns. The nurses and doctors portrayed in soap operas are almost always supposed to be competent, and usually superior, practitioners of their profession; but they are not infallible, nor are they immune to temptations and weakness. Good doctors in soap operas occasionally turn to alcohol to escape from family or professional pressures; sometimes they fail to save lives; and some have been known to abandon their profession in response to some failure. Because of the wide range of virtues and weaknesses, the nurse characters are often shown to be stronger or superior to a doctor in some ways. Thus Audrey March, a nurse on *General Hospital,* found herself trying to save a once fine surgeon from killing himself with alcoholism. Young nurse M. J. Match on *The Doctors* was shown to be the source of moral regeneration for a skilled cardiovascular surgeon but known womanizer, Dr. Colin Wakefield, who unfortunately died before his full reformation. Certainly Jessie Brewer of *General Hospital* did all she could to sustain her errant physician husband Phil Brewer through all of his personal difficulties.

The structure and values found in soap opera drama are consistently found throughout all of the series. Thus it is possible to gain a rather comprehensive understanding of the role nurse characters play in soap opera by examining but a few of them in depth. Of course, *General Hospital* and *The Doctors* demand analysis because so many of their cast members are nurses and doctors; in addition, *All My Children* and *Another World* will be reviewed in order to show how nurses fit into the non-health care oriented daytime dramas.

General Hospital premiered April 1, 1963 on ABC. The background for the series has been a large hospital in Port Charles, Anywhere U.S.A., especially the seventh floor, Internal Medicine, where the lives and careers of many nurses, doctors, and their family and friends, meet in front of the nursing station and elevator. When the series began, attention focused upon the current crises of a group of doctors and nurses who would form the nucleus of this long-running soap opera, and by 1979, after numerous marriages, divorces, rapes, murders, and betrayals, the younger generation became the focus.

The entire dramatic conflict of such daytime series as *General Hospital* is predicated upon the complications arising from the search for true love. "True love" must describe the deep, eternal love between two characters, from whom no amount of distraction can shake their single-minded devotion to each other. Murder, rape, fornication, adultery, seduction, kidnapping, lying, cheating, stealing, or marriage to another may cloud one of the lover's judgment for a time, but never for long. In addition to this eternal, unchanging dimension of true love, the lovers themselves must be "good people." The romance and/or marriage between a good woman and a bad man or vice versa can never be true love. Thus, *General Hospital*'s Rick and Monica's long-standing sexual/romantic involvement never acquired the sympathy invoking quality of true love, because Monica was a conniving, scheming woman. Lesley's marriage to Cameron Faulkner never convinced the viewer of its sincerity, because Lesley was a good woman and Cam an evil, manipulative, scheming, and rich man. Dr. Mark Dante, married at one time to a mentally ill woman, dallied with another woman, Rick and Jeff's sister Terri; although both Terri and Mark were good people, and the viewer was not offended by their extramarital romance, their love lacked the eternal quality. However, later on Mark fell in love with Katie Corbin, wife of a rich financier; this time, because their love was true and they were both good people (helped by Lamont Corbin's bad image), the two lovers found happiness. Perhaps the greatest example of true love to be followed through its ups and downs has been the longstanding romance between Steve Hardy and nurse Audrey March Hardy.

The worst obstacle to successful union of true lovers has always been the intervening demands of children. The only higher value than true love has been true motherhood or fatherhood. Thus, Audrey abandoned her hopes of happiness with Steve in order to be with her son Tommy. Diana Maynard Taylor repeatedly jeopardized her marriage to Peter in her obsessive concern for her child's welfare.

The health care setting and professional identification of the characters on *General Hospital* remain incidental to the show's domestic, romantic focus. Although physicians often go through professional crises—disabling physical informities, loss of objectivity, frustrated ambitions—the storyline emphasizes the personal repercussions of these professional problems. Thus, although Rick Webber struggled in his career to be named director of a new cardiac wing, the important result of these professional problems was to weaken his marriage to Lesley and make him vulnerable to another woman's wiles. Dr. Gina Lansing, an attractive female research scientist, stood at an important point in her research, but the upshot of her professional interest was that she jeopardized her marriage to Gary by putting her work before his demands. Student nurse Bobbie Spencer made her priorities clear; she wanted to catch a rich husband. Her nursing duties were often subverted to help her seek her goal.

The show does not even attempt to portray hospital life in a realistic setting. Although the series does have a medical advisor, his duties must be limited to advising the script writers on the possibilities of disease states and the actors on the pronunciation of three syllable words. In most episodes considerable action takes place in and around the nursing station of the seventh floor of a supposedly big, urban hospital. However, there is none of the hustle and bustle of activity usually associated with hospital corridors. Patients are rarely seen in the hallways, and few aides appear. A brief look at the show would suggest that *General Hospital* has about ten doctors to each patient. A 1979 episode depicted a young female car accident victim after her car went off the side of a mountain. Three physicians hovered around her in the exam room, and all three looked at X-rays. No nurse entered the picture. The victim looked pretty well for having gone off a mountaintop: her hair was neatly combed and artfully arranged around her calm, unmarred face. The only sign of medical intervention was a tube attached to her arm: The tube hung from an I.V. pole to which there was no visible bottle of I.V. solution of blood. Later, although the doctors pronounced the young woman comatose, she conveniently and articulately muttered the words "engagement ring . . . Scotty . . ." which revived a slightly dormant true love.

Shift rotation for nurses is left very sketchy; Jessie Brewer always seems to be on duty whenever real tragedy happens, no matter what time of day. Bobbie Spencer, the hot-to-trot student nurse, carries books and wears an odd blue uniform to show she is a student; otherwise she has the same duties as the other staff nurses. The nurses most often appear at the nursing station doing unidentified paper work and answering the phone. Occasionally they prepare or pick up medication. Once Jessie told Bobbie to check on the patients and make sure they were comfortable. Very little interaction between patients and nurses occurs on the screen, and very little is referred to off the screen; patient care is generally left to the physicians.

Despite the lack of realism which pervades the show, the viewer is led to believe that some of the characters are good nurses or doctors and others bad ones. Professional competence usually correlates exactly with personal values; rarely are evil persons good nurses or doctors, and vice versa. Brief character sketches of the more famous or infamous nurse characters from *General Hospital* will reveal the range of character types available.

Jessie Brewer, R.N. Jessie Brewer has assumed a quasi-matriarchal stature in the series because she was one of the original characters (always played by actress Emily McLaughlin). For sixteen years Jessie has been in and out of love, never guilty of faithlessness, and her romantic involvements have usually placed her in almost maternal roles, although she has never had a child survive infancy. During her tenure as a central character, Jessie has often given a home to young people. First she sheltered the niece and nephew of her dead brother; in 1979 she has housed student nurse Bobbie Spencer. Jessie is one of the few characters who trusted Bobbie, most of the others seeing through her sweetness to her opportunism. But Jessie always gives people the benefit of the doubt and sees their best qualities first. Jessie appears to have financial resources sufficient to maintain a comfortable standard of living, but she continues to work at the hospital as a staff nurse (sixteen years without a promotion). Other characters trust Jessie and confide in her; she is considered a top-notch professional (despite little evidence of her nursing ability) and a good friend.

Audrey March, R.N. Audrey began her nursing career after her experiences in a Vietnamese orphanage. Clearly Audrey's maternal instincts and her overwhelming love of children led her into nursing. She often places the welfare of others before her own fulfillment. She placed her love of Steve Hardy after her desire for her son's welfare; she preferred to attempt a loveless marriage with Tom Baldwin rather than jeopardize her child's home. Audrey has usually been a self-confident character; however, after her disastrous marriage to James Hobart, she attempted suicide. She married the man out of pity (a surgeon, he lost the use of his hands) and tried relentlessly to help him adjust to his decreased professional capacity; her pity turned the man sour, and he eventually rejected her for another woman. One way out of her emotional depression and loss of self-confidence was provided by Steve Hardy. In addition to his personal support, he appointed Audrey the supervisor of student nursing in order to give her a new lease on life. (There was no evidence that Audrey had had any experience in nursing education.) Audrey and Steve have finally remarried, but the course of their marriage has not always been smooth. In 1979, during an epidemic of Lassa fever in General Hospital, Steve Hardy hovered near death. Although Audrey had promised Steve never to reveal a closely guarded secret, in the anguish and concern at Steve's imminent death she told Jeff Webber that he was, in fact, Steve Hardy's natural son. Audrey felt that Jeff ought to know his real father, especially as his real father was dying. Audrey's maternal motives were, unfortunately, not well received. Jeff ran away from Port Charles, in the throes of an anguished identity crisis, and Steve Hardy, upon his recovery, blamed Audrey for breaking a confidence and ruining Jeff's life.

Diana Maynard Taylor. Diana (in 1980 played by Brooke Bundy) began life in Port Charles as a waitress in the restaurant where Dr. Phil Brewer worked incognito as a dishwasher. At some point in the past sixteen years, during which time Diana had two out-of-wedlock pregnancies, rocky marriages, and one murder charge, she became a professional nurse. Her problems have centered upon her jealousy of her husband and her concern for her children. After losing her two natural-born children, she developed fanatical ideas about safeguarding her remaining, adopted son. For all her self-sacrificing and loving qualities, Diana remains the series' least stable character.

Bobbie Spencer. Bobbie is not a good woman. She comes from a distant city and reveals little about her past, for good reason since she worked as a call girl in Florida before coming to Port Charles and entering nursing school. Her brother Luke, who owns a discotheque controlled by organized crime, helps his little sister when he can; for example, he will order his bartender to slip drugs into the drinks of Bobbie's friends upon request. In early 1980 Bobbie's main goal in life is to catch a rich husband and she will stop at nothing to attain her purpose. For quite some time Bobbie has felt that Scotty Baldwin, stepson of wealthy attorney Lee Baldwin and soon to be graduated law student, would be the perfect candidate. Unfortunately for Bobbie, Scotty has been enamored of Laura for many years. Bobbie lies, cheats, spreads rumors, and endangers the well-being of others. Other nurses repeatedly chide Bobbie about gossiping with patients. However, few of the regular characters suspect the extent of Bobbie's selfishness; she always appears to be so nice and sweet. Jessie has taken the girl into her home. Rick Webber and Lesley suspected Bobbie's intentions when she tried to set Laura up as a violent and vicious girl in order to have her sent to reform school. The other nurses appear to be sober, serious individuals, but Bobbie wears elaborate makeup and a full, sexy hairdo; her appearance is both inappropriate to her position as a nursing student and very unprofessional looking; off duty her wardrobe, usually suggestive and flamboyant, reflects her manhunting intentions. (Of course her arch enemy, Laura, the good woman, wears the clothing of a high school senior and exudes naivete, even after having had a couple of torrid affairs and committing murder.)

Dorrie Fleming, R.N. Dorrie (another staff nurse on Jessie's floor) is an attractive, young English woman who plays a limited role. She appers to be a basically good woman and therefore a good nurse. She often reminds Bobbie of her nursing duties, namely the need to keep her mouth shut about the patients' problems.

In the past, nurse characters have contributed enormously to the storyline, but for one reason or another the characters were discontinued. Lucille March, R.N. (Lucille Wall) was the sister of Audrey and head nurse for many years; she too was a mother figure with no romantic involvements but at least one child who returned to Port Charles as a nurse. Lucille was more sharp-tongued than was Jessie, and she ran a tighter ship on the seventh floor; but in general, she was perceived as a sympathetic character. For several months or years Janie Dawson, R.N. (Shelley Hiatt) received quite a bit of attention because of her troubled marriage to physician Dr. Howard Dawson. Janie wanted a family and Howie did not. To prove his point, he had a vasectomy. Some time later Janie and Howie had a baby, after overcoming their disagreements and, presumably, the effects of a vasectomy. Augusta McLeod (Judith McConnell) was a nurse character introduced to dissolve the Taylors' marriage; she seduced Peter Taylor, became pregnant, and killed Phil Brewer. Despite Augusta's determination to snare Peter, she did not want to do so on the basis of pity; because Phil threatened to reveal her pregnancy to Peter, she murdered him. Thus, Augusta's pride outweighed her desire to break up the Taylor's marriage.

The main qualities valued by characters on *General Hospital* and revealed by major nurse characters are maternal concern and self-sacrifice. This brief review also suggests that nurses frequently become involved in adulterous relationships and have illegitimate children. This impression is somewhat corrected by the fact that the other major female characters, doctors and non-professionals, also have irregular romantic and marital relationships. Furthermore, most of the nurse characters are perceived as sympathetic, positive women who suffer for the sake of higher motives: true love or motherhood. Five rapes within loveless marriages also explain the high incidence of children born to nurses and female doctors. Thus, through no fault of their own, female characters find themselves pregnant by the wrong man in terms of the true love index. Except for Monica and Bobbie, the remaining regular female characters, mostly nurses, never knowingly enter into adulterous liaisons. Despite the seemingly huge number of out-of-wedlock children and adulterous relationships, the female protagonists rarely appear promiscuous or bad.

The male characters also remain surprisingly upstanding and honest in their reputations despite their myriad involvements and romances, although one or two bad characters can taint many good characters. Thus, evil actions are usually attributable to a very few characters.

General Hospital does not focus very much on the professional ambitions of nurses. On the other hand, the image of nursing emerges rather positively in this series. For the most part nurse characters are good, honest women who enjoy their work and who suffer personal trauma through no fault of their own or through their own acts of self-sacrifice. Nurses are not held in less regard than are physicians. The female physician characters do perhaps appear more glamorous and sophisticated than their nursing counterparts, but the personal lives of all the characters on the show are not distinguished on the basis of professional identification. A doctor would be as likely as would a nurse to be an adulterer, an unwed mother, or a murderer. Most of the nurses do not appear to work for money; that is, they have other means of financial support. Thus nurses do not appear to be in a lower class than are doctors; the intermarriage between doctors and nurses from differing backgrounds reinforces the assumption of social equality.

The viewers' impression of any nurse character is absolutely related to the character's personal qualities rather than to his or her professional skills or experience. Except for such notable villainess types as Bobbie Spencer, the nurses in *General Hospital* display very generous, loving natures. Jessie, Audrey, Diana, and Dorrie nearly always put the needs of others before their own; often their self-sacrifice causes them great suffering and grief. But the intentions and motives of most of these nurse characters are always honorable and kind. The loyal viewer of *General Hospital* would have to conclude that while nursing may possibly harbor such scheming and ambitious women as Bobbie Spencer, the typical nurse represents an admirable mixture of noble idealism and human frailties. Yet, in the last analysis, the image of nursing is probably very little affected by the nurse characters who come and go on *General Hospital*. These characters (like the female physicians) are first and foremost women, wives, mothers, lovers, and only secondarily nurses.

The second major health care soap opera, *The Doctors,* premiered on NBC April 1, 1963, the same day as did *General Hospital* on ABC, both as daytime attempts to enter the newly popular health care drama trend. The series began as a one-story-a-week drama, but after about a year it was transformed into a continuing serial. *The Doctors* has never had tent-pole characters, although the duos of Matt and Maggie Powers and Steve and Carolee Aldrich have given, over a period of time, a sense of stability and continuity to the series.

Nurses and nursing play a much less important role in *The Doctors* than they do in *General Hospital;* since the series' inception, the emphasis has been on the personal interactions of male and female doctors with occasional romantic forays into the world beyond medicine. The only recurrent, important nurse character has been Carolee Simpson Aldrich, whose marriage to Dr. Steven Aldrich has often been the source of much dramatic conflict. Carolee's most important personality traits are her maternal instincts, her role as counselor and advisor to friends, and her sincerity and devotion to her family; however, despite Carolee's preoccupation with personal problems, she has never neglected her career as a nurse.

More than any nurse character on *General Hospital,* the major nurse character on *The Doctors* has evolved not only personally but also professionally. When the program began, Carolee was a staff nurse who seemed especially at the beck and call of Dr. Matt Powers. After her marriage to Steve, Carolee kept working—even with a house full of children—and she became the director of nursing of the supposedly large Hope Memorial Hospital. Often she was seen in street clothing while at work, to emphasize her changed occupation. At one point in the narrative Carolee began experiencing an identity crisis in which she questioned her role in life; part of her crisis involved her career and she explored other job opportunities. In 1979 Carolee began training herself as a nurse–midwife; in a dramatic episode about the birth of Greta and Billy's child, Carolee supervised the birth in very unfavorable circumstances. Apparently, Carolee also offered advice and counseling to Billy and Greta about the birth process and about their lives as well. Sometime thereafter Carolee took up a new position in the hospital which allowed licensed nurse–midwives to perform prenatal examinations. Carolee's character has reflected, to some extent, the changing opportunities for nurses since the early 1960s when the series began.

Compared to the female physicians, Carolee is portrayed as less glamorous and sophisticated. Much was made of Carolee's humble background and plain looks, and when Steve's wealthy mother heard of the marriage, she wanted Steve to return to his marriage with the more suitable Dr. Ann Larimer. Again, as in *General Hospital,* nurse characters are not presented as socially or even intellectually inferior to the doctors. The tangled web of romantic relationships has often bound doctor to nurse, doctor to doctor, doctor to cabaret singer, doctor to lab assistant, and so on.

On the basis of visual evidence, *The Doctors* is more realistic than *General Hospital*. Two 1980 scenes of emergency care indicated *The Doctors'* higher standard of realism. In *General Hospital* a young girl was rushed into the emergency room after driving off the top of a mountain. There was not a scratch on her, and she was very well groomed. She was examined in an almost empty treatment room, where three M.D.s examined her X-rays; no other personnel were in evidence. The girl's only treatment was an unconvincing I.V. On *The Doctors*, however, Steve and Carolee's son Billy was rushed into the emergency room following a motorcycle accident. It was busy and frantic; the boy looked as if he had been in a wreck and sported convincing, seeping bandages and tubing. In the intensive care unit, he was surrounded by all the appropriate blinking and bleeping equipment and was attended by a special nurse.

Of course both series subordinate professional issues to personal ones; Carolee's proposed career change some seasons back was important because of the strain it placed on her marriage rather than because it represented a professional issue for her. Carolee's nurse–midwifery skills have been important to the story because they have brought her deeply into the personal problems of her son and his girlfriend Greta. Steve and Carolee have often had disagreements on professional matters, usually regarding the effect that job pressures or changes in working situations would have on their family life.

Although viewers see fewer nurses in *The Doctors* than in *General Hospital*, the image of nursing is stronger and more positive in the former. The character of Carolee has always presented the duties and responsibilities of her nursing position with a certain care and detail. In addition, in 1980 the story focused on some very real problems facing hospital nurses who work in understaffed institutions. The nurses on *General Hospital* have rarely been developed professionally.

Nurse characters in other soap operas follow these same established patterns. The good nurse characters are always extremely sympathetic women who suffer a variety of personal problems, usually romantic in nature. Also, these good nurses generally reveal a very strong maternal instinct and serve as mother figures both to their own children and to others in search of comfort. An examination of two nurse characters, in non-health care soap operas, supports these ideas.

Another World, which premiered in 1964, has revolved around the Matthews, an affluent, middle-class family composed of father Jim, an accountant, mother Mary, a housewife, and their three children: Pat, a pretty but troubled young woman, Alice, a pretty young nurse, and Russ, a young doctor. Young Alice (Jacqueline Courtney) who radiated innocence, purity, and kindness, at first studied art but later changed her mind and became a nurse. Stephen Frame, a handsome local businessman, fell in love with beautiful Alice; the story of their romance was the focal point for almost the first decade of the series' life, until the actor who played Steve Frame left the show in 1975. The main complication in Alice and Steve's love turned out to be Alice's sister-in-law Rachel, who decided that Steve Frame was really the man for her.

Alice worked at the hospital as a nurse and gradually fell in love with Steve. After her marriage, Alice quit her work as a nurse in order to live in the beautiful home that Steve had built for her; her entire life revolved around her husband, and the knowledge (false, as it was planted by Rachel) that he was involved with Rachel destroyed her self-confidence. She ran away to New York where she got a job as a private nurse–companion to a boy with a cardiac defect. Eventually, of course, she returned to her family and continued to work in the hospital, as if to protect herself from the total emotional dependence upon her husband that she experienced before. Yet her true goal was to give Steven a child of their own. When at long last she became pregnant, she quit her job; unfortunately, she lost the baby in an accident. As a result of this, the knowledge that she could never have children, and Steve's legal problems, Alice nearly lost her mind and entered a sanatorium for several weeks. Though well again, Alice has never returned to nursing, although her adopted daughter Sally has decided to become a nurse.

Another World has never had an abundance of nurses and physicians, but there are always enough to keep the hospital background a recurrent feature. Alice's brother Russ has been the most important physician character throughout the series, with two other physician characters entering the story in 1979.

Nursing has never been an important focus for this series, but because the character of Alice was made to be a nurse, the implications of her nursing identification must be considered. For years, Alice was the show's true heroine; she was not only beautiful and pure but concerned about others. She was presented as the absolute antithesis of Rachel, a beautiful but selfish and self-centered bitch. Rachel never tried to do anything for others; she never sought to work at a job; she preferred to be supported in style by wealthy men. Alice, on the other hand, who could expect a life of leisure, given her upperclass standing, dedicated herself to nursing, a job which allowed her to concentrate on helping others. Given the comparison between Alice's goodness and Rachel's evil, the nursing profession emerged as a sign of moral superiority and virtuous living.

The technical side of nursing, and medicine for that matter, never mattered very much to the storyline of the show. When Alice went off to New York, she worked as a nurse–companion to a boy with cardiac problems; however, nothing ever transpired to indicate that the boy needed a registered nurse. Mainly Alice provided the mother love sorely missed by the boy, whose own mother was a jet set traveller, never at home. Just as unrealistically, it turned out that the only physician who could correct the boy's problem was Russ Matthews, Alice's brother, who worked in Bay City; no doctor in New York could handle the operation. Alice also became involved in a one-sided romance with the boy's father, an important international journalist. When she returned to nursing after her second marriage to Steve, the focus of her professional and personal life turned upon her desire for a child. After she miscarried her own baby, she discovered an orphan in the hospital whom she decided to adopt. Again, after Steve's death and her adoption of the child, she quit nursing. Thus, nursing has never seemed very important to Alice; she repeatedly fell back on her nursing to provide her with outlets for her maternal concerns and her general empathy for others, but she never concentrated on her professional career. Like so many soap opera heroines, Alice's priorities included motherhood and family responsibilities. Unlike the nurse-heroines of *General Hospital* and *The Doctors,* Alice had displayed no long-term interest in her professional identification. Ruth Brent Martin (Mary Fickett), another nurse character in a non-health care soap opera, *All My Children,* has revealed a more permanent commitment to nursing than has Alice.

All My Children, created in 1970, revolved around two families in fictional Pine Valley: the wealthy Tyler clan and the affluent Martin family, both families having numerous nurses and physicians related by either blood or marriage. The only apparently stable marriage in this story has been Dr. Joe Martin and his wife Ruth Martin; even they had some rough moments when Ruth found herself attracted to a younger man. Despite this brief interlude, Joe and Ruth have had a solid marriage; recently, they had their first child together, Joseph Henry.

Ruth Martin can be compared to Jessie Brewer *(General Hospital)* and Carolee Aldrich *(The Doctors)* in terms of her character's role and personality. Ruth is essentially a mother figure and friend to the troubled members of Pine Valley. Since she and her husband have between them several grown children—Tara, Jeff, and Phil—they are frequently embroiled in the more turbulent romantic upheavals of the younger generation. Ruth constantly worries about the safety and happiness of her children. Children have always been important to Ruth. She adopted her sister's illegitimate son Phil, has served as a loving stepmother to her husband Joe's two children, has adopted Tad, the son of the now convicted man who raped and assaulted her, and just recently has given birth to her first natural child, complicated by fears about her age. Through all her domestic problems, Ruth has continued to work as a nurse at the hospital. There she can also serve as a sympathetic friend and counsellor to the other troubled mothers of the Pine Valley community. Ruth stands as the maternal counterweight to Phoebe Tyler, female head of Pine Valley's leading family who seeks only to keep up appearances and pursue the glittery social whirl. Phoebe cares not a scrap for true love or people's real worth. She is taken in by appearances. Ruth, on the other hand, seeks to give support to her family and friends, and she loyally stands by them through all their misfortunes. Ruth offers sympathy but does not try to interfere in others' lives. Furthermore, Ruth works as a nurse, a sign of her earnest nature and desire to help others.

Ruth has frequently held aloft the standard of decency and justice in the show. Creator Agnes Nixon used the show in its early months as a vehicle to express anti-Vietnam war sentiments. When Phil Brent was drafted and presumed killed, Ruth gave a moving mother's testimonial against the war and won a daytime Emmy as a result of her role. *All My Children* has not continued to promote political opinions, but Ruth has continued to be a character who experiences many events, both cruel and joyous, much discussed in women's magazines these days. She was raped and recovered, although presumably she went through all sorts of emotional crises as a result. In 1979 she delivered a late-in-life baby and had to go through all the agonies of worry about the baby's health and normalcy. Some of her friends, namely Phoebe, advised her to have an abortion, and Ruth had to fully consider her own feelings on the subject; she decided against it at any price.

Ruth's nursing identification has always provided her with an outlet for her charity and concern, although she has always had plenty to do for the members of her immediate family. The fact that she has continued to work as a nurse through all her problems suggests to the viewer that nursing is very important to this character. If Ruth rarely performs skilled nursing tasks on the show and never really talks about her feelings about her profession, the audience must assume that she is very dedicated to have stayed with her work for so long.

The other nurse characters to be featured on *All My Children* have generally displayed very positive personal characteristics. Sweet nurse Mary Kennicott who married Dr. Jeff Martin was generally perceived as a wonderful young woman, full of love for her husband. The only cloud on her horizon was the fact that she could not bear children, an extremely heavy burden for soap opera females to bear. However, she was brutally murdered, leading to her subsequent canonization by friends who recall her. Perhaps her younger sister Betsy is meant to step into her role. Nurse Caroline, the black woman who is married to Dr. Frank Grant, has been very troubled. She loves her husband very much, but knows that his love for her is not as great. She knows that Frank wants a child and desperately wants to give him one, to no avail. She is very jealous of his continuing interest in his ex-wife Nancy, and their marriage suffers as a result of Caroline's jealousy and unhappiness that she is not pregnant. However, Caroline's virtues seem to outweigh her vices, and she decides to abandon the field to her husband and Nancy. She accepts the fact that she could not hold onto her husband if he really still loves another woman. The only other nurse to appear, albeit infrequently, is the scheming and ambitious Sybil who has tried to capture handsome Dr. Cliff Warner; Cliff loves Nina, but Sybil does not care about anything but her own gratification. The overall image of nursing on *All My Children* would have to be judged positive because the good nurse characters heavily outweigh the bad nurse characters.

In fact, in the entire world of daytime drama, the profession of nursing is generally regarded as a worthy and fitting occupation for good, strong, maternal women who not only serve their families but also seek to help others. The range of nurse characters is rather limited in the soap opera world. The dominant nurse type is an empathetic, middle-aged, attractive woman who serves as a mother figure within her familial and professional roles. Jessie Brewer, Audrey March Hardy, Carolee Aldrich, and Ruth Martin personify this important image. These women work as nurses because they obviously feel a commitment to their profession—obvious because they continue to work without needing the money. Nursing is but a professional mirror for their familial role; in other words, their work and family life are totally integrated. Only Carolee has shown problems in coping with both career and family, but she has managed to overcome obstacles to her professional growth. It is difficult to imagine an occupation better suited for these soap opera heroines than nursing. Not only does nursing allow them to interact in the emotionally charged world of the hospital, but it also allows them to extend their maternal sympathies and counselling skills to strangers.

There is a younger nurse type frequently found in daytime drama; she is generally a beautiful, kind, young woman who becomes involved in all sorts of romantic complications and maternal situations. Alice Matthews of *Another World,* Caroline and Mary of *All My Children,* and M. J. Match of *The Doctors* have all experienced true love, heartache, and a yearning for children, often thwarted by their inability to bear children. Again, nursing seems the natural professional identification for these noble and long-suffering young women.

A distinct but important minority of soap opera nurses are the scheming, conniving bitches who often undermine the happiness of the truly deserving heroines. Sybil of *All My Children,* doomed Kathy Ryker of *The Doctors,* and, of course, Bobbie Spencer of *General Hospital* use their nursing role to further their selfish schemes. However, no matter to what depths they descend in their dirty work, they rarely bring dishonor to their profession. For the most part they aim their barbs at their healthy colleagues, and they seem to competently perform their duties. In addition, the minimal attention to any nurse's specific professional role ameliorates any viewer reaction to the image of the nursing profession.

Nurse characters in daytime drama, and, for that matter, all the female characters, reveal the same set of values and beliefs. With the exception of the few schemers and villainesses, soap opera women hope for romantic love with its base in a solid marriage. Furthermore, these women all yearn for children, and once mothers, they sacrifice all their personal desires to their child's welfare. Often they allow themselves to be exploited by a husband whom they do not love in their attempt to provide a secure home for their children. They often go insane at the thought of being unable to have children or in the aftermath of losing a child. The most revered and positive nurse characters also serve as mothers and counsellors to other members of their community. Jessie Brewer, Carolee, and Ruth do not limit their self-sacrificing efforts to blood kin. Yet, if leaders of the feminist movement in America were to scorn these fictional women for their stereotypic and traditional views on marriage and children, it would be misplaced scorn. The female characters in daytime drama, as seen in the professional nurse characters, offer one of the few examples of women who not only work at a profession over an extended period of time but also have to juggle their family duties and cope with emotional problems all the while. All the memorable prime-time nurses—Consuelo, Dixie, Liz Thorpe, Hot Lips, and others—have always been single women, it being the story's odd assumption that somehow nursing and family life were incompatible. The unrealistic storylines of soap operas must be balanced by the very realistic presentation of contemporary social arrangements. In fact, a huge percentage of middle-class mothers and wives work for a living; a large number of professional, working nurses are married and have families. Only the world of soap opera has attempted to dramatize the lives of ordinary, middle-class women. In general daytime drama society's nurse characters emerge as influential women and greatly respected members of their communities. These nurse characters do not exist in a vacuum, nor do they live in the wake of a powerful physician like the prime-time nurses. Rather they have full community and family relationships. The producers and creators of nighttime programming could profit from looking at the rich world of daytime serials.

10
Perspectives on the Image of Nursing on Television

Since the 1950s nurse characters have appeared in a wide variety of television shows. The dramatic, comedic, public service, and action–adventure series discussed in the preceding chapters having provided hundreds of nurse characters revealed only a handful of stereotypes that have recurred throughout the years. A description of some of these common stereotypes reveals that more often than not nurse characters serve some plot function for the writers, either by providing a quick laugh or by providing an unsympathetic foil to the hero. None of these categories is exclusive of the others; together they provide a composite of the fictional television nurse. A brief survey of these character types quickly exhausts the manner in which nurses have usually been portrayed.

One stereotype is the nurse as a stern disciplinarian, usually middle-aged or older, who exacts unquestioning obedience from both her patients and her subordinates. Usually the nurse represented high standards, rigorously applied, but frequently she was seen lacking in sympathy and compassion. To her, good nursing signified neatly made beds and well arranged schedules. Very often this type of nurse was used as a foil to the doctor-hero because her regulation abiding regime threatened to obstruct the doctor's altruistic and compassionate behavior. For example, on *Medical Center* a nurse called Ernestine Hull (a name which conjures up a repressed spinster) vigorously objected to Joe Gannon's demands on her nursing staff because he evaded the proper channels and expected too much while she resented his unorthodox handling of a patient. Nurse Hatch on *The Bold Ones* complained about the young doctors' frivolous disregard of her supply system and worried terribly over the number of aspirin pills for which she could

---

References to awards and award shows throughout this chapter are from Kaplan, Mike (ed.). *Variety international show business reference.* New York: Garland Publishing, Inc., 1981, pp. 773–915.

not account. An emergency room nurse on *Quincy, M.E.* contributed to the acquittal of a rapist because of her inability to tolerate a change in her established procedures. An unfeeling nurse in a *Dr. Kildare* episode refused to admit a patient in need of care because the patient did not meet the standard bureaucratic qualifications for admission to the institution; the patient died as a result of the nurse's action. Elements of Hot Lips' character in *M*A*S*H* have been built upon the viewer's automatic and negative response to an authoritarian nursing figure. Sometimes these law abiding and demanding nurses have been introduced as purely comic elements designed to evoke the great guffaw; for example the head nurse character of *The Nurses* was named Major Charlotte Hinkley but called "Big Momma," or "B.M." by her less-than-admiring staff.

The not so subtle message being broadcast about nursing was that for nurses to advance in their profession, they had to subordinate all human emotions to a mechanical insistence upon observation of rules and regulations. In addition, the stern disciplinarian view of the nurse indicated that nurses have been unable to develop much in the way of critical faculties; they follow rules because they cannot think for themselves.

Nursing students, candy-stripers, and recently graduated nurses have often been presented as very naive and clumsy rookies who need constant supervision to keep them from harming their patients. Gail Lucas of *The Nurses,* although purportedly an altruistic, idealistic, energetic, and promising young nurse, very often made glaring errors and misjudgments in her work. Miss Hakopian in *Dr. Hudson's Secret Journal*, a very young nurse, appeared very girlish and forgot her basic duties and responsibilities when she was taken with a romantic crush or involved in some private project. Harriet Barnes, "The Scarlet Woman in White" on *Hennessey,* displayed great naivete and immaturity despite her attempts to play the femme fatale. These nurses frequently developed personal problems with which they could not cope; their inability to handle their own problems brought them into the omnipotent range of the physician-heroes. Drs. Jim Kildare, Ben Casey, and Joe Gannon often found distraught young nurses in need of guidance or rescue. The damage to the image of nursing in these presentations of immature students was limited, in that usually the audience would take into account the troubled nurse's age and lack of experience. As a point of comparison, medical students in television drama and comedy, although frequently presented as untested or overconfident, have rarely emerged as silly or dependent. Perhaps the worst feature of these presentations of rookie nurses has been the fact that nursing supervisors or teachers have rarely been used to help the young nurse with her problem. With the exception of *The Nurses,* almost all rookie nurses have been rescued or reformed through the offices of a physician character. The presence of disaster-prone young nurses, without the countervailing presence of experienced and helping older nurses, placed the nursing profession in a position of being the ward of the medical profession.

The writers of health care drama have often resorted to using nurse characters as victims in need of rescue, almost always by a physician character: nurses as the victims of rape; unmarried, pregnant nurses; nurses jilted by their husbands or boyfriends; nurses exploited because of their compassion or their naivete; alcoholic nurses. Nurse Lydia Mitchell on *Ben Casey* was a middle-aged, lonely divorcee who found herself pregnant by a man unable to marry her. Student nurse Diana on *Medical Center* allowed her husband to use her to support him. Nurse Pamela on *The Lazarus Syndrome,* raped by an unknown assailant, found it difficult to recover her emotional stability without the help of a doctor friend. Although nurses as victims cannot be said to share any particular traits other than bad luck, the recurrent use of nurses as victims suggests to the viewer that nurses are especially powerless to direct their lives or to change their fate.

In the last decade nurse characters have frequently been used as objects of sexual attention. Especially in the 1970s with the relaxation of network censorship, nurse characters have been used for a variety of purposes dependent upon their sexual attractiveness, usually in a comic vein. The linen closet joke is apparently de rigueur for all contemporary drama or comedy involving hospital life. Whether or not nurses are even present on the screen, they are often referred to in passing as being readily available for a sexual tryst in the linen closet, supply room, or other available dark corner. In the early years of *M*A*S*H*, the physicians often made such remarks or appeared in active pursuit of a willing nurse. Suspicious wives have often accused their physician husbands of having affairs with nurses. When such passing remarks have not been sufficient to establish the sexual tension for some series, the writers resort to introducing attractive nurse characters into the background or into the main action. The shapely nurses aboard the submarine on *Operation Petticoat*, most of the nurses at the M.A.S.H. 4077, the nurses attendant at the air force base of the *Black Sheep Squadron,* nurse Rhonda of *A.E.S. Hudson St.,* or nurse Amanda of *Temperature's Rising* existed solely for the provision of sexual interest. Feminist viewers might find the presentation of these nurse characters offensive for the simple reason that the nurses were clearly exploited for their instant sexual appeal. The damage to the image of nursing goes beyond mere disaffection for the playboy philosophy inherent in the roles. The use of nurses as objects of sexual attention implies that the profession itself is something of a sideline for the young woman portrayed. Nurses are not only promiscuous but are also willing to walk away from their responsibilities for a few passionate moments in the linen closet. The presence of the gorgeous nurses in non-health care oriented military situations, in *Black Sheep* and *Operation Petticoat,* suggests that in wartime nurses were so plentiful and dispensable that the Army or Navy could allow them to frolic for years as mascots of some isolated unit. *M*A*S*H* has made an obvious and successful effort to undo the demeaning sexual stereotypes of the nurses from its first few seasons, but unfortunately, the new *M*A*S*H* has found no imitators; its second cousin,

Trapper John, introduced in the 1979–1980 season, hewed to the old line with the inclusion of a shapely blonde nurse named Ripples.

An antecedent of the sexually exploited nurse character common to the 1970s is the nurse as girlfriend of the hero. Just as nurse characters are used today for sexual interest, young and attractive nurse characters appeared in the role of girlfriend in the 1950s and 1960s. These nurses again performed few nursing tasks; mainly they served as secondary characters in non-professional roles. Miss Nancy Remington of *Mr. Peepers,* a school nurse, was Mr. Peeper's girlfriend for two seasons and married him in the third year. Martha Hale of *Hennessey* had a longer courtship with Chick, but ended up marrying her Navy doctor at the end of the series' three year run. Elements of Julia's character in *Julia* followed this romantic presentation of the nurse. Of course Zoe Lawton, Dr. Kildare's girlfriend in that series' final year, was introduced solely to allow the hero to have an adoring romantic sidekick readily available. Many one-time-only nurse characters have served this function in all the health care dramas. The image of the nursing profession gleaned from these nurse–girlfriends is much more sympathetic and positive than that emerging from the more sexually explicit characterizations. At least, the nurse–girlfriends appear to be morally upright and worthy of a hero's interest. However, as in the use of nurses as sexual objects, the use of nurses as simple romantic partners dulls the viewers' perceptions of nursing as a career and leads to the belief that nursing is a temporary occupation for young women who will quit once they have found their man.

Perhaps the most common stereotype of the nurse on television has been the all-around doctor's helper, the Girl Friday who has devoted her life to the service of a single physician. The presentation of nursing as an outlet for maternal feelings has been a well established route to the creation of a sympathetic nurse. Consuelo Lopez of *Marcus Welby* comes to mind as the most consistently maternal of all regular nurse characters, although she herself did not have any children. Many other nurse characters have brought their motherly urges to their nursing work. Often Liz Thorpe of *The Nurses* found herself playing mother hen to her students or instead playing tigress mother for unfortunate patients. Hannah Yarby and Julia Baker of *Julia* both served in maternal roles; Hannah played a grandmotherly role in relationship to Julia and her son, and Julia's relationship to her son was a very strong component of her character. Soap opera nurses have frequently complicated their own lives because of their overwhelming devotion to their own or someone else's children. Jessie Brewer, Audrey Hardy, and Diana Maynard Taylor of *General Hospital* all mixed strong maternal motives with their nursing identification. Carolee Simpson Aldrich of *The Doctors* demonstrated strong maternal feelings for both her own children and for the unfortunate patients that occasionally came her way. *Medic*'s Clara Mary Gallegher, an over-sixty nurse who had lost her only child, devoted herself to the comfort of her patients—new mothers and their babies; in her finest hour, she sacrificed her own retirement travel plans in order to give shelter to a homeless new mother and her infant. The image of nursing derived from the myriad nurse mothers can only be judged positive; but the recurrent identification of nursing with motherhood carries the very clear message that good nursing depends not upon education, not upon intelligence, not upon skill. Good nursing is an inborn trait; either a woman is by nature self-sacrificing and maternal, or she is not. If she is not, no amount of training can make her a worthy nurse. The episode of *Marcus Welby* in which an older sister, generous and loving by nature, was an excellent nurse and a younger sister who received outstanding marks in nursing school was a poor nurse because she lacked the innate motherly drive to put the needs of others first made this notion explicit. By lulling viewers into believing that good nurses are simply motherly women in white, the profession's claim to being an academic discipline on the same footing as medicine and other professions is undercut.

All the nameless television nurses seen scurrying down hallways with charts, carts, or stretchers fall into the category of handmaidens. As a means of establishing realistic backgrounds, producers always use nurse characters in the background of health care series' hospital settings. These nurses rarely address a physician or speak unless spoken to. Their duties are only indirectly related to patient care. Nurses deliver medicine and food, monitor equipment, make notations in charts, push wheelchairs and carts, answer the phones, file things at the nursing station, and take orders from doctors. They never appear to be teaching their patients or talking with them, except perhaps in light conversation. They never appear to be discussing patient care with other nurses or to be involved in developing nursing care plans for the patients. Frequently these handmaiden nurses have had minor continuing roles on long-running doctor shows. The colorless Miss Wills of *Ben Casey* appeared in every episode for five years; the viewer never learned her first name or anything about her personal life. She existed for the sole purpose of taking direct orders from Ben or Dr. Zorba, for answering the phone, and for delivering messages. Three nurses on *Medical Center,* Nurse Chambers, Nurse Holmy and Nurse Wilcox, appeared in almost all the shows; their parts were completely interchangeable. Again, their first names were unknown. The good doctors of *Medical Center* even admitted that nurses were a lot like the equipment; as long as they worked, one tended not to notice them. The overwhelming impression of the work of hospital nurses on television has been that they are valuable to patients only insofar as they carry out the doctor's orders. Unless they put a cool hand on the occasionally fevered brow, they provide no other nursing service to the patient. Beyond this indirect service to the patients, nurses serve mainly as a clearinghouse for information. They answer the phone and deliver messages to busy doctors. They stand and wait for the doctor to tell them to do something. They keep files of information at hand in order to answer doctors' inquiries. The frequency and consistency of the handmaiden nurses is perhaps the most damaging of all television images of nursing. Because their presence is unquestioned and unexamined, the viewer tends to accept at face value the limited nature of their role in the hospital, and the true nature of nursing in the modern hospital is eroded. These nurse characters give no evidence as to the existence of a nursing profession with independent standards and a separate administrative structure. Good nurses are judged by the doctors and not by their peers.

When one reviews the three decades of television broadcasting in search of developments or trends in the presentation of the nursing profession, it is soon obvious that there has been little development. The nursing profession per se is presented to the television audience of the 1980s in much the same manner as it was shown in 1950, despite revolutionary changes in the profession itself. Furthermore, the attributes of quality nursing care, that is, those areas in which nurses are acknowledged as valuable, have not changed or expanded. Good nursing in the 1970s still means to the producers and writers the same womanly treasurehouse of virtue identified in the 1950s: Nurses are compassionate, self-sacrificing, gentle, and motherly. Most of the stereotypic presentations of nurses discussed above began in the 1950s. (Actually these stereotypes began in earlier works of fiction, film, and radio.) Authoritarian and rigid nurses appeared in *Medic, Dr. Kildare, The Nurses, The Bold Ones, Medical Center,* and most recently in *Trapper John.* Naive nursing students have been around as long as health care drama, and the nurse as the epitome of mother love has been explicitly recognized in many shows, from *Medic*'s Clara Mary Gallagher to *Marcus Welby*'s Consuelo Lopez. The Girl Friday nurse perhaps began with *Dr. Hudson's Secret Journal* but has since been repeatedly seen, most recently in "Starch" of *Trapper John.*

The physical appearance of nurses on television has changed very little in thirty years. The typical nurse on television in the 1950s wore a longsleeved, starched, white cotton uniform, cap, white stockings, and white duty shoes. The typical nurse shown on television in the 1970s was almost identical, although the uniform dress usually appeared to be shortsleeved and made from a synthetic material. Some few nurses wore white pantsuits, but almost all of them still wore their nursing caps. The fact that hospitals have drastically changed their requirements for nursing uniforms (in some places nurses do not need to wear the traditional uniform at all) has never been shown on television. The only nurse characters not usually shown in traditional white have been those assigned to military units; in these cases the producers have opted for the sexier look of t-shirts and well-fitted fatigue pants.

The work done by television nurses in hospital settings has not changed at all since the beginning of health care drama on television. Nurses still function as handmaidens, standing behind a nursing station and answering the phone, delivering phone messages to busy physicians, or filing cards. When nurses leave the safety of their nursing station, they almost always seem to have some mobile object to move with them: a drug cart, a wheelchair, a gurney, an I.V. pole. It is as if nursing personnel must always be associated with some mechanical device needed for a patient's care or comfort. At the very least a nurse must carry a chart or a tray. These ubiquitous props, noted in all television presentations of the work of the professional nurse, emphasize that the nurse is being used as the instrument needed to operate machinery or monitor equipment or administer drugs ordered by the physician.

The work of nurses in an office setting has also remained static. The office nurse, according to the understanding of television writers, serves primarily as a receptionist–secretary. Ann Talbot, in *Dr. Hudson's Secret Journal* from the mid-1950s, although working in a hospital, actually worked as a private secretary for Dr. Hudson. Julia Baker in *Julia* frequently performed secretarial functions. Vera *(Rafferty)*, Kelly *(Having Babies/Julie Farr)*, Tully *(Doc)*, Puni *(Brian Keith)*, and of course Consuelo *(Marcus Welby)* were all registered nurses who spent most of their professional lives presiding over the waiting room, answering the phone, filling out insurance forms, and keeping the books. No one ever questioned this obviously inefficient use of registered nurses. Perhaps, once upon a time, registered nurses did run all aspects of a physician's office, but there are few physicians these days willing to pay a registered nurse's salary in order for her to answer his phone.

Notably absent from the presentation of the nursing profession has been any consistent recognition of the recently expanded role of professional nurses. In the entire thirty year span of television programming, the instances of nurses shown in truly professional roles can be counted on one hand, despite the well-known development in the nursing profession. Portraying nurses as secretaries or meek executors of doctors' orders in the 1950s was much closer to reality than it is today. Liz Thorpe and her colleagues on *The Nurses* were presented as true professionals who were concerned with the preservation of nursing standards and ethics as they were perceived in the early 1960s. These nurses were not shown in expanded roles calling for semi-independent or autonomous judgment about the delivery of health care.

There have been only occasional exceptions. One episode of *Medic* did explain the role of the public health nurse who visited her patients at home and instituted rehabilitative regimens for them. One episode of *Marcus Welby* featured Consuelo's involvement with a pilot project for the training of nurses in prenatal care and midwifery. Carolee on *The Doctors* has recently been certified as a nurse–midwife and allowed to practice in the hospital. Mary Ellen Walton of *The Waltons* has been shown in the role of a horsebackriding, public health nurse in the mountains of Virginia in the 1940s. *M*A*S*H* has made a fairly obvious attempt to present its nurse characters as capable of expanded responsibilities in the late 1970 seasons; in one episode, Major Houlihan instituted a training program to teach her nurses to handle triage, thereby freeing the physicians for surgery. On other occasions, Margaret delivered babies for local women and conducted a prenatal class for Korean women in the area. Although these presentations of nurses involved in work requiring judgment and initiative have been important milestones in the story of nurses on television, there has been no general trend to imitate these cases. The average viewer would never be able to infer from these limited examples that the nursing profession has undergone a significant change in the recent past.

The most evident change in the presentation of nursing and nurse characters on television has been in the romantic or sexual role assigned to the nurse characters. The nurse has been transformed from a sweet and innocent girlfriend/wife type to a rather promiscuous young woman more interested in a love affair than in marriage. Obviously sexual mores and network censorship of the 1950s and 1960s played a role in the rather innocent portrayals of nurses, but the recent depiction of nurses has been an exaggerated one, designed to exploit the nurse as an object of sexual excitement in a hospital or military camp. As mentioned earlier, the proliferation of tasteless and unwarranted linen closet humor has branded the nurse as promiscuous. Interestingly, the number of young, married, or engaged nurses, typical of the 1950s and early 1960s, has also declined. It is almost as if television writers are saying that nurses make good playmates but are not worthy of marriage. None of the nurse characters on *Operation Petticoat, Black Sheep Squadron,* and the early seasons of *M*A*S*H* appeared to be involved in a serious romance; at best the nurses appeared engaged in selective promiscuity. Hot Lips' hypocritical affair with Frank Burns on *M*A*S*H* was perhaps the most damning example. Jill Danko of *The Rookies* has been about the only example of a chaste, young, married nurse to be found in recent television depictions of nursing. The doctor-heroes of contemporary health oriented drama and comedy do not choose nurses as marriage partners or even as serious contenders. As early as *Ben Casey* it appeared that nurses were not quite good enough for the important physician. Ben dated a series of attractive professional women, but never a nurse. Jim Kildare's most passionate and seemingly important romances were not with nurses, although a romance with a young nurse was created for him in the final season. Joe Gannon of *Medical Center* never dated a nurse, although he pursued female doctors and other beautiful women. The doctors of *The Bold Ones* showed no permanent romantic interest in nurses. Steve Kiley of *Marcus Welby* occasionally dated a nurse character, but he married a sophisticated and glamorous public relations director of the hospital, as if a traditional nurse were not quite strong enough to hold down the role of Steve's career-minded wife. Charlie Nichols, the hero of *House Calls,* had been looking for a mature and intelligent woman, and although he dated lots of nurses, not until a new female hospital administrator arrived on the scene did he find what he had been looking for. Gonzo, the surgeon hero of *Trapper John,* has made explicit his understanding that the nursing staff serves an important role in his life: to provide leisure time sexual diversion. However, neither he nor his mentor Trapper has ever become seriously interested in a nurse character. Even the doctor-heroes of *M*A*S*H* have rarely had an important romance with a nurse. Hawkeye, the only unmarried doctor until Winchester arrived, had only one serious affair with a nurse who happened to be his old girlfriend. Otherwise he has seemed genuinely attracted to a Korean woman and to a Swedish doctor. The strict association of nurses as good wives and mothers in the 1950s may have been a bit distorted and naive, but the blatant presentation of nurses as promiscuous in the 1970s is rather more damaging to the image of the profession. If young nurses are consistently portrayed as amenable to the casual sexual encounter, it makes it difficult for the average viewer to accord them their rightful measure of professional respect.

Writers have never tried to deal with nurse characters as well-rounded, career-minded, and intelligent women, with, of course, the exception of *M*A*S*H* and, to some extent, *The Waltons*. As noted above, nurses have been consistently treated on television over the past thirty years in terms of the way in which their professional responsibilities have been depicted. The creative directors of *M*A*S*H*, undoubtedly stimulated by Alan Alda, have consciously revamped their attitudes to female characters in the series; and since nurses appear more than any other female type, the nursing profession has profited enormously from the sympathetic and yet unromantic view of nurses in wartime. However, *M*A*S*H* aside, when producers have attempted some nodding acknowledgment of the women's movement, they have generally aimed their attention at women in traditionally male roles—doctors, lawyers, and police.

Health care drama and comedy have experienced a huge increase in the number of female physicians seen in the recent past, especially the 1970s. Nursing has suffered indirectly because of the obvious, if unexplored, differences between typical nurse characters and typical female doctor characters. It must be said that in general the female physician characters have been more intelligent, more ambitious, more articulate, more glamorous, and more sophisticated than have been nurse characters in the same show. The unstated premise of these divergent presentations is that nursing has remained an undeveloped profession, attracting only the traditional handmaiden type of woman who is willing to subordinate all her goals to the service of a doctor or a hospital. It strongly suggests that the most intelligent women interested in the field of health care will automatically enter medicine rather than nursing if they have any choice at all. Even before female doctors appeared on television with any frequency, writers often showed extremely talented and intelligent nurses as women who entered nursing because they could not enter medicine for lack of opportunity. *Doctors Hospital, The Interns, Westside Medical,* and *Julie Farr* all featured regular female physician characters. *Medical Center* also showed female doctors with some frequency, but *Marcus Welby* much less often. *Doctors' Private Lives* and *Women in White* featured extremely ambitious and beautiful female doctors. *Women in White* presented the most damaging image of nurses and female physicians shown to date. The female doctors were physically, morally, and professionally superior to the nurses shown. The physicians were objective, while the nurses were incapable of overcoming their personal feelings. The physicians were glamorous and wore chic, tailored clothing; the nurses wore dowdy or uninspired wardrobes. The physicians had professional goals; the nurses did not. Again, the female physician characters in all of these shows appeared as more worthy of the romantic attention of a successful male physician than were the nurses shown. In addition in some shows the writers used female physicians to replace nurses. In *The Interns* and *Westside Medical* the female physicians seemed to perform functions more in line with traditional nursing than did their male colleagues. *Doctors Hospital* was perhaps the only series to attempt some parity between female doctors and nurses, but this was never too consistent. For example, in one episode, the female neurosurgeon Norah comforted a distraught nurse and noted that they were both "two working broads." However, in another episode, a former nurse who had become a doctor experienced a serious lack of cooperation from the nursing staff, who resented her for deserting the ranks.

As has been noted above, there has been an incredible consistency in the presentation of nursing programs on television. One reason for this sameness is that they have been created and produced by a very few men. Approximately four teams of writers and producers have been responsible for the majority of television health care dramas and some comedy. James Moser, later in association with Matthew Rapf and Jack Laird, created and wrote *Medic,* produced *Ben Casey,* and created *Doctors Hospital.* David Victor, with later associations with David J. O'Connell and Norman Felton, created and produced *Doctor Kildare, Marcus Welby, M.D., The Eleventh Hour, Women in White,* and *Operation Petticoat.* Frank Glicksman produced *Medical Center* with Al Ward and created and produced *Trapper John* with Don Brinkley. Finally, William Blinn and Jerry Thorpe have collaborated on *The Rookies, The Lazarus Syndrome, The Interns, Rafferty,* and *The Little People/Brian Keith Show.* In addition to these creative production teams, about fifteen to twenty scriptwriters have contributed stories for all the health care shows since the 1950s. The same men wrote the plots and dialogues for *The Nurses, Ben Casey, Medical Center, Marcus Welby,* and many others. Thus, it is no surprise that the world of television nursing and medicine has exhibited rather consistent if distorted assumptions about the nature of health care in the United States and that the images of nursing have undergone little genuine change.

All of the observations made on the image of nursing so far do not attempt to weigh or measure the strength of any given image of the profession. Such easily forgotten television efforts as *The Fighting Nightingales* or *Rafferty* cannot be compared to such important shows as *Medical Center* or *Ben Casey.* In order to examine which images of the profession have been the most influential, it is important to identify those health care shows with regular nurse characters that have been the most successful in terms of longevity, ratings, and critical acclaim. The ten most influential television shows are listed in Table 10–1, below. In only two of these series, *The Nurses* and *Julia*, did nurse characters play leading roles. A separate rank must be accorded the two long-running daytime serials, *The Doctors* and *General Hospital*, each of which has broadcast approximately 4,420 episodes to date.

A corollary to the number of episodes produced is the potential of the series to enjoy a second life in syndication. The rule of thumb for syndication is that a series must have one hundred episodes in order to be suitable for stripping in syndication; that is, it must be shown five days a week (*Emmy*, p. 40). Of all nursing/medical series ever produced, only about six have had much success in syndication. It is impossible to measure the impact of a series after it begins its rounds as a syndicated series. *M*A*S*H* of all the health care theme shows available, promises to be the show repeated most often, namely because the thirty-minute comedy fits more readily into the type of scheduling used by local stations during their five to eight time slots and because the half-hour comedy has proven a more durable item for repeat viewing. It would seem a fair guess that Major Margaret "Hot Lips" Houlihan will be the most influential nurse character produced by television in its entire history.

The fact that the above listed ten series survived the networks schedule cuts for several seasons indicates, also, their relative strength in the Nielsen ratings. The cutoff mark for a show apparently stands at about a 15 percent rating. That is, a show which does not attract over 15 percent of the total television families stands no chance of renewal and possibly may not finish a season. Usually, the shows

Table 10–1
The Ten Most Influential Television Shows

Title	No. of Episodes	Length of Episode	No. of Seasons
M*A*S*H	225 plus	30 minutes	11
Marcus Welby	172	60 minutes	7
Medical Center	169	60 minutes	7
Ben Casey	153	60 minutes	5
Dr. Kildare	190*	60 minutes*	5
Emergency	130	60 minutes	5
The Nurses	103	60 minutes	3
Hennessey	92	30 minutes	3
Julia	86	30 minutes	3
The Rookies	68	60 minutes	3

**Dr. Kildare*'s last season changed from a sixty-minute, weekly episode format to two thirty-minute weekly episodes, which accounts for the high number of episodes.

ranked 50 and below constitute these doomed series. The rating of 15 to 16 percent is a marginal one; if the network thinks such a series has a chance of gradually building an audience, the show may be given a second chance, but not for long. For example, *Operation Petticoat,* ranked 53 at the end of the first thirteen weeks of the 1977 season, with a 15.6 percent rating. The network gave the series another chance, but by the following year, ranked 54 with a rating of only 15.7 percent, the show was cancelled. Any show with a rating of 18.5 percent or above stands a very good chance of remaining on the network schedules, as these shows rank between the 30 and 40 most popular series. The rating represents the percentage of "households tuned to a given program in a time period from the universe of households equipped to receive television" (Brown, 1977, p. 352). Much about the impact of television is said in the fact that even a very unpopular, failed series, with a rating of 13 percent represents a television audience of 9.27 million viewers. The top ranked series usually draw a rating of between 26 and 31 percent, representing average audiences of between 18.5 and 22.1 million viewers. Very few health theme series have ranked in the top ten Nielsen ratings for extended periods of time. Most of the successful ones have enjoyed rather brief periods of extreme popularity and have gradually slipped in the ratings.

The first television shows featuring nurses and doctors to have swept the Nielsen's were *Doctor Kildare* and *Ben Casey* in the years 1961–1963. *Dr. Kildare* peaked in popularity during its first season, and thereafter slipped gradually out of the top ranked shows until its cancellation after an unsuccessful fifth season, 1965–1966. *Ben Casey* peaked in the second season of its life, 1962–1963, and then followed the slide experienced by its rival, *Dr. Kildare*. The next health theme series to attract large audiences was *Julia,* the situation comedy introduced in 1968. During the show's first season it finished as the number six show, garnering an average rating of 24.8 percent. Thereafter, the series did not appear in the top ten of the Nielsen ratings, indicating that the novelty of using a black leading lady had worn off very quickly. *Marcus Welby* shot to the top of the Nielsen's in its first season, ranking as the number one program for the 1969–1970 season, rating 25 percent of the total possible audience, and drawing a 47 percent audience share of televisions actually in use. After two or three seasons in the top ten, *Marcus Welby* began an inexorable decline, ranking 45 in its sixth season. *Medical Center* never enjoyed the kind of peak reached by *Marcus Welby,* but the CBS series remained a perennial contender in the top twenty most popular shows throughout its seven year run. Even in its final two seasons, the show ranked number 17 and number 16 respectively.

In 1972 *M*A*S*H* aired on CBS. Although the series was not an immediate hit, it gradually built a loyal audience and has, since its second season, remained in the top twenty programs, and usually within the top ten. It consistently earns a rating of between 21 and 26 percent; the ups and downs of its ratings no doubt stem from the network's tendency to shift the program from one time slot to another, and from rival networks' counter-programming challenges. In its seventh season, when most long-running shows begin to show the signs of imminent collapse, *M*A*S*H* ranked as the number seven show of the season, with an average rating of 25.4 percent, and an audience share of 37 percent. In the 1979–1980 season, *Lazarus Syndrome,* which promised success after a respectable 23.1 percent rating for its pilot episode, failed to attract a consistent audience and was cancelled after four weeks. On the other hand, *Trapper John* was deemed a success in the ratings and was retained on the schedules for 1980–1981. *House Calls,* introduced in December 1979, also was doing well in the ratings and was renewed for a second season.

Series such as *Emergency, The Rookies,* and *The Nurses* which lasted for several seasons, did not distinguish themselves in the Nielsen ratings. *The Nurses* never quite reached the status of a top twenty show, although its producer Herb Brodkin noted that it was cancelled with ratings that were higher than other shows that remained on the schedules. *Emergency*'s ratings ranged from 18.1 percent to 20.2 percent throughout its five year run, and similarly, *The Rookies* could count on ratings from 19.4 percent to 20.9 percent. These ratings were sufficient to keep them on the schedule for several seasons, but were not outstanding.

Thus the five most influential series, in terms of their ratings and the length of their runs on television would appear to be: *M*A*S*H, Marcus Welby, Medical Center, Ben Casey,* and *Dr. Kildare.* These five series not only enjoyed several seasons of prime-time broadcasting but also appeared in the top rated shows for several seasons of their lifetimes. The influence of these series also derives from their critical acceptance. The value of an Emmy award, presented annually since 1948 by the National Academy of Television Arts and Sciences, for a television series does not equal that of an Oscar for a feature film; many have been the Emmy winners from cancelled series. That is, on television critical approval often does not go hand in hand with popularity and success. Unlike the Oscars, the Emmy Awards represent the opinions of those outside as well as within the industry. The Quigley Publications Awards, 1948–1972, never carried the cachet of the Emmy as they represented only a polling of television critics by *Motion Picture Daily* and *Fame.* Furthermore, many of the award categories of the Quigley Awards, such as "most unique new program" and "most promising new male star," reflected a concern with accidental phenomena rather than with the aesthetic quality of current productions. A review of the way in which health care theme series and specials have fared in the award department can contribute to an understanding of these series beyond the simple listing of Nielsen ratings.

The major medical–hospital–nursing shows fall into three main rankings with regard to their showing among the Emmy and Quigley winners. The lowest rank includes those long-running series remarkable for their lack of critical appeal: *Dr. Kildare, Medical Center, Emergency,* and *The Rookies.* The middle range includes those series that can be associated with better than average production qualities although the series never won major award recognition: *Medic, Ben Casey, The Nurses, Mr. Peepers, Hennessey,* and *Julia.* The final and highest rank is for the select group of shows that have been honored with generous and/or frequent acclaim: *The Hallmark Hall of Fame, Marcus Welby, M.D.*, and *M*A*S*H*.

Several of the longest running and most popular health care series received virtually no notice from the Emmy Award process. *Dr. Kildare* never won an Emmy; only twice was someone associated with the series even nominated—Suzanne Pleshette in 1961 for her single performance in an episode and Adrian Spies for a 1963 script. The Quigley Awards did accord Chamberlain the honor of being the second "most promising new male star" of 1961 (following his rival Vince Edwards); in 1965, the Quigley poll cited *Dr. Kildare* as the third "best half-hour drama" of 1965, an unimpressive notice since few half-hour dramas were on the air that year and since *Kildare* never placed in previous citations for its sixty-minute format. *Medical Center,* which ran for seven years, never earned so much as a glance from the Emmy judges or from the less discriminating Quigley poll. Chad Everett did not even rate "most promising new male star" status in the 1969 Quigley poll, although James Brolin of *Marcus Welby* did. *Emergency* and *The Rookies,* aimed at the preteen and adolescent viewer, not surprisingly never received an Emmy award.

Health care shows in the second category never received overall commendation but did receive several nominations and some of the lesser Emmy awards. *Medic,* the granddaddy of medical shows, won the Sylvania Grand Award for 1954 (an award never repeated) and the Quigley "Best New Drama" for 1954. Although no one associated with *Medic* won an Emmy, in 1954 there were six nominations for the series, including "best actor" (Richard Boone) and "best drama series." (The best drama series of that season was *The U.S. Steel Hour,* no mean competitor for a half-hour medical show.) Although *Ben Casey* now seems almost synonymous with *Dr. Kildare,* in fact the James Moser series received much more positive critical response than did its rival. In 1961 *Ben Casey* was nominated in the Emmy competition as "best dramatic program" and Vince Edwards for "outstanding continuing performance by an actor in a series." Furthermore, four other actors received nominations for their work in the series that season, as did the cinematographer for his contribution. "Outstanding writing" and "outstanding directing" nominations went to series' participants in 1962. Kim Stanley and Glenda Farrell won 1962 Emmys for their leading and supporting performances in the *Ben Casey* episode "A Cardinal Act of Mercy." The Quigley poll recognized *Ben Casey* and Vince Edwards in several categories in 1961.

The Nurses, Herbert Brodkin's 1962 entry into the hospital drama field, garnered two nominations in 1963 for guest stars who appeared in the show. None of the series regulars was ever nominated for an Emmy, but the Quigley poll cited both Zina Bethune and Shirl Conway as "most promising new female star of tomorrow" in 1962. The competition among dramatic series was especially keen in these years, with Brodkin's other series, *The Defenders* and *East Side/West Side,* consistently taking nominations and awards in several categories.

Situation comedies featuring nurse characters have received respectable critical notice. *Mr. Peepers* and *Hennessey*—both low-keyed, soft comedy—were nominated several times for Emmy's. *Mr. Peepers,* competing with *I Love Lucy,* was nominated as the "best situation comedy" for each of its three seasons. Jackie Cooper was nominated twice for his portrayal of the ineffectual doctor, Chick Hennessey; and Abby Dalton, as his wisecracking nurse Lieutenant Martha Hale, was nominated for her supporting role in 1960. *Julia,* 1968–1971, received three Emmy nominations after its first season, and the Quigley poll listed Diahann Carroll as the "most promising new female star." Probably much of this early attention was more of a reward to the producers for daring to use a black leading lady than for any inherent qualities in the series.

Only a handful of health care theme shows have been more than once honored with the major Emmy Awards. In a special category, *Hallmark Hall of Fame* in its productions of "Little Moon of Alban" (1958 and 1963) won five Emmys. The 1958 version won, for its leading lady Julie Harris, the "best single performance by an actress" award for her portrayal of a nursing sister, as well as awards for "best single dramatic program," "best writing," and "best directing." The 1963 version won for Ruth White, who played Miss Harris's mother, an award for her "outstanding performance in a supporting role." In 1964 Miss Harris was one of twelve nominees for "outstanding individual achievement in entertainment" for her interpretation of Florence Nightingale in *Hallmark Hall of Fame*'s "The Holy Terror."

Only two series that featured nurses and physicians have received major Emmy Awards. In 1969 *Marcus Welby, M.D.* swept the drama field with four major awards, including "best drama series," and awards for the two stars, Robert Young and James Brolin. After 1969 the best dramatic awards went to *The Bold Ones,* to several PBS entries, and to *The Waltons.* The comedy series *M*A*S*H* has received more critical acclaim than has any other health care series. Interestingly, the awards keep coming, reflecting sustained critical approval of the show rather than a fleeting acknowledgment of distinction as in the 1969 *Marcus Welby* winnings. *M*A*S*H* has won most of the major Emmy awards. In 1973 the series won the "best comedy" distinction, and Alan Alda won the "actor of the year" award and "best lead actor in a comedy" distinction that year. Gary Burghoff won a supporting actor award in 1976. The series has won the "best directing in comedy" citation for several years—for different directors—1973, 1974, 1975, and 1976, and two film editing awards in 1975. Alan Alda also won an award for "best writing, comedy" in 1978. For the 1978–1980 season Loretta Swit won the award for best supporting actress and Henry Morgan won the best supporting actor award for a comedy, variety or music series.

With specific attention to recognition of nurse characters, the Emmy record is not very edifying, reflecting the generally limited scope given to the role of nurses in most health care series. With the exception of Julie Harris and Loretta Swit, no male or female actor has won an Emmy for playing a nurse. Abby Dalton received a nomination in 1960; Harold J. Stone and Ruby Dee received nominations in 1963 for their guest appearance as nurse characters on *The Nurses;* and in 1968, Diahann Carroll was nominated for her role in *Julia*.

The more influential series depicting nurses, through their longevity and likelihood of being seen again and again in syndication, have stamped a very few seemingly indelible impressions of nursing and medicine upon the viewing public. There is one and only one physician character allowed in television medicine. This physician can be easily described: He is an attractive, white male; he is unmarried; he devotes himself heart and soul to the care and welfare of his patients; he downplays the importance of payment for his services; and he knows or learns all the important circumstances of his patient's life so as to better help him. Frequently these physicians operate in teams or in partnership with other doctors who exhibit all the same characteristics; most often, there is a noticeable age difference between the doctors who work together, so as to allow for the interplay of constraining wisdom and youthful enthusiasm. Though these heroes may look different on screen, one could not distinguish one from the other on the basis of their dialogue in a script.

Nurse characters cannot be lumped into such a singular and obvious category, but there are very few ways in which nurses have been treated in these most important television shows. Four major treatments of nurse characters on television can be found in ten programs already identified:

The Nurse as Nonentity: This mode of treatment describes the presentation of nurse characters in: *Ben Casey; Dr. Kildare;* and *Medical Center*.
The Good Nurse: Consuelo Lopez of *Marcus Welby,* and, to a lesser degree Dixie McCall of *Emergency* personify this image.
The Nurturing Nurse: Martha Hale of *Hennessey;* Julia Baker of *Julia;* and Jill Danko of *The Rookies* comprise this grouping.
The Professional Nurse: The least imitated category of all, this type finds only two exponents in all of television broadcasting: Liz Thorpe of *The Nurses* and Margaret Houlihan of *M*A*S*H*.

Although there have been many other images of the nursing profession noted in the review of television programming, these four images not only predominated the most influential television series but have been repeated and imitated dozens of times in less successful series. Each of these categories deserves some discussion.

The Nurse as Nonentity

Ben Casey, Dr. Kildare, and *Medical Center* each included regular nurse characters in their casts, though the names of these characters and the actresses who played the roles do not come readily to mind. Miss Wills (Jeanne Bates) of *Ben Casey;* Nurse Conant (Jo Helton) and Nurse Fain (Jean Inness) of *Dr. Kildare;* and Nurse Chambers (Jayne Meadows), Nurse Holmby (Barbara Baldavin), and Nurse Wilcox (Audrey Totter) of *Medical Center* appeared in hundreds of episodes of these series and yet remain virtually unknown. These nurse characters served essentially as messengers and always remained extremely minor characters, without first names. Nothing of the personal lives of the nurse characters ever emerged in the entire life of the series. To say that these nurse characters were appreciated by the doctor-heroes would be saying too much; although they would be generally perceived as good nurses, the physician-heroes took the services of these nurses for granted.

The professional duties of these nurses remained firmly in the handmaiden category. They were willing minions, ever ready to leap to the doctor's terse command. They staffed the nursing stations and appeared in the corridors of the hospital, involved in unidentifiable duties. They never discussed patient care with anyone. These nurses existed in something of a vacuum; they did not appear to have friendships with anyone on the staff. Occasionally, one might indicate her esteem or affection for a physician, but these gestures were never reciprocated. For example, scenes in which one or more of the staff nurses would arrange a surprise party for a doctor, go out of her way to deliver a message she knew the physician would like to hear, or offer a personal remark about the doctor's appearance, often recurred in these series. Never did a physician character offer a similar personal remark to a nurse; nurses never looked tired, overworked, never had birthdays, and never needed a pat on the back for encouragement.

In all three of these series, when a guest star nurse character received more than passing attention, the attention almost always had to do with the way in which the physician character was called upon to help the nurse solve a personal problem. The heroic physicians, pressed by the responsibilities of their work, could always find time to assist a distraught nurse, especially if the nurse's personal problem interfered with her ability to efficiently obey his orders. The range of personal problems was legion with these benighted nurses. They were alcoholics, former alcoholics, daughters, wives, or girlfriends of alcoholics. They were pregnant and unmarried or pregnant and married but unhappy. They were intolerant because of dismal personal experiences that clouded their judgment. They were raped. They were crazed. They murdered out of love; they loved murderers, felons, and escaped convicts.

Despite these occasional forays into the world of troubled nurses, these three doctor shows should be remembered more for how they ignored nurses than how they treated them in infrequent featured roles. The treatment of the registered nurse as a non-person, a piece of hospital equipment, has been the most frequent depiction of the profession. Because these regular nurse characters appeared so frequently with such little examination of their role, they existed in an almost subliminal space in the viewer's mind. Unexamined and unemphasized, these nurses nevertheless have exerted a tremendous influence on the audience's perception of the role of nursing in contemporary hospital routine. The health care shows with regular, major nurse characters, have offered different but similar views of the nursing profession.

The Good Nurse

The characteristics of this nurse are most clearly delineated in the character of Consuelo Lopez. The Good Nurse is unmarried, past the first blush of youth, and has dedicated herself to the professional success of a single doctor. Her role in the series is primarily identified in her professional capacity, but this professional identification is clearly tied to and dependent upon a particular doctor. This nurse enjoys a familial, even domestic coziness in her relationship to her employer. She serves the role of lady of the house, accompanying her boss to social events, preparing a snack or a meal for him; she is privy to both his professional and personal problems. The viewer might often wonder why the Good Nurse is not married to her doctor. In some variations on the Consuelo role, the writers hint at her desire for such a position. Generally these Good Nurses have long accepted that the doctor is already married—to his work. Her virtues are strictly feminine; she is compassionate, self-sacrificing, gentle, and intuitive. The doctor lauds her for being a fine nurse and recognizes that she complements his practice of medicine with her warmth, loyalty, and patience.

It is important to emphasize that this presentation of nursing is extremely positive, and the nurse characters in this category receive great audience sympathy. There is a clear sense that the Good Nurse is very capable and deserving of the doctor's confidence; however, both she and the doctor have come to realize that she can be of more use to the world in her assistance to the doctor than she could if she were to work in a hospital or pursue her own goals. This Good Nurse does not make mistakes; however, she rarely has the opportunity to do so. Often she does assist the doctor in saving a life or finding the cause or cure for a particular problem. But she never takes the lead, never demonstrates initiative. She may be able to follow through on a doctor's request with terrier-like determination, persevering in difficult tasks to a final successful conclusion, but she does not initiate the effort on her own judgment.

The Good Nurse has been presented in many formats, both comic and dramatic. *Dr. Hudson's Secret Journal, Doc, The Practice, Emergency, Rafferty,* and *Trapper John* have all had such devoted, Good Nurses as regular cast members. In general, the Good Nurse has no personal ambitions; she has arrived at the role in life she enjoys, even if this role is subordinate to both physicians and to those who have less education than she. Her personal admiration for the men in the series as well as her respect for their work make her content in her position of assistant.

The Nurturing Nurse

In this television version, the nurse's professional identification is incidental. Her major role in the series is defined by her nurturing relationship with other characters. Martha Hale of *Hennessey* worked as a nurse in the naval dispensary, but her most important role was as girlfriend of the series' protagonist, physician Chick Hennessey. Her nursing role served primarily to put her into contact with her boyfriend. Again, her virtues and faults were peculiarly feminine. She could be compassionate and gentle, expressing concern for the downtrodden or weak. She could also be jealous, prone to gossip, and subject to frequent change of heart, a woman's prerogative. Her main strength came from her intuition, not her knowledge of nursing. Her responsibilities appear to have been in the handmaiden category; she served as Chick's assistant and did not seem to have any work to do independent of the doctor. In keeping with her womanly, romantic role, Martha eventually married her doctor–boyfriend and presumably retired from her profession and her naval career. In *Julia,* the leading character worked as a nurse in an industrial health office, but her more important identification was as a black, widowed mother of a young son, and friend to her colleagues. Julia did very few professional tasks and, like Martha Hale, seemed to have no function independent of the physician who ran the office. Although she took initiative in dealing with personal problems, both her own and those of her friends, she did not demonstrate any ambition or leadership in her professional role. Jill Danko of *The Rookies* worked as a staff nurse in a large general hospital, but her most important role in the series was as wife and sounding board of one of the policeman protagonists and friend to the others. Her nursing, although frequently shown, remained a secondary function of her character. Although Jill performed many more professional tasks than did either Martha or Julia, she could have been working in any other profession without changing the tenor of the series to any great degree. The producers merely found it convenient to make Jill a nurse, as it placed her in more frequent contact with the rookie policemen who often brought injured criminals or policemen into the hospital and just as often landed in the hospital as patients themselves.

These marriage- and family-oriented nurses were all treated with respect by their co-workers and appeared to be appreciated as good nurses. They exhibited the same strengths and virtues as their colleagues, the Good Nurse. There have been several of these Nurturing Nurses beyond those discussed: Donna Stone of *The Donna Reed Show;* Nancy Remington of *Mr. Peepers;* Jessie Brewer of *General Hospital;* Zoe Lawton of the final season of *Dr. Kildare.* In all, both the Good Nurse and the Nurturing Nurse have always subordinated their nursing identity to the greater professional demands of a doctor, or group of doctors, or to a personal or familial relationship. They have always been presented in positive terms, and have thereby received great audience sympathy. These nurses, with their ignored colleagues on *Dr. Kildare, Ben Casey,* and *Medical Center,* account for almost all television nurse characterization. Nevertheless, there has been a radically different presentation of nursing on television, albeit limited and rarely imitated.

The Professional Nurse

Liz Thorpe of *The Nurses* and Major Margaret Hot Lips Houlihan of *M*A*S*H* complete the roster of nurse characters who have been developed as professional nurses. It is a short but distinguished list, important not so much for the impact, although arguably Hot Lips may be the most memorable nurse character in all of television history, but for the proof that intelligent producers and writers can conceive of strong and independent minded nurses and can present them with subtlety and style. On the surface, Liz Thorpe and Hot Lips have little in common. Liz is older, ladylike, reserved, and presented as the head nurse in a large hospital in New York in the early 1960s, and as such is subject to the constraints on both the profession and on women in general. Margaret is younger, brasher, often tawdry, sexually free in the manner of the 1970s, and employed in an unusual professional position, as head nurse of a mobile army surgical hospital during the Korean war, a position which frequently allows her to work in an expanded capacity. Beneath these superficial differences, the two women share many of the same traits. First, both characters' professional identity is at least as important as any other of their roles; Liz's nursing identity is clearly the most important, and for Margaret it is as important as her role as an officer in the Army, as paramour to some, and as friend to others. In both instances, the audience clearly perceives that nursing is a profession separate from medicine, possessing its own standards and ethics. These women work at jobs in which the agenda of their day is not totally dependent upon the whim or order of a physician character. Clearly Liz, in her capacity as head nurse, supervises the nursing staff on her floor for an eight-hour shift; doctors come and go, but she and her nursing staff remain. Liz frequently takes a special interest in one or more of her patients and offers them support or help on her own initiative. Margaret, while ruled to some degree by the vagaries of the war which also determine the schedule for the doctors, operates out of her own understanding of the nurse's job. Margaret supervises her nurses, trains them when necessary, supplies the operating room, inventories supplies, and schedules her nurses for coverage of the post-op ward, independent of any physician's order. Both of these nurses take direct orders from physicians, usually without question and with great efficiency; they execute these orders not because they are mere handmaidens but because they recognize this as part of their nursing responsibility, and they also appear to understand the medical imperatives behind the doctor's order.

In their professional relationships with doctors, these two nurses frequently volunteer their opinions and are asked for their impressions by the doctors. They are trusted by the physician characters because of their intelligence, their skill, and their experience, not merely because of their loyalty and compassion. Both of these nurses enjoy relatively smooth professional relationships with physicians. Margaret unendingly feuds with most of the doctors during the series' early years, less so recently, but these feuds arise from her personality differences with the doctors, from challenges to her military authority, and from the antagonistic role given her in the first few years of *M*A*S*H*. She has almost never had a genuine professional disagreement with the doctor-heroes; concomitantly, the doctors harrass and ridicule her in every area but her nursing. Liz experienced fewer personal problems with her medical colleagues because her character was less differentiated than was Margaret's.

Both nurses had love affairs with physician characters; they were clearly deemed worthy of this romantic position, a role not always accorded to nurses in the other important health care shows. Martha Hale did manage to marry her doctor–boyfriend in *Hennessey,* but otherwise Good or Nurturing Nurses did not have romances with their doctors. Liz's steady boyfriend for the better part of two seasons was Dr. Anson Kiley; their relationship was serious, although prevailing standards of censorship did not allow the writers to make explicit their sexual activity. Anson and Liz respected each other professionally and presented a rather balanced romantic pair. Chick Hennessey dominated the relationship he shared with Martha Hale; and certainly Jim Kildare dominated the romance with Zoe Lawton. Margaret Houlihan, in an interesting about face, dominated her somewhat ridiculous love affair with Frank Burns; often she spoke for him and prodded him into trying to assume a leadership role in the camp. This pair was very unbalanced. Although Margaret would defend Frank from the jeers of the other doctors, deep down she did not respect him. When she suffered an attack of appendicitis, she wanted Hawkeye to do the surgery and forbid Frank from putting a gloved finger on her. At the end of this love affair, Hot Lips married another military officer, though not a medical man. After her marriage ended in divorce, Margaret attempted to find a man who was somewhat closer to her in intelligence and skill. In a very brief and humorous love affair with Hawkeye, Margaret at last found a man who, although totally unsuited for her personality, matched or exceeded her in intelligence and strength of character. As things stood in the series as of the beginning of the 1980–1981 season, it seemed unlikely that Margaret would fall in love again with someone vastly inferior to her.

Both Liz and Margaret appeared to be very strong-minded women. These two nurses were never smiling ciphers, grinning and shuffling around a physician's ego. Liz possessed an often caustic wit, usually reserved for incompetent staff or outrageous patients. Liz scrupulously obeyed the physicians' orders, although at times she was seen biting her tongue to avoid a sarcastic response. Liz was a mature woman who knew how to control her temper. Margaret Houlihan, on the other hand, has had to go through a process of maturation during the series' long life. Short-tempered by nature, Margaret unleashed her considerable outrage on all those around her, especially on those less able to defend themselves, enlisted men for example. As the series has developed, the audience has been brought to the realization that much of Margaret's anger and blustering verbal assaults are born of her insecurity. The new Margaret Houlihan, emerging during and after her marriage to Donald Penobscott, has been much more able to control her temper and to save her indignation for the truly deserving. She still lets loose in occasional bursts of anger, but she apologizes later to those she has abused.

The virtues of these two nurse characters include such traditionally feminine virtues as gentleness, compassion, and maternal feelings, but also those more masculine traits such as wit, intelligence, aggressiveness, and keen judgment. Both Margaret and Liz have demonstrated their concern for motherless orphans and patients in need of special care. Even at the height of Margaret's authoritarianism, she energetically pitched in to accommodate displaced orphans and pregnant women. But more important to their professional image, these two nurses repeatedly demonstrated their ability to make decisions and their aggressive promotion of the nursing profession. Liz Thorpe was a stickler for perfection in her nursing students, not because of her innate authoritarianism but because she had a clear vision of the type of young women needed in the nursing profession. She would defend her young nurses from unwarranted insults or discipline, and she offered them sympathy and help when they faced personal problems. She made it clear that nurses helped their own and did not depend on the medical profession for protection. Margaret Houlihan has frequently been at odds with her nursing staff, especially in the earlier years of the series; the carefree but skilled young nurses did not appreciate their Major's often arbitrary discipline and sharp tongue. Yet even at her worse, Margaret kept her nurses' best interests in mind and tried, in her way, to promote the nursing profession. She simply wanted the nurses to hold up their end of the struggle and to earn the reputation of being good soldiers as well as good nurses. She has attempted in the last few seasons to gain for her nurses the right to perform such expanded duties as directing the triage operation on incoming wounded.

The most important characteristic of these two professional nurse characters is that they have demonstrated that nursing is a separate profession with its own standards and ethics, a profession that works in close but not dependent association with medicine. They have shown that nurse characters can be well developed human beings, with faults and strengths. These two nurse characters were strong women who were nurses; they were proud of being nurses. They had not become nurses because they could not become doctors. Liz Thorpe and Margaret Houlihan have proved that nurses can be sympathetic characters because of their strength and intelligence rather than simply because of their generosity and compassion.

The question remains: Why have television producers and writers clung to their stereotypes of the Good and Nurturing Nurse and so ignored the role of professional nursing in contemporary health care? The limited number of producers and writers of medical drama mentioned earlier, has obviously contributed to the narrow and unrealistic portrayal of nurses and nursing. However, perhaps the most important reason behind the stilted portrayal of nursing is simply the fact that a mythic and simplistic assumption about the nature of health care in the United States overrides all other production values in television health care programming.

Since the 1950s with *Medic,* television producers have taken great pride in their realistic medical shows. Collaborative efforts with real medical specialists, a resident technical consultant, and medical script reviewers have guaranteed an overvaunted authenticity for these shows—overvaunted because this authenticity has been strictly limited to technical jargon, to the placement of equipment, and to the handling of surgical instruments. There has been no successful attempt to present authentic portrayals of physicians. Such recent shows as *Lazarus Syndrome* and the earlier *Medical Story* flouted the conventions regarding the omnipotent role of the doctor and promptly disappeared from the schedule. The only type of physician character to appeal to television audiences has been the doctor-hero, the man who combines medical–surgical expertise with a tenacious personal concern for his patients.

In all of the long-running series the doctors have been male, handsome, altruistic and idealistic, dedicated to their patients' welfare, confident of their skills, aggressive in the treatment of disease, and crusaders against injustice, ignorance, or stupidity. All have been unmarried or at least been considered eligible because of the absence of their wives. For example, not all of the doctors in *M*A*S*H* have been unmarried, but they all have been developed, on several occasions, as romantic objects. In addition, their unmarried status imbues their role with the priestly tone of a man who serves but one mistress—his work. Furthermore, the doctor-heroes of these shows have exhibited universal lack of interest in money or monetary compensation for their work. In the 1960s much was made of the financial sacrifices made in pursuit of a medical career, and little attention was paid to the future dividends. In the 1970s doctors appeared much more affluent but still never paid the slightest attention to fees or money.

In their relationships with their patients these physicians have demonstrated a standard of medical practice that rarely exists in fact. In most of the doctor–patient encounters, the physicians were either friends of their patients or else soon became their confidantes and friends. These fictional doctors spent hours of time with each patient and never appeared to be in a hurry or to have other business to attend to. The doctor-heroes of these shows have traditionally applied their talents and energies not only to the solution of medical and surgical problems but also to a wide range of emotional and social difficulties faced by their patients. These doctor-heroes made routine the practice of visiting their patients at home or at work in order to discover missing bits of information needed for a diagnosis or to ensure compliance with a prescribed regimen.

Finally, the television portrayal of the physician has reinforced the notion that the doctor always knows best. Although in recent years, the doctor-heroes have paid lip service to the notion that a patient might legitimately desire a second opinion, in no case were the doctor-heroes proven mistaken or even misguided in their initial diagnoses or prescriptions. With some exceptions noted in *Marcus Welby,* all the other series suggested that the patient had little role in his own treatment beyond blind obedience to the doctor's orders. Rarely have fictional physicians brought their patients into a discussion of their treatment, and rarely have a patient's desires been considered. The dramatic narrative of an episode would most often find the doctor pitted against a recalcitrant patient in a struggle to see whose decision regarding treatment would prevail; invariably the doctor-hero had his way.

The pervasiveness of this single image of the physician bespeaks its origin in a collective longing for a god-like figure in our lives. People need to believe in a person whom, they perceive, has their lives in hand. Even a witch doctor is revered, and great knowledge and power are ascribed to him, probably not so much because he possesses those powers as because he represents the only hope for his patients. Hence not only do people believe that those powers are real; they tend also to exaggerate them.

The rise of medical technology has offered people fresh assurance that their doctors do indeed have special knowledge and has further reinforced the notion of the physician's mastery of these new, miraculous techniques. The dark side of technological knowledge, of course, is that it, like other kinds of power, has the potential for misuse. Because our lives literally depend upon both the physician's skill and his good will, our good image of the doctor exaggerates his technical knowledge and his capacity for compassion and dedication to our welfare. Instances of doctors forgetting their oaths and using their technological knowledge for twisted ends have produced memorable fictional monsters of the mad scientist persuasion. The unsettling knowledge that in real life doctors have perverted their knowledge to inhumane ends, for example, the experiments of Nazi doctors, establishes a nagging doubt, often deeply buried, in our relationships with real life doctors and other technocrats in control of our lives.

Thus our pride in technological advances, in miracle drugs, in fantastic computerized medical equipment goes hand in hand with our fear of the misuse of these marvels of science. The fictional doctor-hero seen in television drama and comedy persuades us that there is nothing to fear.

The image of nursing in this view of medicine and health depends exclusively upon this image of the good doctor. Compared to such a paragon of wisdom, skill, and charity, no one can compete for audience sympathy. In order to keep the doctor-heroe's image intact, he must not depend upon anyone else for substantive help. A kindly nurse might keep his office tidy and make sure he gets his meals; she might keep his patients calm while they wait for him; but she will never provide the comprehensive and aggressive care his patients have come to expect.

Bibliography

Action for Children's Television. *TV and teens: Experts look at the issues.* Reading, Mass.: Addison-Wesley, 1982.

Adler, R., and Cater, D., eds. *Television as a cultural force.* Palo Alto, Calif.: Aspen Institute of Humanistic Studies, 1976.

Adler, R., ed. *Television as a social force: New approaches to TV criticism.* New York: Praeger, 1975.

Aronoff, C. "Old age in prime time," *Journal of Communication,* 1974, 24(4): 86–87.

Baran, S. J. "Sex on TV and adolescent sexual self-image," *Journal of Broadcasting,* 1976, 20(1), 61–68.

Barnouw, Erik. *Tube of plenty: The evolution of American television.* New York: Oxford University Press, 1975.

Bedell, Sally. "Behind the scenes at 'Lifeline'," *TV Guide* 26(October 7, 1978), 26–31.

Berk, L. M. "The great middle American dream machine," *Journal of Communication,* 1977, 27(1), 27–31.

Beuf, A. "Doctor, lawyer, household drudge," *Journal of Communication,* 1974, 24(2), 142–145.

Bird, Caroline. "What's television doing for 50.9% of Americans?," *TV Guide,* 19(February 27, 1971), 5–8.

Brooks, T., and Marsh, E. *The complete directory to prime time network TV shows 1946–present.* New York: Ballantine Books, 1979.

Brown, L. *The New York Times encyclopedia of television.* New York: New York Times Book, 1977.

Brown, L. *Television: The business behind the box.* New York: Harcourt Brace Jovanovich, 1971.

Brown, R., ed. *Children and television.* Beverly Hills, Calif.: Sage, 1976.

Busby, L. J. "Sex-role research on the mass media," *Journal of Communication,* 1975, 25(4), 107–131.

Cantor, M. G. *Prime time television: Content and control.* Beverly Hills: Sage Publications, 1980.

Cassata, M. B., Anderson, P. A., and Skill, T. D. "The older adult in daytime serial drama," *Journal of Communication,* 1980, 30(1), 48–49.

Castleman, H., and Podrazik, W. J. *Watching TV: Four decades of American television.* New York: McGraw-Hill Book Company, 1982.

Christ, C. "Marcus Welby or Archie Bunker: Will the real chauvinist pig please stand up?," *Christian Century,* 1975, 92,260–262.

Christiansen, J. B. "Television role models and adolescent occupational goals," *Human Communication Research,* 1979, 5(4), 335–337.

Churchill, G. A., and Moschis, G. P. Jr. "Television and interpersonal influences on adolescent consumer learning," *Journal of Consumer Research,* 1979, 6(1), 23–35.

Cole, B. G. "Women on the screen," *Television.* New York: Free Press, 1970, pp. 265–266.

Comstock, G. *Television in America.* Beverly Hills: Sage Publications, 1980.

Comstock, G., and Fisher, M. *Television and human behavior: A guide to the pertinent scientific literature.* Santa Monica, Calif.: The Rand Corporation, 1975.

Comstock, G., and Lindsey, G. *Television and human behavior: The research horizon, future and present.* Santa Monica, Calif.: The Rand Corporation, 1975.

Comstock, G.; Chaffee, S.; Katzman, N.; McCombs, M.; and Roberts, D. *Television and human behavior.* New York: Columbia University Press, 1978.

Davidson, B. "Jack Klugman of 'Quincy'," *TV Guide,* 25(March 26, 1977), 29–34.

Davidson, B. "Medical Center," *TV Guide,* 19(July 17, 1971), 12–16.

DeFleur, M. L. "Occupational roles as portrayed on television," *Public Opinion Quarterly,* 1964, 28, 57–74.

DeFleur, M., and DeFleur, L. "The relative contribution of television as learning source for children's occupational knowledge," *American Sociological Review,* 1967, 32, 777–789.

Downing, Mildred. "Heroine of the daytime serial," *Journal of Communication,* 1974, 24(2), 130–137.

Durdeen-Smith, J. "Daytime TV: Soft soaping the American woman," *The Village Voice,* February 8, 1973, 19.

Edmondson, M., and Rounds, D. *The soaps: Daytime serials of radio and TV.* New York: Stein and Day, 1973.

Efron, E. "Is television making a mockery of the American woman?" *TV Guide,* 18(August 8, 1970), 7–9.

Efron, E. "The soaps—anything but 99–44/100 percent pure," *TV Guide,* 13(March 13, 1965), 6–11.

Eliot, M. *American television: The official art of the artificial.* Anchor: Doubleday, October, 1981.

Elliott, P. *The making of a television series: A case study in the sociology of culture.* New York: Hastings House, 1973.

Elliott, W. Y. *Television's impact on American culture.* East Lansing: Michigan State University Press, 1956.

Franzblau, S., Sprafkin, J. N., and Rubinstein, E. A. "Sex on TV: A content analysis," *Journal of Communication,* 1977, 27(Spring), 164–171.

Franzwa, H. H. *The image of women in television: An annotated bibliograpy.* Washington, D.C.: U.S. Commission on Civil Rights, 1976.

Franzwa, H. "The image of women in television: An annotated bibliography," in G. Tuchman, A. K. Daniels, and J. Benet (eds.), *Hearth and home: Images of women in the mass media.* New York: Oxford University Press, 1978.
Friedan, B. "Television and the feminine mystique," *TV Guide,* 12(February 1, 1964), 6–11 and 13(February 8, 1964), 19–24.
Frueh, T., and McGhee, P. E. "Traditional sex role development and amount of time spent watching television," *Developmental Psychology,* 1975, 11(1), 109.
Gade, E. M. "Representation of the world of work in daytime serials," *Journal of Employment Counseling,* 1971, 8,37–42.
Gehman, Richard. "Caseyitis," in Jay S. Harris (ed.), *TV Guide: The first 25 years.* New York: Simon and Schuster, 1978.
Gerbner, G., and Gross, L. "The scary world of TV's heavy viewer," *Psychology Today,* 10, 1976, 41–46, 89.
Gerbner, G., Gross, L., Morgan, M., and Signorielli, N. "Health and medicine on television," *The New England Journal of Medicine,* 1981, 305, 901–904.
Gerbner, G., Gross, L., Signorielli, N., and Morgan, M. "Aging with television: Images on television drama and conceptions of social reality," *Journal of Communication,* 1980, 30(1), 37–47.
Gerbner, G., and Signorielli, N. "Women and minorities in television drama, 1969–1978." Unpublished manuscript, The University of Pennsylvania, 1979.
Glennon, L. M., and Butsch, R. "The family as portrayed on television 1946–1978," in D. Pearl, L. Bouthilet, and J. Lazar (eds.), *Television and behavior: Ten years of scientific progress and implications for the eighties.* Washington, D.C.: United States Government Printing Office, 1980.
Goethals, Gregor T. *The TV ritual: Worship at the video altar.* Boston: Beacon Press, 1981.
Goldberg, M. "A doctor examines TV's health shows," *TV Guide,* 25(May 14, 1977), 4–8.
Goldsen, R. K. *The show and tell machine: How television works and works you over.* New York: Delta, 1978.
Graves, S. B. "Psychological effects of black portrayals on television," In S. B. Withey, and R. P. Abeles (eds.), *Television and social behavior: Beyond violence and children.* Hillsdale, N.J.: Lawrence Erlbaum Associates, 1980.
Greenberg, B. S. "Television and role socialization," in D. Pearl, L. Bouthilet & J. Lazar (eds.), *Television and behavior: Ten years of scientific progress and implications for the eighties.* Washington, D.C.: United States Government Printing Office, 1980.
Greenberg, B. S. *Life on Television: Content analyses of U.S. TV drama.* Norwood, N.J.: Ablex Publishing, 1980.
Greenberg, B. S., and Reeves, B. "Children and perceived reality of television," *Journal of Social Issues,* 1976, 32(4), 86–97.
Gross, L. "Why can't a woman be more like a man?," *TV Guide,* 21(August 11, 1973), 6–8.
Gutcheon, B. R. "Look for cop-outs on prime time, not on 'Soaps'," *New York Times,* December 16, 1973, p. D–21.
Gutcheon, B. "There isn't anything wishy-washy about soaps," *Ms.,* 1974, 3(2),42–43.

Halberstam, M. J. "An M.D. reviews Dr. Welby of TV," *New York Times Magazine,* January 16, 1972, pp. 12–13, 30, 32, 34–35, 37.

Harvey, S. E., Sprafkin, J. N., and Rubinstein, E. "Prime time television: A profile of aggressive and prosocial behaviors," *Journal of Broadcasting,* 1979, 23(2), 179–189.

Hawkins, R. P., and Pingree, S. "TV influence on social reality and conceptions of the world," in D. Pearl, L. Bouthilet, and J. Lazar (eds.), *Television and behavior: Ten years of scientific progress and implications for the eighties.* Washington, D.C.: United States Government Printing Office, 1980.

Johnston, D. "Teamwork M*A*S*H-style," *TV Guide,* 28(January 5, 1980), 22–26.

Johnston, J., Ettema, J., and Davidson, T. *An Evaluation of "Freestyle: A television series designed to reduce sex role stereotypes."* Ann Arbor, M.I.: Institute for Social Research, 1980.

Kalisch, P., Kalisch, B., and Scobey, M. "Reflections on a televised image: The nurses, 1962–1965," *Nursing and Health Care,* 1981, 2(5), 248–255.

Kalisch, P., and Kalisch, B. "Nurses on prime time television," *American Journal of Nursing,* 1982, 82, 264–270.

Kalisch, P., and Kalisch, B. "Sex role stereotyping of nurses and physicians on prime time television: A dichotomy of occupational portrayals," *Sex Roles,* in press.

Kalisch, P., Kalisch, B., and Clinton, J. "The world of nursing on prime time television, 1950–1980," *Nursing Research,* in press.

Katzman, N. "Television soap operas: What's been going on anyway?," *Public Opinion Quarterly,* 1972, 36,200–212.

Kaufman, L. "Prime time nutrition," *Journal of Communication,* 1980, 30(3), 37–46.

Kilguss, Anne F. "Using soap operas as a therapeutic tool," *Social Casework,* 1974, 55,525–530.

Kinzer, N. S. "Soapy sin in the afternoon," *Psychology Today,* 1973, 7,46–48.

Klavan, E. *Turn that damned thing off: An irreverent look at TV's impact on the American scene.* New York: Bobbs–Merrill, 1972.

Klein, P. "The men who run television aren't that stupid . . . they know us better than you think," *New York Magazine,* January 25, 1971, 20–31.

Klemesrud, J. "TV's women are dingbats," *The New York Times,* May 27, 1973, D–15.

La Guardia, R. *The wonderful world of TV soap operas.* New York: Ballantine Books, 1974.

Lemon, J. "Dominant or dominated? women on prime time television," in G. Tuchman, A. K. Daniels, and J. Benet (eds.), *Hearth and Home: Images of Women in the Mass Media.* New York: Oxford University Press, 1978, pp. 51–68.

Liebert, R., Neale, J. M., and Davidson, E. S. *The early window: Effects of television on children and youth.* New York: Pergammon Press, 1973.

Lopate, Carol. "Daytime television: you'll never want to leave home," *Feminist Studies,* Spring/Summer, 1976, 3(3/4),69–82.

Lull, J. "Girls favorite TV females," *Journalism Quarterly,* 1980, 57, 146–150.

Mannes, M. "Everything's up-to-date in soap operas," *TV Guide,* 17(March 15, 1969), 16–21.

Margulies, Lee. "The Second time around," Emmy: The Magazine of Television Arts and Sciences, 1(Fall, 1979), 39–40, 55–56.

McGhee, P. E., and Frueh, T. "Television viewing and the learning of sex-role stereotypes," *Sex Roles,* 1980, 6(2), 179–188.
McLaughlin, J. "The doctor shows," *Journal of Communication,* 1975, 25(3),182–184.
McNeil, J. C. "Feminism, femininity and the television series: A content analysis," *Journal of Broadcasting,* 1975, 19,259–271.
"The medium is macho," *Human Behavior,* August, 1975, 4(8),71.
Miles, B. *Channeling children: Sex stereotyping in prime time TV.* Princeton, N.J.: Women on Words and Images, 1975.
Miller, M. M., and Reeves, B. "Dramatic TV content and children's sex-role stereotypes," *Journal of Broadcasting,* 1976, 20,35–50.
Mills, K. "Fighting sexism on the airwaves," *Journal of Communication,* 1974, 24(2),150–153.
Moody, K. *Growing up on television.* New York Times Books, 1980.
Northcott, H. C., Seggar J. F., and Hinton, J. L. "Trends in TV portrayal of blacks and women," *Journalism Quarterly,* 1975, 52,741–744.
Peevers, B. N. "Androgeny on the TV screen?: An analysis of sex-role portrayal," *Sex Roles,* 1979, 5(6), 797–809.
Raddatz, L. "Let's play father image," *TV Guide,* 12(May 23, 1964), 24–27.
Raddatz, L. "The destiny of the bold ones," *TV Guide,* 17(October 25, 1969), 40–46.
Ramsdell, M. L. "The trauma of television's troubled soap families," *Family Coordinator,* 1973, 22,299–304.
Real, M. R. "Marcus Welby and the medical genre," in *Mass-Mediated Culture,* Englewood Cliffs, N.J.: Prentice-Hall, 1977, p. 118–139.
Rock, G. "Same time, same station, same sexism," *Ms.,* 1973, 2(6),24–26.
Roiphe, A. "The Waltons," *New York Times Magazine,* November 18, 1973, 40.
Rosen, D. "TV and the single girl," *TV Guide,* 19(November 6, 1971), 13–14.
Schorr, T. "Nursing's TV image," *American Journal of Nursing,* 1963, 63, 119–121.
Schwartz, Tony *Media: The second god.* New York: Random House, 1981.
Seggar, J. F. "Imagery of women in television drama: 1974," *Journal of Broadcasting,* 1975, 19(3), 273–282.
Seggar, J. F. "Women's imagery on TV: Feminist, fair maiden or maid? Comments on McNeil," *Journal of Broadcasting,* 1975, 19(3), 289–294. (b)
Seggar, J. F., and Wheeler, P. "World of work on TV: Ethnic and sex representation in TV drama," *Journal of Broadcasting,* 1973, 17,201–214.
Silverman, L. T., Sprafkin, J. N., and Rubinstein, E. A. "Physical contact and sexual behavior on prime-time TV," *Journal of Communication,* 1979, 29,33–43.
Skornia, H. J. *Television and society: An inquest and agenda for improvement.* New York: McGraw-Hill, 1965.
Smythe, D. W. "Reality as presented by television," *Public Opinion Quarterly,* 1954, 18,143–156.
Somers, A. R. "Violence, television, and the health of American youth," *New England Journal of Medicine,* 1976, 294(15), 811–817.
Sternglanz, S. H., and Serbin, L. A. "Sex role stereotyping in children's television programs," *Developmental Psychology,* 1974, 10(5), 710–715.

Tedesco, N. S. "Patterns in primetime," *Journal of Communication*, 1974, 24(2), 119–124.
Terrace, V. *The complete encyclopedia of television programs 1947–1976*, 2 vols. New York: Barnes, 1976.
"There's a doctor in the house," *TV Guide*, 18 (April 18, 1970), 41–44.
"Through the Years with Dr. Kildare," *TV Guide*, 21 (January 20, 1973), 15–18.
United States Commission on Civil Rights. *Window dressing on the set: Women and minorities in television*. Washington: Government Printing Office, 1977.
United States Congress, House Committee on Interstate and Foreign Commerce, Subcommittee on Communications. *Sex and violence on TV*. Hearings, 95th Congress, 1st Session, 1977. Washington, D.C.: United States Government Printing Office, 1977.
United States Congress, Senate Committee on Commerce, Subcommittee on Communications. *Surgeon General's Report by the Scientific Advisory Committee on Television and Social Behavior*. Hearings, 92nd Congress, 2nd Session, March 21–24, 1972. Washington, D.C.: U.S. Government Printing Office, 1972.
United States Congress, Senate Committee on Commerce, Subcommittee on Communications. *Impact of television on children*. Hearings, 94th Congress, 2nd Session. Washington, D.C.: United States Government Printing Office, 1976.
U.S. Public Health Service, Surgeon General's Scientific Advisory Committee on Television and Social Behavior. *Television and social behavior, volume I: Media content and control*. Washington, D.C.: Government Printing Office, 1972.
Volgy, T., and Schwarz, J. "Television entertainment programming and sociopolitical attitudes," *Journalism Quarterly*, 1980, 57, 150–154.
Wahl, O. "TV myths about mental illness," *TV Guide*, 24 (March 13, 1976), 4–8.
Welch, R. L., Huston-Stein, A., Wright, J. C., and Plehal, R. "Subtle sex-roles cues in children's commercials," *Journal of Communication*, 1979, 29(3), 202–209.
Werner, A. "The effects of television on children and adolescents: A case of sex and class socialization," *Journal of Communication*, 1975, 25(4), 45–50.
Wexler, M., and Levy, G. "Women on television: fairness and the 'fair sex'," *Yale Review of Law and Social Action*, 1971, 2, 59–68.
Whipple, T. W., and Courtney, A. E. "How to portray women in TV commercials," *Journal of Advertising Research*, 1980, 20(2), 53–60.
"Who Runs America," *U.S. News and World Report*, 92(May 10, 1982), 34–45.
Wilk, M. *The golden age of television: Notes from the survivors*. New York: Delacorte Press, 1976.
Williams, C. T. "It's not so much 'You've come a long way, baby' as 'You're gonna make it after all,'" Journal of Popular Culture 7(1974), 981–989.
Winick, C., and Winick, M. P. "Courtroom drama on television," *Journal of Communication*, 24(1974), 67–73.
Winick, M. P., and Winick, C. *The television experience: What children see*. Beverly Hills, Calif.: Sage Publications, 1979.
Winn, M. *The Plug in Drug*. New York: Viking, 1979.

Appendix: Television Series and Series Pilots Pertaining to Nurses and Physicians

A.E.S. Hudson Street (30 minutes, Comedy) ABC, March 17, 1978 to April 20, 1978, 5 episodes. Nurses in regular cast: Nurse Rosa Santiago (Rosana Soto); Nurse Rhoda Todd (Julienne Wells); Nurse Newton (Ray Stewart)

Amanda Fallon (60 minutes, Medical–Drama Pilot) NBC, March 5, 1972, 1 episode. Nurse in regular cast: Nurse Crawford (Lillian Lehman)

Annie Flynn (30 minutes, Comedy Pilot) CBS, January 21, 1978, 1 episode. Nurse in regular cast: Annie Flynn (Barrie Youngfellow)

Ben Casey (60 minutes, Medical Drama) ABC, October 2, 1961 to March 21, 1966, 153 episodes. Nurse in regular cast: Nurse Wills (Jeanne Bates)

The Black Sheep Squadron (60 minutes, Adventure) NBC, December 14, 1977 to September 1, 1978 (As *Baa Baa Black Sheep* September 21, 1976 to August 30, 1977), 34 episodes. Nurses in regular cast (The Fighting Angels): Nancy Gilmore (Nancy Conrad); Samantha Greene (Denise DuBarry); Captain Dottie Dickson (Katherine Cannon); Ellie Farrell (Kathy McCullem); Sue Webster (Brianne Leary); Anne Wilson (Leslie Charleson); Cheryl (Sharon Ullrick)

The Bob Crane Show (30 minutes, Situation Comedy) NBC, March 6, 1975 to June 19, 1975, 14 episodes. No regular nurse characters.

The Bold Ones: The Doctors (60 minutes, Medical Drama) NBC, September 14, 1969 to June 23, 1973, 44 episodes. No regular nurse characters.

Breaking Point (60 minutes, Medical Drama) ABC, September 16, 1963 to September 7, 1964, 30 episodes. No regular nurse characters.

Calling Dr. Storm, M.D. (30 minutes, Comedy Pilot) NBC, August 25, 1977, 1 episode. No regular nurse characters.

City Hospital (30 minutes, Medical Drama) CBS, March 25, 1952 to October 1, 1953, 72 episodes. No regular nurse characters.

Doc (30 minutes, Comedy) CBS, September 13, 1975 to August 14, 1976, 23 episodes. Nurse in regular cast: Beatrice Tully (Mary Wickes)

Doc (30 minutes, Comedy) CBS, September 25, 1976 to October 30, 1976, 6 episodes. Nurse in regular cast: Janet Scott "Scotty" (Audra Lindley)

Doc Elliot (60 minutes, Medical Drama) ABC, October 10, 1973 to August 14, 1974, 15 episodes. No regular nurse characters.

The Doctor (30 minutes, Medical Anthology) NBC, August 24, 1952 to June 28, 1953, 36 episodes. No regular nurse characters.

Doctor Christian (30 minutes, Medical Drama) Syndicated, 1956, 39 episodes. Nurses in regular cast: Nurse (Jan Shepard); Nurse (Cynthia Baer); Nurse (Kay Faylen)

Doctor Simon Locke (30 minutes, Medical Drama) Syndicated, 1971, 39 episodes. Nurse in regular cast: Nurse Louise Wynn (Nuala Fitzgerald)

The Doctors (30 minutes, Serial) NBC, Premiered April 1, 1963, 5,000 plus episodes. Nurses in regular cast: Nurse Kathy Ryker (Nancy Barrett, Holly Peters); Carolee Aldrich (Carolee Campbell, Jada Rowland); Lauri James (Marie Thomas); Nurse (Susan Adams); Nurse Brown (Dorothy Blackburn); M. J. Carroll (Kathy Glass)

Doctors Hospital (60 minutes, Medical Drama) NBC, September 10, 1975 to January 14, 1976, (The two-hour pilot film, "One of Our Own," aired on NBC on May 5, 1975) 12 episodes. Nurses in regular cast: Nurse Connie Kimbrough (Elisabeth Brooks); Heather Stanton, admissions nurse (Adrian Ricard); Nurse Forester (Barbara Darrow); Nurse Wilson (Elaine Church)

Doctors' Private Lives (60 minutes, Medical Drama) ABC, March 5, 1979 to April 26, 1979, (The two-hour pilot film aired on ABC on March 20, 1978). 4 episodes. Nurse in regular cast: Nurse Diane Curtis (Eddie Benton)

The Donna Reed Show (30 minutes, Situation Comedy) ABC, September 24, 1958 to September 3, 1966, 274 episodes. Nurse in regular cast: Donna Stone (Donna Reed)

Dr. Kildare (60 minutes, Medical Drama) NBC, September 27, 1961 to August 29, 1966, 190 episodes. Nurses in regular cast: Nurse Zoe Lawton (Lee Kurty); Nurse Conant (Jo Helton)

Dr. Hudson's Secret Journal (30 minutes, Medical Drama) Syndicated, 1955–1957, 78 episodes. Nurse in regular cast: Nurse Ann Talbot (Frances Mercer)

The Eleventh Hour (60 minutes, Medical Drama) NBC, October 3, 1962 to September 9, 1964, 62 episodes. No regular nurse characters.

Emergency! (60 minutes, Medical Drama) NBC, January 22, 1972 to September 3, 1977, 115 episodes. Nurses in regular cast: Nurse Dixie McCall (Julie London); Nurse Carol Williams (Lillian Lehman); Nurse (Deidre Hall); Nurse (Ginny Golden)

The Fighting Nightingales (30 minutes, Comedy Pilot) CBS, January 16, 1978, 1 episode. Nurses in regular cast: Maj. Kate Steele (Adrienne Barbeau); Lt. Angie Finelli (Livia Genise); Capt. "Irish" McCall (Erica Yohn); Lt. Hope Phillips (Stephanie Faracy).

The First 36 Hours of Dr. Durant (90 minutes, Medical Drama Pilot) ABC, May 13, 1975, 1 episode. Nurses in regular cast: Nurse Katherine Gunther (Katherine Helmond); Nurse Olive Olin (Karen Carlson)

The Flying Doctor (30 minutes, Adventure) Syndicated, 1959, 39 episodes. Nurse in regular cast: Mary (Jill Adams)

General Hospital (30 minutes, April 1, 1963 to July 23, 1976; 45 minutes July 26, 1976 to January 13, 1978; 60 minutes January 16, 1978; Serial) ABC, Premiered April 1, 1963, 5,000 plus episodes. Nurses in regular cast: Audrey March (Rachel Ames); Nurse Iris Fairchild (Peggy McCay); Nurse Jessie Brewer (Lois Kibbee, Emily McLaughlin, Aneta Corsaut); Nurse Kendell Jone (Joan Tompkins); Nurse Lucille March (Lucille Wall); Nurse Linda Cooper (Linda Cooper); Bobbi (Jackie Zeman–Kaufman)

Handle With Care (30 minutes, Comedy Pilot) CBS, May 9, 1977, 1 episode. Nurses in regular cast: Liz Baker (Marlyn Mason); Jackie Morse (Didi Conn); Major Hinkley (Mary Jo Catlett); Shirley "Scoop" Nichols (Betsey Slade); Turk (Jeannie Wilson)

Hennessey (30 minutes, Comedy/Drama) CBS, September 28, 1959 to September 17, 1962, 92 episodes. Nurse in regular cast: Martha Hale (Abby Dalton)

House Calls (30 minutes, Comedy) CBS, December 17, 1979 to September 13, 1982, 58 episodes. Nurses in regular cast: Head Nurse Bradley (Aneta Corsaut); The Admissions Nurse (Sharon DeBord); Nurse (Peggy Frees); Nurse (Terri Berland); Nurse (Georgia Jeffries)

The Interns (60 minutes, Medical Drama) CBS, September 18, 1970 to September 10, 1971, 24 episodes. Nurse in regular cast: Nurse (Jenny Blackton)

Janet Dean, Registered Nurse (30 minutes, Nursing Drama) Syndicated, 1953–1955, 39 episodes. Nurse in regular cast: Janet Dean (Ella Raines)

Julia (30 minutes, Comedy) NBC, September 17, 1968 to May 25, 1971, 86 episodes. Nurses in regular cast: Nurse Julia Baker (Diahann Carroll); Hannah Yarby, head nurse (Lurene Tuttle)

Julie Farr, M.D. (Having Babies) (60 minutes, Medical Drama) ABC, March 28, 1978 to April 18, 1978; June 12, 1979 to June 26, 1979; March 7, 1978 to March 21, 1978, 8 episodes. Nurse in regular cast: Nurse (Deborah Green)

The Lazarus Syndrome (60 minutes, Medical Drama) ABC, September 11, 1979 to October 9, 1979, 6 episodes. Nurse in regular cast: The Admissions Nurse (Christina Alvila)

Lifeline (60 minutes, Medical Profile) NBC, October 8, 1978 to December 30, 1978, 10 episodes. No regular nurse characters.

The Little People (30 minutes, Comedy) NBC, September 15, 1972 to September 7, 1973, as *The Brian Keith Show* September 21, 1973 to August 30, 1974, 48 episodes. Nurse in regular cast: Puni (Victoria Young)

The March of Medicine (30 minutes, Documentary) ABC, July 8, 1958 to July 29, 1958, 3 episodes. No regular nurse characters.

Marcus Welby, M.D. (60 minutes, Medical Drama) ABC, September 23, 1969 to May 11, 1976, 172 episodes. Nurses in regular cast: Consuelo Lopez (Elena Verdugo); Nurse Kathleen Faverty (Sharon Gless)

M*A*S*H (30 minutes, Comedy Drama) CBS, September 17, 1972 to date, 225 plus episodes. Nurses in regular cast: Major Margaret "Hot Lips" Houlihan (Loretta Swit); Nurse (Lt.) Maggie Dish (Karen Philipp); Nurse (Lt.) Ginger Ballis (Odessa Cleveland); Nurse (Lt.) Leslie Scorch (Linda Meiklejohn); Nurse (Lt.) Jones (Barbara Brownell); Nurse Louis Anderson (Kelly Jean Peters); Nurse Maggie Cutler (Marcia Strassman, Lynnette Metty); Nurse Bigelow (Enid Kent); Nurse Abel (Judy Farrell); Nurse Baker (Jean Powell, Lynne Marie Stewart, Linda Kelsey); Nurse Mary Jo Walsh (Mary Jo Catlett); Nurse Gaynor (Carol Locatell); Nurse Preston (Patricia Sturges); Nurse (Shari Saba); Nurse Memdenhal (Shelly Long); Nurse (Jennifer Davis); Nurse (Gwen Farrell); Nurse (Connie Izay)

Matt Lincoln (60 minutes, Medical Drama) ABC, September 24, 1970 to January 14, 1971, 15 episodes. No regular nurse characters.

Medic (30 minutes, Medical Drama) NBC, September 1954 to November 1956, 60 episodes. No regular nurse characters.

Medical Center (60 minutes, Medical Drama) CBS, September 24, 1969 to September 6, 1976, 169 episodes. Nurses in regular cast: Nurse Chambers (Jayne Meadows); Nurse

Holmby (Barbara Baldavin); Nurse Courtland (Chris Huston); Nurse Higby (Catherine Ferrar); Nurse Murphy (Jane Dulo); Nurse Wilcox (Audrey Totter); Nurse Crawford (Virginia Hawkins); Nurse Bascomb (Louise Fitch); Nurse Loring (Nancy Priddy)

Medical Horizons (30 minutes, Public Affairs) ABC, September 12, 1955 to March 5, 1956, 26 episodes. No regular nurse characters.

Medical Story (60 minutes, Anthology) NBC, September 4, 1975 to January 8, 1976, 11 episodes. No regular nurse characters.

Mother and Me, M.D. (30 minutes, Comedy Pilot) NBC, June 14, 1979, 1 episode. Nurse in regular cast: Lil Brenner (Rue McClanahan)

Mr. Peepers (30 minutes, Situation Comedy) NBC, July 3, 1952 to June 12, 1955, 96 episodes. Nurse in regular cast: Nancy Remington (Patricia Benoit)

The New Healers (60 minutes, Medical Drama Pilot) ABC, March 27, 1972, 1 episode. Nurse in regular cast: Nurse Michelle Johnson (Kate Jackson)

The New Operation Petticoat (30 minutes, Comedy) ABC, September 25, 1978 to October 19, 1978; June 1, 1979 to August 3, 1979, 9 episodes. Nurses in regular cast: Lt. Dolores Crandall (Melinda Naud); Lt. Catherine O'Hara (Jo Ann Pflug); Lt. Betty Wheeler (Hilary Thompson)

Nurse (60 minutes, Nursing/Medical Drama) CBS, April 1981 to May 21, 1982, episodes. Nurses in regular cast: Nurse Mary Benjamin (Michael Learned); Nurse Toni (Hattie Winston); Nurse Penny (Bonnie Hellman); Nurse Betty LaSada (Hortensia Colorado); Nurse Bailey (Clarice Taylor)

The Nurses (The Doctors and The Nurses) 60 minutes, Nursing/Medical Drama) CBS, September 27, 1962 to September 17, 1964; as *The Doctors and The Nurses* September 22, 1964 to September 7, 1965, 103 episodes. Nurses in regular cast: Nurse Liz Thorpe (Shirl Conway); Nurse Gail Lucas (Zina Bethune); Nurse Ayres (Hilda Simms)

The Nurses (30 minutes, Serial) ABC, September 27, 1965 to March 31, 1967, 390 episodes. Nurses in regular cast: Liz Thorpe (Mary Fickett); Gail Lucas (Melinda Plank); Brenda (Patricia Hyland); Nurse Dorothy Warner (Leonie Norton)

Operating Room (60 minutes, Comedy Pilot) NBC, October 4, 1979, 1 episode. No regular nurse characters.

Operation Petticoat (30 minutes, Comedy) ABC, September 17, 1977 to August 25, 1978, 22 episodes. Nurses in regular cast: Major Edna Hayward (Yvonne Wilder); Lt. Dolores Crandall (Melinda Naud); Lt. Barbara Duran (Jamie Lee Curtis); Lt. Ruth Colfax (Dorrie Thompson); Lt. Claire Reid (Bond Gideon)

Police Surgeon (30 minutes, Crime Drama) Syndicated, 1972, 76 episodes. No regular nurse characters.

The Practice (30 minutes, Comedy) NBC, January 30, 1976 to August 6, 1976; October 13, 1976 to January 20, 1977, 22 episodes. Nurse in regular cast: Molly Gibbons (Dena Dietrich)

Quincy, M.E. (60 minutes, Crime Drama) NBC, February 4, 1977 to date, 126 plus episodes. No regular nurse characters.

Rafferty (60 minutes, Medical Drama) CBS, September 5, 1977 to November 28, 1977, 10 episodes. Nurses in regular cast: Vera Wales (Millie Slavin); Beryl Kaynes (Joan Pringle)

The Rookies (60 minutes, Crime Drama) ABC, September 11, 1972 to June 15, 1976, 68 episodes. Nurse in regular cast: Jill Danko (Kate Jackson)

Scalpels (30 minutes, Comedy Pilot) NBC, October 26, 1980, 1 episode. Nurse in regular cast: Connie Primble (Kimberly Beck)

The Specialists (90 minutes, Medical Drama Pilot) NBC, January 6, 1975, 1 episode. No regular nurse characters.

Stat! (30 minutes, Medical Drama Pilot) CBS, July 31, 1973, 1 episode. Nurse in regular cast: Nurse Ellen Quayle (Marian Collier)

Temperatures Rising (30 minutes, Comedy) ABC, September 12, 1972 to August 29, 1974, 42 episodes. Nurses in regular cast: Nurse Ann Carlisle (Joan Van Ark); Nurse Mildred MacInerney (Reva Rose); Nurse Ellen Turner (Nancy Fox); Wendy Winchester (Jennifer Darling); Miss Tillis (Barbara Cason); Nurse Kelly (Barbara Rucker)

Trapper John, M.D. (60 minutes, Medical Drama) CBS, September 23, 1979 to date, 59 plus episodes. Nurses in regular cast: Nurse "Starch" Willoughby (Mary McCarty); Nurse Gloria "Ripples" Brancusi (Christopher Norris); Nurse (Jennifer Davis); Nurse (Brenda Elder); Scrub Nurse Ernestine Shoop (Madge Sinclair)

The Waltons (60 minutes, Drama) CBS, September 14, 1972 to March, 1981, 208 episodes. Nurses in regular cast: Mary Ellen Walton (Judy Norton-Taylor); Nora, the county nurse (Kaiulani Lee)

Westside Medical (60 minutes, Medical Drama) ABC, March 15, 1977 to April 14, 1977, 5 episodes. No regular nurse characters.

Where's Poppa? (30 minutes, Comedy Pilot) ABC, July 17, 1979, 1 episode. Nurse in regular cast: Louise Hamelin (Judith-Marie Bergen)

Women in White (60 and 120 minutes, Drama) NBC, February 8, 1979 to February 22, 1979, 3 episodes. Nurses in regular cast: Nurse Cathy Payson (Patty Duke Astin); Nurse Lisa Gordon (Sheree North); Nurse (Gloria Delaney); Nurse Jean Robinson (June Witney Taylor); Admitting Nurse (Janet Winter)

Young Doctor Kildare (30 minutes, Medical Drama) Syndicated, 1972, 24 episodes. Nurses in regular cast: Nurse Marsha Lord (Marsha Mason); Nurse Ferris (Dixie Marquis); Nurse Newell (Olga James)

Index

Note: Characters in dramas/series appear under their full names, not under their surnames.

Action-adventure series, 42, 97, 101–113, 178, 183, 185, 186, 188, 189, 191, 193, 194
A.E.S. Hudson Street, 98–100, 178, 207
All My Children, 161, 163, 171–174
Amanda Fallon, 207
Annie Flynn, 97, 207
Another World, 163, 170–172
Armstrong Circle Theatre, 2
Audrey March, 166
Awards, 188–191

Baa Baa Black Sheep, 109, 110
Baby Time, 2
"Behind the Mask," 6–7
Ben Casey, 7, 18, 19–22, 25, 26, 39–40, 58, 60, 177, 180, 183, 185, 186, 187, 188, 191, 192, 195, 207
Best of Broadway, 3–5
Blacks, 15, 35–36, 106. See also *Julia*
The Black Sheep Squadron, 42, 97, 101, 109–113, 178, 183, 207
Blinn, William, 185
Bobbie Spencer, 166–167
The Bob Crane Show, 85–86, 207
The Bold Ones: The Doctors, 41, 42–43, 58, 176, 181, 183, 190, 207
Breaking Point, 18, 25, 26, 40, 207
The Brian Keith Show (Little People), 84–85, 182, 185
Brinkley, Don, 185

Calling Dr. Storm, 207
City Hospital, 1, 7, 8–9, 138, 207
Consuelo Lopez, 50–51, 54–57, 179, 182, 191, 193

Daytime dramas, 159–175
The Defenders, 27, 28
Diana Maynard Taylor, 166

Dixie McCall, 107–109
Doc, 86–90, 93, 100, 182, 193, 207
Doc Elliot, 63–64, 208
The Doctor, 7, 9, 208
The Doctors, 160, 161, 163, 169–170, 172, 174, 179, 182, 186, 208
The Doctors and The Nurses, 28–29, 40, 177, 210. See also *The Nurses* (CBS)
Doctors Hospital, 64, 66–69, 80, 184, 185, 208
Doctors' Private Lives, 75, 80, 184, 208
The Donna Reed Show, 12–13, 16, 195, 208
Dorrie Fleming, 167
Dr. Christian, 8, 138, 139, 208
Dr. Hudson's Secret Journal, 138, 139–141, 177, 181, 182, 193, 208
Dr. Kildare, 7, 18–20, 23–25, 26, 39–40, 58, 177, 181, 185, 186, 187, 188, 189, 191, 192, 195, 208
Dr. Simon Locke, 141–143, 208

"An Echo of the Past," 3, 5–6
The Eleventh Hour, 18, 25–27, 40, 185, 208
Emergency!, 42, 101, 105–109, 113, 186, 188, 189, 191, 193, 208
Emmy Awards, 188–191

Felton, Norman, 185
The Fighting Nightingales, 97–98, 185
The First Hundred Years, 159
The First 36 Hours of Dr. Durant, 208
The Flying Doctor, 208
Ford Theatre, 6–7

Gail Lucas, 28, 29–30, 31–34, 177
Galard-Terraube, Genevieve de, 2
General Hospital, 160, 163, 164–169, 170, 172, 174, 179, 186, 195, 208
"Girl Friday" nurse, 179–180
Glicksman, Frank, 185

212

Index

"The Glorious Red Gallegher," 9, 10–11
Good nurse, 16, 68, 191, 193–194. See also *Emergency!; Marcus Welby, M.D.*

The Hallmark Hall of Fame, 36–39, 189, 190
Handle with Care, 157–158, 208
Having Babies, 75, 77, 182
Hennessey, 1, 11, 13–15, 16, 40, 177, 179, 186, 189, 190, 191, 194, 209
"The Holy Terror," 36–39, 190
Hospital-medical dramas
  in the 1950s, 1–17
  in the 1960s, 18–40
  in the 1970s, 41–59, 60–80
House Calls, 130, 135–136, 183, 188, 209

The Interns, 61–63, 102, 184, 185, 209

Janet Dean, R.N., 138–139, 141, 209
The Jayne Wyman Show, 3, 5–6
Jessie Brewer, 165–166
Jill Danko, 102–105, 113, 183, 191, 194
Julia, 18, 34–36, 40, 179, 182, 186, 187, 189, 190, 191, 194, 209
Julie Farr, M.D., 75–77, 182, 184, 209

Laird, Jack, 185
The Lazarus Syndrome, 130, 133–135, 136, 178, 185, 188, 198, 209
Lifeline, 75, 209
Life with Baby, 2
"Little Moon of Alban," 190
Little People (The Brian Keith Show), 84–85, 114, 185, 209
Liz Thorpe, 27–31, 33–34, 40, 179, 182, 191, 195–198
The Loretta Young Theatre, 3

Made-for-TV movies, 137, 147–156
Mann, A., 64
"The Man Who Came to Dinner," 3–5
The March of Medicine, 2, 16, 209
Marcus Welby, M.D., 41, 42, 50–58, 60, 64, 77, 93, 179, 180, 181, 182, 183, 184, 185, 186, 187, 188, 189, 190, 191, 193, 199, 209
Margaret "Hot Lips" Houlihan, 42, 119, 123–130, 177, 182–183, 186, 191, 195–198
Martha Hale, 13–15, 16, 179, 191, 194
Mary Ellen Walton, 42, 114–117, 182

M*A*S*H, 42, 96, 97, 100, 114, 117–130, 136, 177, 178, 182–183, 184, 186, 187, 188, 189, 190, 191, 195–198, 209
Matt Lincoln, 60–61, 209
Medic, 2, 8, 9–11, 16, 17, 18, 19, 179–180, 181, 182, 185, 189, 198, 209
Medical Center, 41, 42, 43–50, 53, 58, 60, 64, 131, 176, 178, 180, 181, 183, 184, 185, 186, 188, 189, 191, 192, 195, 209
Medical dramas, see Hospital-medical dramas
Medical Horizons, 2, 16, 75, 210
Medical Story, 64–66, 80, 198, 210
Meeting of Minds, 157
"Mercy Wears an Apron," 10, 11
Moser, James, 19, 185
Mother and Me, M.D., 210
Movies, TV, 147–158
Mr. Peepers, 11–12, 16, 40, 179, 189, 190, 195, 210
Mystery of the Week, 148

Negative images of nursing, 7, 15, 23–24, 25, 56, 85, 112, 146–147, 148. See also Nurse(s); Stereotypes
The New Healers, 210
The New Operation Petticoat, 210
Nielsen ratings, 14, 186–188
"Night Cries," 148
Nightingale, Florence, 36–39, 157
Nonentity, nurse as, 22, 26, 70, 75, 84, 121, 145–146, 191, 192–193. See also *Ben Casey; Dr. Kildare; Medical Center*
Non-network programs, 137–158
Nova, 156–157
Nurse(s)
  disciplinarian, 176–177
  as Girl Friday, 179–180
  the good, 16, 68, 191, 193–194
  as handmaiden, 68, 180–182, 192–193
  in 1950s programs, 1–17
  in 1960s programs, 18–40
  in 1970s programs, 41–113
  as nonentity, 22, 26, 70, 75, 84, 121, 145–146, 191, 192–193
  nurturing, 11, 54–55, 191, 194–195
  physical appearance of, 24, 181
  professional, 191, 195–200
  as protagonist, 25, 54, 75–80, 124, 134
  as sexual object, 14–15, 123, 128, 174–175, 178–179, 183–184

in situation comedies, 81–100
stereotypes of, 5, 14, 17, 176–185, 191–200
Nurse, 148–153, 210
"Nurse Killer," 147–148
The Nurses (ABC), 96–97, 210
The Nurses (CBS), 3, 18, 27–34, 40, 153, 177, 179, 181, 182, 185, 186, 188, 189–190, 191, 195–198, 210
"Nurse Will Make It Better," 148
Nurturing nurse, 54–55, 191, 194–195. See also *Hennessey; Julia; The Rookies*

O'Connell, David J., 185
Operating Room, 210
Operation Petticoat, 93–96, 97, 178, 183, 185, 187, 210

Physicians, female, 53, 69, 75–80, 182, 184–185
Playhouse 90, 2, 3, 27
Police Surgeon, 141, 143–144, 210
Portrait of a Rebel: Margaret Sanger, 148, 153–157
Positive images of nurses, 6, 23, 26, 29–34, 37–38, 56, 96, 112–113, 114–130, 141, 148–153, 162–163. *See also* Nurse(s)
The Practice, 86, 90–93, 100, 193, 210
Producers of health care TV programs, 185
Professional nurse, 191, 195–200. See also *M*A*S*H; The Nurses* (CBS)
Protagonists, nurses as, 25, 54, 75–80, 124, 134. *See also* Margaret "Hot Lips" Houlihan; *The Nurses*
Public television programs, 137–138, 156–158

Quigley Publication Awards, 188–189
Quincy, M.E., 69–70, 177, 210

Rafferty, 72–75, 182, 185, 193, 210
Rapf, Matthew, 185
Ratings, 14, 186–188

Realism, 9–10, 28, 62, 65, 102, 131, 148–153
The Rookies, 42, 101, 102–105, 113, 183, 185, 186, 188, 189, 191, 194, 210

Sanger, Margaret, 148, 153–157
Scalpels, 210
"Scarlet Woman in White," 14–15, 16, 177
Sexual exploitation, 14–15, 123, 128, 174–175, 178–179, 183–184
Short-lived dramas, 60–80
Simon Locke, 63
Situation comedies, 11–15, 41, 81–100, 114, 177–179, 183, 186–191, 194–195. *See also M*A*S*H*
Soap operas, 159–175
The Specialists, 211
Stat!, 211
Stereotypes, 5, 14, 17, 176–185, 191–200
Studio One, 2
Sylvania Grand Award, 189
Syndicated series, 137, 138–147, 177, 181, 182, 193

Temperatures Rising, 81–84, 85, 114, 211
Thorpe, Jerry, 185
Top Plays of 1954, 3
Trapper John, M.D., 41, 130–133, 136, 179, 181, 183–184, 185, 188, 194, 211

Victor, David, 185

The Waltons, 42, 114–117, 136, 182, 184, 190, 211
Ward, Al, 185
Westside Medical, 70–72, 184, 185, 211
Where's Poppa?, 211
Woman, 157–158,
Women in White, 75, 77–80, 184–185, 211
Writers of health care TV programs, 185

Young Dr. Kildare, 141, 144–147, 211